This is the Lord's Doing

A MODERN-DAY JOB STORY, OR SO I THOUGHT

Leeta Bigbee, MSM

TRILOGY CHRISTIAN PUBLISHERS

TUSTIN, CA

Trilogy Christian Publishers
A Wholly Owned Subsidiary of Trinity Broadcasting Network
2442 Michelle Drive
Tustin, CA 92780

This Is the Lord's Doing: A Modern-Day Job Story, Or So I Thought

For information about special discounts for bulk purchases, please contact Trilogy Christian Publishing.

Manufactured in the United States of America

10 9 8 7 6 5 4 3 2 1

Library of Congress Cataloging-in-Publication Data is available.

ISBN: 979-8-88738-109-1

E-ISBN: 979-8-88738-110-7

Dedication

Thanks to All of You

I went through a lot of difficult times, and there were many people who helped me throughout the years. For that help, I am truly grateful. The lists of names are not in any particular order. I want to give special thanks to my family, who helped me in spite of not understanding what was going on and how erratic and irrational my behavior had become at times. Thank you:

Barbara Thomas, Tyler Hutchinson, Trelyn Shannon, Yelena Brackney, Charles Brackney, Tia Coleman, Glenn Coleman (RIP), Reece Coleman (RIP), Evan Coleman (RIP), Arya Coleman (RIP), Christopher Martin, Tiffany Martin, Gregory Emmanuel II, Tyree Miller, Gloria Collins, John (RIP) and Sarah Boyd, Alisia Gray, Pamela Grays, Billy Grays, Juan Geralds II., Sierra Grays, Denina Sharp, Renée Edwards, Sarah Lowe, Sarah (Ludy) Lowe, Patsy Newson, Lisa Lowe.

There were several others who helped and stood by me, even during the tough times, and I just wanted to say thanks to them as well, no matter how large or small the part played. Once again, the names are in no particular order:

Gary Sr. and Sally (RIP) Burt, Michael Jones Sr. (RIP), Jessie Jones (RIP), Michael II and LaShonda Jones, James and Reneé White, A. Janice Dalton, Toni Martin (RIP), Toni Burt, Regina Majors, Trina and Kevin Davis, Beth Hearn-Brooks, Jeremie and Joyce Bell, Melissa and Barry Brown, Mary and Nathaniel Grandberry, Tina Blackwell, Jason and Mika Chambers, Marcetta Davis, Cassandra (Missy) Howard-Adams, Sabrina Burt, Teresa and L. Jay Jones, Dawn Alvies (RIP), Melita Davis, Don Juan Cooley, Carlissa Donaldson, Rhegan Gilmore, Rhonda Alvies, Milo and Anitra Green, LaTonya Har-ris-Swint, Angela Jones, Shirley Bowens, Evan and Marilyn Kimble, Renita Minor (RIP), Gregory and Josephine Quick, Starla Raine, Octavia Reed, Deborah and Paul Ross, Bernice Rutledge, Rashida Taylor, Je'Lisa Brown, Alissa Thomas, Horatio Brown (RIP), Donna Mason, Patrice Mason, Juan Geralds Sr., Thomas Griffith Sr., Denise Griffith (RIP), Amy Wimbleduff, Viola Smith (RIP), Lela Davis, Shanae Johnson, Tyree Sr. and Tonya Harris, Cynthia Folson, Talethia Folson, Jacquelyn Wells-Dodson, Gertrude Olloway, Janice Mays, Theresa Geist, James Blaine, Theresa Starks, Anntoinette Taylor, Christine Scott (RIP), Jan and Vincent Ash Sr., Jeanette Edwards (RIP), Courtney Demery, Jori Hargrove, Michelle and Brian Starks, Monique Ragland,

Nadja McCloud, Nicole Dukes, Sharesse Underwood, Priscilla Williams (1), Priscilla Williams (2), An-drea Johnson, LaDonna Bland, Alexis Elliott, Tasha Pittman, Christine King, Lisa Forrest, LaTwana Presswood, Tommy Love, Frankie Pinner, Anna Davenport, Wayne Burt, Lydia Harriston (RIP), Robert and Susan (RIP) Harriston, Jason Harriston, Kim Weathered, Erica Robinson.

Acknowledgements

Jessica Whitaker with Jessica Rene Photography.

Methodist Hospital and staff, Community North Hospital and staff.

Contents

Preface

When thinking about this book, it reminds me of a song by Kevin Davidson titled "Fight On." The song is an excellent reminder that we should not become defeated when we go through tests and trials. If we are doing our best, we should not be discouraged but encouraged because God is the one that fights for us. These past few years would truly be considered the fight of my life, or should I say my Euroclydon.[1] I was fighting against an enemy that I knew nothing about and was also totally unequipped to fight against. I hadn't been taught how to fight like him, move like him, or to even think like him. No one instructed me on what to do when he did this or what to do when he did that. It was kind of like getting in a boxing ring with Muhammad Ali, and no one had ever taught me how to box. It was almost a TKO.

There was a time in my life when I became aware that the fight I was in was not a carnal, natural, or fleshly fight. But the fight I was fighting was a spiritual fight (battle) just like

---

1 A violent agitation, a tempestuous wind or hurricane, cyclone, on the Mediterranean, and very dangerous; now called a "levanter." This wind seized the ship in which St. Paul was ultimately wrecked on the coast of Malta. It came down from the island and therefore must have blown more or less from the northward (Acts 27:14). Available: http://www.websters-online-dictionary.org/definitions/Euroclydon

Paul spoke about in Ephesians 6:12 (KJV), which states, "For we wrestle not against flesh and blood, but against principalities, against powers, against the rulers of the darkness of this world, against spiritual wickedness in high places."

When thinking about the book of Job, there was a point in Job's life when he became afflicted in his body. However, Job did not have a natural medical condition, sickness, or medical affliction. Job had several medical symptoms but no medical condition. Job was in a spiritual battle, which manifested itself as the symptoms of several medical ailments. You don't believe me when I say he was in a spiritual battle? Read Job 1:6–12 and Job 2:1–7. Job was totally unaware that God (spirit) and Satan (spirit) were having a conversation about him. After the conversations, God allowed Satan to go immediately to wreak havoc on Job's life and body.

I believe if Job were around today, and those same conversations took place with God and Satan, Job would rush to the emergency room and try to get answers to why his body was doing the things it was doing. I'm sure Job would want to know why he was in so much pain and what's up with all the boils.

However, I don't believe Job would get any answers because blood tests, X-rays, EKGs, or any other medical machine or test could not then; and never will be able to detect or pick up the presence of a spirit. I believe the doctors would have told Job they did not find anything wrong with him. Nevertheless, I do believe they would have started him on a series of medications in an attempt to treat his symptoms. Job found himself in the fight of his life, a spiritual battle, which showed forth via fleshly symptoms. Job wasn't in the fight because of any sin he had committed, but just because God allowed it to happen so that He could show Satan and Job just how faithful a servant Job was unto God. Also, to show Job just how excellent God was and still is.

We, as spirit-filled people, need to be able to recognize if we are in a natural battle or a spiritual battle. It is my belief if you go to the doctor and he draws blood, runs tests, and finds a legitimate problem (disease, diabetes, high blood pressure, a malignant tumor, or whatever), then I believe you probably have a natural medical condition. However, I still believe that God is the God of all flesh, and He can and will heal and deliver if it is His will. On the other hand, if you are experiencing symptoms and the doctors have drawn blood and/or ran all the tests, they can think to run. If the doctors have sent you to every specialist that deals with the condition your symptoms are associated with, and then the doctors still come back with that famous quote, "We can't find anything wrong; all your tests were negative." Please, please, please, people, do not speak death over your own life, such as, "I know I have this disease or that disease because I know my body and something is wrong." Life and death do truly lie in the power of the tongue, and you can speak life or death into your own situation, or in other words, you can speak salvation or damnation unto yourself. Think about it as it says in Proverbs 23:7, "For as he thinketh in his heart, so is he." That scripture basically says if you think it and believe it sincerely in your heart, it will come true—good or bad—and I'll prove it to you. Accordingly, if they say they have found nothing wrong, realize or understand it is conceivable that you may be in a spiritual battle/test.

It took me a long time to realize I was in a spiritual battle because my natural body began to deteriorate very quickly. The stress had become so intense I started to lose weight; I went from 143 pounds down to 103 pounds in two months. I was in and out of the doctor's office every week because I knew my body, and I could tell something was wrong and not normal. Once I realized that every trip to the doctor brought back a bunch of negative test results, no diagnosis, and a bunch of prescription medications, I eventually realized I was in a spiritual battle and not a natural, medical one. I was reminded of the lyrics in the song that says, "The battle is not yours but the Lord's." So, I say to you, recognize who your opponent is and learn his tricks, tactics, strengths, weaknesses, opportunities, strategies, and threats. Because no matter what, the battle really isn't yours. It's the Lord's, and it is for God to get the glory out of your situation.

For that reason alone, you already have the victory. Therefore, prepare yourself for battle and commence fighting! As we see in the book of Job, and even in our own lives, Satan cannot do anything without the permission of the Almighty God. God has allowed every test, trial, and situation that we have faced in life. So, we need to understand, know, and accept, "This is the Lord's doing; it is marvelous in our eyes" (Psalm 118:23).

Introduction

Sometimes when I don't see results or any progress, I begin to feel like what's the use, and I want to quit trying and give up. Then, I see a post on social media, or I receive a telephone call or a text from a friend, which reminds me Rome wasn't built in a day, and any progress is a good thing.

This book is based on actual events that took place in my life. While dealing with the events in this book, I began to do a lot of studying and reading the Bible. Job 1:1 reads, "There was a man in the land of Uz, whose name was Job; and that man was perfect and upright, and one that feared God, and eschewed evil." Then Job 1:6 reads, "Now there was a day when the sons of God came to present themselves before the LORD, and Satan came also among them." Finally, in Job 1:7, it reads, "And the LORD said unto Satan, Whence comest thou? Then Satan answered the LORD, and said, from going to and fro in the earth, and from walking up and down in it."

My point in saying all of this is that scholars believe it is uncertain who wrote the book of Job. But from reading the book of Job, we know God was there, the sons of God were there, and Satan was there, but it must be said that whoever wrote the book of Job had to be there also. How else would he know all that God said about Job and what God said to Satan?

Having nothing else to do but sit around and suffer, I began to calculate how long Job suffered. After calculating for about two months, I completed my calculations and determined that Job suffered approximately thirteen months, according to time as we calculate it today. In 1 Peter 3:8, it reads, "But, beloved, be not ignorant of this one thing, that one day is with the Lord as a thousand years, and a thousand years as one day." Clearly, the Scripture lets us know that God does not mark time the way man marks time. There aren't years, months, days, hours, minutes, or seconds to God. God is timeless; He is from everlasting to everlasting. After calculations were complete, I determined Job suffered approximately thirteen minutes in God's time.

I wrote the first six chapters of this book in one night. Then the attack became more severe. Exactly thirteen months to the day after I passed out in church, I was taken back to the hospital by ambulance when a sister from my old church brought food over for me to eat. The tests started all over again. I ended up back in the hospital and later was transferred to the psych ward. I lost so much weight. I wore a child size 10; my hair was falling out; I lost my first house and my car, later lost my new apartment due to mold (not to mention I'm allergic to mold); I flipped my truck over; I ended up in the psych ward again; I lost my second apartment due to seizures, and then I started working on the book again. Every time I approached the end of the test, Satan attacked me again, and the book was put on hold. I was under attack several times. During the attacks, it seemed as if the process just kept repeating itself.

Around 2015, everything seemed to be going well. Then the tests started all over again. I ended up in the Intensive Outpatient Center and was diagnosed with insomnia, severe depression, and bipolar disorder. After being sick for months, I realized my new home had a severe mold problem. The mold made it feel like I had the flu all the time. I had also been prescribed sleeping pills for the last ten years. If I did not have any sleeping pills, I would purchase over-the-counter sleep aids in order to sleep. Not only would I purchase the over-the-counter sleep aids, such as Tylenol PM, I would take way more than recommended. For instance, if the sleep aid said to take two tablets, more likely than not, I would take four or five. When I was prescribed Ambien for insomnia, the prescribed dosage was one pill per night. I recall a night when I took seven pills. Every time I woke up, I would take another pill just so I could fall asleep and stay asleep. When my son Timmy found me after taking all the sleeping pills, he contacted my mother, my sisters, and my niece because he knew something was wrong. My son Tommy would often question how I received all the bruises on my body. I normally would get them from sleepwalking after taking sleeping pills.

After the last attack, I felt extreme hopelessness and wanted to die. I asked the Lord daily to please take my life. I listened to the book of Job and quoted it frequently. I repented for myself and my children when I knelt to pray. I did not charge God foolishly, nor have I ever been angry with God. I explained it to someone like this: it's like me asking you whether I could borrow twenty dollars, and you told me no. How then can I get mad at you for not loaning me what is yours? It is the same way with God. It's His health. How can I become angry with God if He doesn't share it with me? The only difference between Job and me was that he suffered thirteen months; I suffered thirteen years, and God spared my children.

The meaning of twelve, which is considered a *perfect* number, is that it symbolizes *God's power and authority*, as well as serving as a perfect governmental foundation. It can also symbolize completeness or the nation of Israel as a whole. For example, Jacob, aka Israel, had twelve sons that were princes, and the twelve tribes of Israel descended from Jacob's sons and grandsons. Ishmael, who was born to Abraham through Hagar, also had twelve sons that were princes (Genesis 12:5–15). The number four derives its meaning from creation and/or order. On the fourth day of what is called "creation week," God completed the material universe. On this day, He brought into existence the sun, the moon, and all the stars (Genesis 1:14–19). Their purpose was not only to give light but also to divide the day from the night on earth, thus becoming a basic demarcation of time. They were also made to be a type of signal that would mark off the days, years, and seasons. The number thirteen is symbolic of rebellion and lawlessness. Nimrod, the mighty hunter who was "before the Lord" (meaning he tried to take the place of God, Genesis 10:9), was the thirteenth in Ham's line. (Ham was one of Noah's three sons who survived the flood.) Thirteen represents all the governments created by men and inspired by Satan in *outright rebellion* against the Eternal God. The number six symbolizes man and human weakness, the evils of Satan, and the manifestation of sin. Man was created on the sixth day. Men are appointed six days to labor.[2]

---

2 (retrieved from Biblestudy.org—meaning-of-numbers).

So, I'm going to tell you why I outlined what I did in the meaning of the numbers, and please keep in mind the numbers and the meanings because I will refer back to them before I complete the introduction.

Leeta was a woman who lived in Indianapolis. She was spiritually mature (*perfect #12*), lived a holy life, and hated evil. She had two sons. Leeta was financially stable, had a nice home and a nice car, and she was well respected in the community and at work. Sometimes Leeta's sons didn't always walk according to the ways of the Lord. So, when Leeta would go before God to pray, she would repent for her sons and for herself concerning whatever they have done and/or said that was contrary to the ways of the Lord.

One day, the sons of God came before the Lord, and Satan came also. The Lord asked Satan,

"Where have you been?"

Walking to and fro on the earth, he answered,

"Have you thought about my servant, Leeta? There really isn't anyone like her in all the earth. She is doing all she knows how to do to live right; she hates evil; and she trusts and fears God."

Then Satan answered,

"Does she trust and fear You with everything in life? If she does, it is because You have always blessed her. She has an abundance of everything, and it seems like she has money to burn. I guarantee You if You take away all that she has, she will curse You to Your face. Take your best shot."

God said. "All that she owns is yours, but don't touch her life."

Satan took off running and began to wreak havoc in Leeta's life (God's power and authority #12). Leeta lost her home and her car in bankruptcy; the IRS froze her bank accounts, including her child support checks; and she was no longer getting a paycheck from her job because she had been and continued to be off work sick. Leeta's children began to misbehave in school and at home. However, Leeta continued to serve God and did all that she knew how to do to live a holy life.

Again, there was a day when the sons of God came before the Lord, and Satan came also.

"Where have you been?" God questioned Satan.

"I was on earth walking all around," he answered.

"Have you thought about my servant, Leeta? There certainly isn't anyone like her in all the earth. She is doing all she knows how to do to live right; she still hates evil; she still trusts and fears Me; and she still believes in Me. She never said anything negative about me and surely never cursed me to my face, and she did all of this even though you moved Me against her to destroy her without a reason," God offered. (Order #4—God created everything perfectly and in order).

Satan quickly answered the Lord and said, "Yeah, that's true, she may have held strong, but it was only because You never allowed me to touch her body. People will get over material things, but if You let me make her sick, I know that will surely make her curse You to Your face."

"Fine, you may make her as sick as you want, but do not kill her," God instructed. Satan then left the presence of the Lord quickly and once again began to cause mayhem in Leeta's life. (Satan in outright rebellion #13 against *man* or *mankind* #6). Just as I wrote this book, I know exactly who wrote Job, and please allow me to be the first to tell you. Job wrote the book of Job. Job was there; he talked with God, and God let him know there were some things in his life that God wasn't pleased with and just how he (Job) measured up to the big scheme of things in God's plan.

When I first began to get attacked, I had no idea what was going on or why it was happening. Approximately thirteen months later, I realized I was in a spiritual battle. I began working toward learning all I knew to learn about how to fight in the spirit. I pulled out the church directory and contacted a sister because she is the only person in church I ever heard pray against spirits. After that, I basically refused to allow her to get rid of me. I followed her around like a little puppy, learning all I could about this thing called spiritual warfare.

In 2005, the boys and I moved in with someone because our apartment was filled with mold. During that time, I was a member of Love Apostolic Fellowship (Love), but we attended Living Word Tabernacle Apostolic Faith Church's (Living Word) first reunion for their eightieth church anniversary. That is the church where I received the Holy Ghost and the church where my mother still attends today. Well, during this time, I was deep in the midst of my spiritual battle, and I was suffering greatly. I was off work on medical leave, physically sick, and the boys were acting up in school and at home. During the anniversary service, the Bishop that was preaching began to prophesy. He would go over to people, lay his hand on them, and start telling them what God had spoken about their lives. Before he could even finish what he was saying, they would take off running and dancing around the church. I don't believe even one of them ever heard the full prophecy.

I sat in my seat, and I thought, *Lord, I know what You have spoken to me, but could You please allow him to prophesy to me to confirm Your word. Because You said I would be in the palace, and I feel like I'm in the pit?* The bishop finished prophesying and took his seat without saying a word to me.

Soon it was time for the offering, and the Bishop was asked to take the offering. The bishop began to talk, and he stated that God told him twelve people would sow into the church double. He stood there for a minute, and then he looked around because no one said anything. He repeated what he said, and then he clarified, "What that means is this church is eighty years old, and God told me twelve people would sow double, so that means twelve people are going to give 160 dollars in this offering," he explained. By that time, God said to me, "Give it." I thought, *God, I'm off work, and I don't even have money to give.* Nevertheless, I hesitantly reached into my purse, pulled out my checkbook, and began to write the check.

The bishop went on to say, "I need the twelve people to stand right now." I was still in the midst of writing my check, so I stood with my checkbook placed on the back of the pew in front of me, and I finished writing the check. I was sitting in the second row of the church, so I was unable to see who else had stood. By the time I finished writing the check, the bishop had said, "I need my twelve people to line up right here at the end of this pew." He pointed directly at the end of the row where I was sitting.

I walked to the end of the pew, and I stood in line. It took a little more prodding, but eventually, he got twelve people to give 160 dollars. When all the people lined up behind me, the bishop walked over to me and said, "Since you were the first to stand and sow into this church double, God said, 'I'm going to bless you double.' You will have your own business, and no bank or the Small Business Administration will help you, but you will be able to do it with all your own money. You will be a millionaire, and your family will be blessed because of you." He placed his hand on my head and said, "And I seal it in the name of Jesus; now go take your offering." I walked off and gave my offering.

Later that night, several people came up to me after church and commented about how I was a millionaire and how rich I was, and so forth. I believed God, and I knew He was telling the truth because He said the exact same thing God told me. When the Small Business Administration sent me the information I requested so that I could start my own business over a year earlier in May of 2004, I never even opened the envelope. By the time the envelope arrived, God had already told me they could not help me. However, living in the moment, I knew none of it had happened yet, because I, along with the boys, were still sleeping at my friend's apartment because my apartment had mold. Then an Evangelist came over to me and said, "You already knew that, didn't you, Sister? God already told you that. Didn't He?"

"Yes, ma'am," I replied.

"I could tell when I saw Bishop talking to you," she said. "You have a good evening."

"You too," I said as I walked away. I walked away with a feeling of hope. I thought, *Finally, I am getting ready to get out of this thing.* Thirteen months was the longest I had been in a fiery test like that, where the heat never seemed to let up.

However, you must have guessed that the heat did not stop then. I didn't see the temperature or the flames go down until around 2007, when I was able to purchase another home and I started a different job, but I was still working for the federal government. One time my Sunday school teacher said, "If God promises you something, then get ready to wait for it." We all kind of sat quietly in class after that, and then she went on to say, "Think about it. If you get a blessing, most times, it is a surprise. When God makes you a promise, just like He did Abraham, it takes years for that thing to happen." She was exactly right.

This book is being published in 2022, and as I look back over my life, God did exactly what He said He was going to do. I no longer suffer from those conditions and attacks. One of the conditions I was diagnosed with was cerebral lupus, and that is the reason I was losing the activity of my brain, according to the doctors. I was told by the end of 2004, "Your brain will be mush, and you will be a vegetable. You won't even be able to dress yourself." But as you all know, God delivered me from that condition, and He restored the functions of my brain because not only did it not turn to mush, I was able to complete my bachelor's degree with a 3.89 GPA on a 4.0 scale. I went on to earn my master's degree, and with the help of the Lord, I achieved a 4.0 GPA on a 4.0 scale. By the time this book is published, I will have owned two homes at the same time, owned two cars at the same time, and it was the first time my bank account more than doubled. I'm currently retired, but before

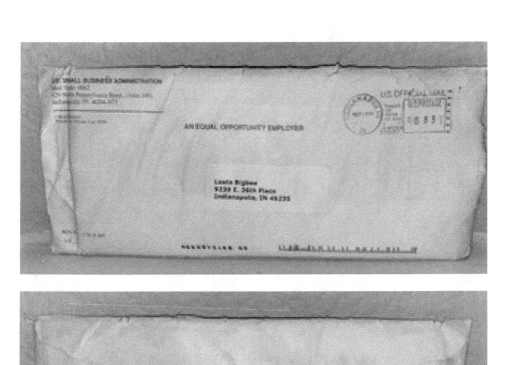

U.S. SMALL BUSINESS ADMINISTRATION

AN EQUAL OPPORTUNITY EMPLOYER

U.S. OFFICIAL MAIL

Lizeta Bigbee
9339 E. 36th Place
Indianapolis, IN 46235

I retired, my salary had more than doubled. Now, I only work for myself if I desire. Additionally, in 2019, I was able to pay off a hundred percent of my debt, including two homes and two cars.

Thank you, Lord. You just keep on doing great things for me. To God be the glory for the things He has done! Therefore, it is true when I think of His goodness and what He has done for me, and when I think of His goodness and how He set me free, I could dance, dance, dance, dance, dance, dance, dance, dance all night!

INDIANA WESLEYAN UNIVERSITY

REGISTRAR'S OFFICE ▲ 4201 S. Washington St. ▲ Marion, IN 46953 ▲ 765-677-2131

Issued To:
Miss Leeta S. Bigbee
4337 Trace Wood Dr
Indianapolis, IN 46254

Transcript Of:
Bigbee
Leeta S.
DOB: 11/11
Student ID: 0529801

Indiana Wesleyan University
Degree Earned: Associate of Science
Awarded: 08/10/2002
Majors: Business

Indiana Wesleyan University
Degree Earned: Bachelor of Science
Awarded: 12/18/2004
Honors: Summa Cum Laude
Majors: Business Information Systems

Indiana Wesleyan University
Degree Earned: Master of Science
Awarded: 04/25/2009
Majors: Management

UNDERGRADUATE COURSEWORK

---------------03/20/2000 to 04/10/2000------------
UNV111   Philosophy and Practice of   2.00 A
          Lifelong Learning I

	Attempt	Earn	GPA Credit	Points	GPA
Cum	2.00	2.00	2.00	7.40	3.70

---------------04/17/2000 to 05/15/2000------------
ENG140   Communications I   3.00 B

	Attempt	Earn	GPA Credit	Points	GPA
Cum	5.00	5.00	5.00	16.40	3.28

---------------05/22/2000 to 06/26/2000------------
ENG141   Communications II   3.00 A

	Attempt	Earn	GPA Credit	Points	GPA
Cum	8.00	8.00	8.00	28.40	3.55

---------------07/10/2000 to 08/07/2000------------
BUS105   Introduction to American   3.00 A
          Business

	Attempt	Earn	GPA Credit	Points	GPA
Cum	11.00	11.00	11.00	40.40	3.67

---------------08/14/2000 to 09/11/2000------------
PHE140   Concepts of Wellness   2.00 A

	Attempt	Earn	GPA Credit	Points	GPA
Cum	13.00	13.00	13.00	48.40	3.72

---------------09/18/2000 to 10/16/2000------------
BIL102   New Testament Survey   3.00 A

	Attempt	Earn	GPA Credit	Points	GPA
Cum	16.00	16.00	16.00	60.40	3.77

Clarian Health
Methodist · IU · Riley

Health Information Mgmt
P.O. Box 1367
DG-402
Indpls, IN 46206-1367

DISCHARGE SUMMARY

Dictated by   Robert J. Alonso, M.D.
Dictated 07/30/2004   000109034 1365696f
Transcribed   08/02/2004 3:20 P   900

 Eigbee, Leeta S.

cc: Marlene A. Aldo-Benson, M.D.
      Robert J. Alonso, M.D.
      Adrienne R. Bowne, M.D.
      Josue Villalta, M.D.

DATE OF ADMISSION: 07/25/2004

DATE OF DISCHARGE: 07/30/2004

ADMISSION DIAGNOSIS: Seizure disorder.

DISCHARGE DIAGNOSES:
1. Seizure disorder.
2. Positive ANA (1:640 homogeneous pattern).
3. Cervical and lumbar spondylosis, status post epidural steroid injection.
4. Endometriosis.
5. Interstitial cystitis.
6. History of depression.
7. History of vasovagal syncope.

COMPLICATION/INFECTION: None.

CONDITION ON DISCHARGE: Improved.

DISPOSITION: The patient was discharged to home in the care of her family in satisfactory condition.

DIET: Regular.

INSTRUCTIONS: Driving has been proscribed. The patient is not to work at heights or in situations where transient lapses of consciousness place her or others at risk.

DISCHARGE MEDICATIONS:
1. Dilantin 100 mg t.i.d.
2. Tylenol 1 or 2 p.o. q.4 to 6h. p.r.n.

HOSPITAL COURSE: The patient is a 36-year-old, female, admitted through the Methodist Hospital emergency room for evaluation and treatment of a series of 3 generalized tonic clonic seizures. The patient was in usual state of satisfactory health until she noted the onset of dull aching bitemporal headache 3 to 4 days prior to admission.

While at church, she experienced an abrupt episode and loss of consciousness followed by tonic clonic seizures which was repeated in route to the Methodist Hospital emergency room. She received Ativan and Dilantin for prophylaxis. CT scan of the head revealed no abnormalities. MRI scan of the head revealed no abnormalities.

COPY TO: Josue Villalta, M.D.

Diagnostic lumbar puncture revealed no evidence of acute or chronic senescent infection. Screening evaluation for occult vasculitis, CNS/systemic infection resulted in positive finding of ANA at 1:640 homogeneous pattern.

Rheumatology consultation was obtained and several additional collagen vascular serologies have been drawn, the results of which are pending for workup of the latter disorder. Toxicology screen revealed no abnormalities. EEG and likewise revealed no abnormalities.

On 7/29/04, the patient experienced several "seizures" characterized by generalized tremulousness with no post ictal phase, no tongue biting or incontinence.

Psychiatric consultation was obtained in view of the history of anxiety and depression, with recommendation for administration of Effexor therapy, though this was declined by the patient.

FOLLOW-UP: She is to be seen in follow-up evaluation in neurology clinic in 1 month, by endocrinology in 1 month, and by her endocrinologist in 1 month.

LABORATORY DATA: Dilantin level 14.8, West Nile titer 0.29 (normal less than 1.3), WBC 11,500, hemoglobin 14.6, hematocrit 43.1, platelet count 263,000, sedimentation rate 5, sodium 137, potassium 4.0, chloride 107, bicarbonate 19, anion gap 11, BUN 7, creatinine 0.9, glucose 148, calcium 9.3, alkaline phosphatase 55, ALT 28, AST 24, bilirubin of 0.3, albumin of 3.5, CK 90, CK-MB index less than 1. Urine toxicology screen, cocaine, opiates, cannabinoid, benzodiazepine, barbiturates, amphetamines negative. CSF xanthochromia negative. CSF WBC 1, CSF RBC 760, CSF glucose 65, CSF protein 50. Urine culture no growth, CSF culture no growth. ANA positive 1:640 homogeneous pattern. VDRL nonreactive. EKG reveals normal sinus rhythm, rate 90 per minute, within normal limits. Cardiac telemetry, sinus rhythm, sinus tachycardia, rate 80-130. Echocardiogram normal.

END OF REPORT

STAFF/ATTENDING PHYSICIAN - Robert J. Alonso, M.D.

Electronically Signed By
Robert J. Alonso, M.D. 08/04/2004 07:24

COPY TO: Josue Villalta, M.D.

No More Fear

The dreams I had for my life seem to have taken a backseat to fear. When I think of how I allowed fear to control my life, I realize I really didn't have anything to be afraid of at all. The things I feared the most were all in my head, and I personally created them with each and every dream I had for myself.

My past experiences, let-downs, and disappointments helped me to slowly put my dreams on the back burner, with thoughts of defeat, rejection, procrastination, and, most of all, fear. No one had to tell me I couldn't do it because I continued to tell myself daily. However, today is the day I decided not to allow procrastination, feelings of defeat, rejection, insecurity, and, yes, even fear to control my life anymore. Today is the day I actually wake up, stop dreaming, and begin moving toward the person God ordained me to be with *no more fear*.

Normally, I don't look at things the same way as everyone else. I realize this, and I just call it Leeta's Logic. I also realize it is good to hear how others view topics and get different ideas and have conversations with diverse people. I'm the type of person who will get on the elevator and just start talking to whoever is on the elevator about whatever topic is on my mind.

However, in doing so, I've also come to realize that the mind is a powerful tool. When I was a child, I remember a commercial that would come on television that said, "The mind is a terrible thing to waste." I really didn't understand it at that time, but now that I am an adult, I understand the meaning behind the commercial. I think back to times when I was in basic training and during physical training (PT), the drill sergeant would yell out, "If you don't mind, it don't matter!" Since I am a thinker, I began to think about what he said, and I would think to myself, *I do mind*, and shortly after, I would stop running or stop whatever other exercise I would be doing at that time. As soldiers, we would also have to yell out the phrase, "More PT, more PT. We like it, we love it, we want more of it. Make it hurt, Drill Sergeant, make it hurt!" And most times, I would just move my mouth and not actually say the words.

When I've gone to physical training, whether with my personal trainer or to a fitness class, during training, I tell myself that I am there to improve myself. I remind myself the trainer is already in shape; he/she can leave anytime he/she wants. Once during a kickboxing class, the trainer yelled out, "I'm here for you all." He said that because he saw the class had begun to slack off. If there is no class, then there is no need for the trainer to be there. Oftentimes when I exercise now, I rehearse the words in my head, *More PT. I like it, I love it. Make it hurt, Drill Sergeant, make it hurt.* Because I realize that exercising is to benefit me, I often try to convince myself that I don't mind doing it.

Don't allow your mind to tell your body/mind that you can't; you're not good enough; that's too big; that's too small, or just to be idle—because an idle mind is the devil's workshop. Don't allow the devil to create or work on anything in your mind.

I said this to say, sometimes, when things come up that I feel are too hard, too long, too wide, or too deep, I remind myself that if you don't mind, it doesn't matter. Therefore, I must convince myself that whatever the situation is, it isn't as bad as it seems. I exercise my mind so that it thinks positive thoughts and not negative ones. Just as with any exercise, it takes time to build up strength. Practice makes perfect.

God has given us a great tool called the mind, but it can also be a deadly one if we don't use it properly. Consequently, today and every day, use your mind to remind yourself how great God is; how happy you are; how the situation isn't impossible; how you don't mind doing this or that; how you don't mind waiting on the Lord; how God has brought you through many tough times before, and He can do it again and again. Always remember—if you don't mind, it doesn't matter.

CHAPTER 1

Whatever It Takes, Lord

January 2006

"Mommy, are you okay?" A small voice called out from the backseat as I went in and out of consciousness.

"Are you all right, lady?"

"Are you able to talk?"

"Can you hear me? I'm a nurse!" the voice cried out from inside the car.

I can hear what you're saying, but I'm unable to answer, I thought to myself as my body lay tangled up in the airbags and rubbish. *What's going on?* I thought as my hands began to wave uncontrollably through the fog and smoke.

"She's deaf; does anyone know sign language?" the nurse screamed to the onlookers on the outside of the truck. "I'm here to help you. Just hold on; I'm here; just hold on. I have to stabilize your neck—please don't move," she said. "Did anyone call the ambulance? I believe her neck is broken," she said as she placed the stabilizing brace around my neck.

Two years earlier: July 2004

What makes people lose their minds? What exactly is losing your mind? It's not like you don't know where it is. You never really lost it at all; it's still in your head. But what makes people start to think in the peculiar way that they do when they believe or say they are losing, or have lost, their minds? We are supposed to have the mind of Christ, right? So, I guess in order to have the mind of Christ, we all must lose our own minds at some point in our lives, right? If nothing else, we need to decrease our way of thinking and increase in thinking like Christ. These were certainly some of the strangest times of my life, and I really felt like I was losing my mind. Was I gaining the mind of Christ? There were times when I felt like I was, and at other times, well... I just didn't know.

Things seemed to be going great. It was Saturday night, and I had just invited my niece Stephanie and my friend Kevin from my study group over for dinner and a movie. They were both feeling down that day and needed a little cheering up. I enjoy cooking, so I prepared one of my Leeta specials: grilled shrimp and chicken marinated in white wine and olive oil, with tomatoes, bell peppers, mushrooms, and fresh garlic over pasta with Alfredo sauce, parmesan cheese, and cheesy garlic bread on the side.

While we were all eating, the phone rang, and it was my friend Kelly. Kelly and I have been friends for many years. I believe she was returning my call. I had been trying to get in touch with her because I wanted to give my dog away, and I figured she would be the best person to start with. Kelly really loves dogs, and I had given her my dog Badu in the past—that dog was crazy, though. It didn't matter; Kelly loved that dog and treated it well. Badu was extremely hyper, and he ran out into the street, was hit by a car, and he didn't survive. Therefore, I figured she would be looking for another dog by now. "Hey, how are you, Kelly?" I questioned.

"Ah, Leeta Bigbee," she said in a joking voice. She knew from the way I was talking to her that I wanted something. I thought I might be on the phone for a while, trying to convince Kelly about this dog. So, I motioned to Stephanie and Kevin to continue eating and watching the movie without me.

Now you see, I hadn't really kept in touch with Kelly; as we grew older, our diverse lifestyles had us pursuing different paths in life. She had recently been open with her lesbian relationship, and I had received the Holy Ghost, so we just didn't have much in common anymore. "Well, uummmm, remember that cute little dog I brought over a while back?" I asked kind of sheepishly.

"Don't even try it, Leeta Bigbee!" she said in a loud voice.

"But the boys and I are just too busy," I replied as if I was ready to cry. "You are just so much better with pets than we are," I continued to complain.

"I'm not taking him. I just can't right now. I told you to get a cat; they can take care of themselves, or a fish or some type of pet you don't have to take care of," she continued to scold, as she had always done.

"I know, I know," I said as I realized I would be stuck with the dog.

Changing the conversation quickly, she asked, "So, what's going on in your life? You still go to your mother's church?"

"No, I belong to a different church, but we still believe in the same things," I said.

"So, what does that mean? What do you believe in?" she asked.

"We still believe in what Jesus taught the apostles: one Lord, one faith, and one baptism," I replied.

"So, where does lesbianism fit in to all of this?" she said sincerely.

I told her to go to Genesis chapter 19, so I could point out in the Scriptures at how God destroyed Sodom and Gomorrah because the people in that city refused to turn from their ungodly ways, which included homosexuality. It was not that homosexuality was a sin greater than any other sin but that they refused to stop the sin. I began to break down the meaning of the word Sodom in order to help her understand a little better. The word Sodom comes from the words [3]sodomy and/or [4]sodomite, meaning anal or oral copulation with a member of the same or opposite sex, also copulation with an animal. (*Merriam-Webster's Online Dictionary* 2007)

"Homosexuality is something that I was born with," Kelly said, defending her position.

"No, Kelly, homosexualy is a choice; each person was born in the image of God, and we were all born to be with the opposite sex," I insisted.

---

3 "Middle English, from Anglo-French *sodomie*, from Late Latin *Sodoma* Sodom; from the homosexual proclivities of the men of the city in Genesis 19:1–11" (Merriam-Webster's Online Dictionary 2007).*Merriam Webster's Online Dictionary* 2007
4 One who practices sodomy. *Merriam Webster's Online Dictionary* 2007

"Oh, so you think it is a choice?" she asked.

I told Kelly, "I know that homosexuality is a choice because in 2 Peter 3:9, it says, 'He is not willing that any should perish but that everyone should repent.' Homosexuals will not inherit the kingdom of God, according to Galatians 5:19–21. Then, in Ephesians 5:1–3, the Scripture says, 'Don't let any of these things be found among you once you become a saint.' If the Lord destroyed everyone in Sodom and Gomorrah because of their sins, including homosexuality, and if He created them to be homosexuals, then 2 Peter 3 would be a lie because He would have created them just so He could destroy them. Homosexuals, as well as others practicing sin (heterosexual sins as well), have a choice. But let's just say, for argument's sake, you were born that way, and so was everyone else in the LGBTQ+ community. Every one of us was born in sin (regardless of what sin it is), and we all have to be born again and change our behavior from the things we did before Christ came into our lives."

"Thanks, Leeta, if you say so," she said. Understanding some may receive the Word of God and others may not, we said our goodbyes and hung up the telephone. I then grabbed my plate of food and joined Stephanie and Kevin in the family room to continue watching the movie, and there we sat, eating and talking, until the wee hours of the morning. When they left, I was feeling pretty good, so before I went to bed, I picked out my clothes for church in the morning.

"Thank you for waking me up this morning. Thank you for starting me on my way, and thank you for the activity of my limbs. Thank you for food, shelter, and clothing. Thank you for my health and strength. Thank you for watching over me and my children. Thank you for being my protector and for keeping my children and me from dangers seen and unseen. And, Lord, thank you for allowing my shoes to arrive in time to wear them to church tomorrow. Help me to see myself as I really am, Lord. I don't want to just be in the church anymore—I want to be in Christ. I really want to love You and do Your will. Help me to see Your face in peace. Help me to make it to the kingdom. Lord, please forgive me, Tommy, and Timmy for anything that we have said and/or done that is not like you.

"Lord, please allow me to be an effective witness. Allow me to be surrounded by people who want to be saved for real. Help my home to be peaceful. Lord, help me to love everyone the way I am supposed to. Help me to lose weight without making myself sick. Lord, help me not to be sleepy all the time. And, Lord, please, do these things, no matter what. In Jesus' name. Amen."

I prayed to the Lord that night, mostly the same way I had prayed every other night. But this time, I was sincere about praying. I wanted God to change some things in me. I wasn't sure how God was going to change me; I just wanted Him to do it. "Help me, Lord, and do it any way You have to. Just whatever it takes, Lord, please, in Jesus's name, Amen." I spoke those final words before I got up off my knees. At that time, I didn't understand how powerful those words were, but I would soon find out.

The next morning, I woke up on time for church and was ready to start my day, feeling good in my spirit. I could not wait to get to church to tell my sister Sharon how God allowed me to witness to Kelly because I hadn't really witnessed to anyone before. The boys and I got dressed, the birds were singing, and the smell of sunshine was in the air. What a glorious morning it was! Don't get me wrong: Timmy, age eight, and Tommy, age eleven, were doing their normal arguing and running around the house, but nothing could break my spirit. I just felt good in my sanctified soul, as the older folks would say.

I knew I was clean and looking good for going to church. I don't necessarily think I'm a pretty person, but I know one thing for sure; I clean up well when I want to. Today was Family and Friends Day, and I wanted to clean up well. I had on a pair of multicolored shoes and carried the matching purse that I had prayed would arrive in time for this day; and they had arrived in the mail the day before. God is good, and He surely answers prayers. I had been waiting on those shoes for about three months because they were back-ordered. I hate it when items are listed, and they aren't available. But this time, it worked out just right. I knew I was looking good, and no one could tell me different.

The drive to church seemed to be longer that day. "Get the door for me, Tommy," I said as we walked up the church stairs. *Wow! Look at all these people,* I thought as I began to walk into the church. "Come on, boys; stay close so we can find a good seat," I said while I grabbed Timmy by the hand. The boys were walking close to me, kind of crowding me because I was walking a little slower than normal. I wanted everyone to see what I was wearing, so I had to take my time to get to my seat. *Family and Friends Day was just like I thought it would be. I knew the church would be packed,* I thought, as I took my time finding my seat.

I wore a bright yellow dress with a matching jacket. I mean, I thought I was looking good—you should have seen me. I had gone to the African beauty salon the day before to get my hair braided. Did you know they charged at least 180 dollars to do the braids? Most times, they braid extremely fast, and I guess that was part of the reasoning for the high cost. They braided my hair in six hours, and the braids were super small. The smaller the braid, the longer it takes to braid the hair, which means the higher the cost for the customer and the higher the pay for the stylist.

When people go to get their hair braided (*don't lose focus; we are still in church*, I'm just thinking), normally, there will be two stylists braiding at the same time on a person's head. But it was a little different with me. I know they hated to braid my hair. I am overly tender-headed, and I kept scooting down in the chair. You know what I mean? The exact same way most of us did when we were younger, and our mothers kept hitting us in the back of the heads with the brush she had dipped in a cup of hot water. "Sit up, sit up!" Getting my hair braided brought about lots of childhood memories.

The stylists were speaking in a language I couldn't understand; however, they were looking in my direction. So, I felt as if they were talking about me, and I had already interpreted what they were saying in my head. No, I don't speak any other languages, but I have a vivid imagination, and I could imagine them saying, "I hope she doesn't ever come back here with her tender-headed self." It didn't matter, though, because I knew I would be back. Seeing that my hair was looking too good to stay away.

I finally arrived at my seat in church. I sat by my sister Sharon, who was sitting next to her husband, Bob. I began to speak to everyone, you know, "Praise the Lord! Praise the Lord," with that quick side-to-side church hand wave and half-cocked smile. Tommy sat in front of me, and, of course, little Timmy sat right next to me as he always did. "Hey, Sharon, there's Mom," I said as I pointed toward my mother coming down the aisle. Mom doesn't go to the same church as Sharon and me, but today was Family and Friends Day, and she came out to support us. The church was super hyped that day: People were praising the Lord, hands were clappin' and feet were stompin', and testimony service had just started.

I'm not really the testifying type. I didn't really care for testimony service until I started attending Love Fellowship (Love). Before then, testimony service was super long and boring, with a bunch of people standing up and telling all their business. Sometimes it was still that way at Love. It took me a while to realize that testimony service was supposed to be people talking about the goodness of God and the great things that He has/had done. Revelation 12:13 reads, "They overcame by the blood of the Lamb and by the word of their testimony." The people of God need to hear about the goodness of God. It wasn't that God hadn't done anything for me; I was just too scared to testify. Any time I would stand to testify, my knees would start shaking, and my heart would start beating so hard I could feel it in my brain. My legs would get indescribably weak, and my hands would go numb. I mean, God was good and all, but I just couldn't do it. I had testified before, so it wasn't like I had never thanked God for what He had done for me. I just wasn't going to do it all the time.

"Guess who I talked to last night," I said as I leaned over to Sharon.

"Who?" she said.

"Girl, Kelly. You won't believe all the stuff we talked about," I said as I began to replay the conversation with her. "Was she receptive to the Word?" Sharon asked.

"I don't know, but I believe she will think about the conversation," I said as I picked up the tambourine and began to play. That was another thing I knew I could do well; I knew I could play the tambourine. You couldn't tell me that I was not one of the best tambourine players in the church. However, I had begun to have problems with my right arm. It had become weak, prohibiting me from playing for long periods of time. So, usually, I would wait until the choir director would cut the music. Y'all know what I am talking about; when the choir director cuts off the music and the bass drum and bass guitar are kickin', and all the hands are double clappin', and it's feelin' kind of "churchy" in the place. Yeah, that's what I'm talking about.

I would pick up the tambourine, jump to my feet, and start playing as loud as I could, and I would make the tambourine make that hard, poppin' sound. *Whooh, I am tearing up this tambourine,* I thought, as I beat that thing with all my might. There is a Scripture in 1 Corinthians 10:31 that reads, "In all that you do, do it unto the glory of God"; however, as I think back, I really wasn't doing that unto the glory of God. I was doing that so I could be seen and so people could hear how well I could play the tambourine. I guess I was doing it unto the glory of Leeta.

After jamming on that tambourine for a while, I sat back down in my seat. "Wham!" is the only thing I felt. *What the heck was that?* I thought to myself as I tried to focus. *Ouch, there it is again.* It felt as if the Incredible Hulk had reached behind himself as far as he could, threw a punch as hard as he could, and punched me dead smack in my forehead. It felt as if my head was going to explode! I was barely able to see in front of me. My eyes started to tear up.

I felt as though a vice was on my head, and the vice was getting tighter and tighter. I began to pray for myself while rubbing my temples, but it didn't seem to help. My head began spinning, and my vision was getting blurry. *What is going on?* I thought as I felt my body feeling weighed down and heavy. My body felt heavy, and it was hard for me to move. I slowly leaned forward and tapped Tommy on the shoulder. "What?" he snapped as he glanced over his shoulder to look at me.

"Touch Elder Roads," I gasped. I recalled that in James 5:14–15, it says something like we are to call for the elders of the church if anyone is sick, so that is what I was attempting to do.

"What? Who are you talking about?" he said as if I were getting on his nerves.

"Please help me," I whispered as I tried to focus. I pointed to the seat in front of Tommy. "I need your help, Tommy, please. Touch Elder Roads... Uhhhhh, I think that's his name," I said, kind of confused. "Tell him I need him to get some elders and meet me in the back of the lobby to pray. I'm feeling sick."

Now you see, Tommy and I had never gotten along well. I really thought he hated me. Since Tommy was in the second grade, he had an attitude that made me feel as if he really didn't like me, kind of like, *Why did I have to have this person as my mother?* "Him," I pointed, "get him right there in the tan suit," I said with authority as I pointed again to show Tommy who I was talking about. This time, Tommy knew I meant business.

When I saw Elder Roads get up and go to his right, I got up too and went in the opposite direction to meet him in the back of the church. I went in the opposite direction because I didn't want to be a disturbance in the church. I was only about three or four people away from the end of the pew if I went toward the left, so I did. I also didn't want anyone to notice that something was wrong with me; I felt I was looking just a little too cute to be sick, and it was no one's business anyway.

When I got up to leave the church, I felt weights pulling and weighing me back down. I turned around to say, "Let go of me," because it felt like someone was holding on to me and pulling me down. But when I turned around, no one was touching me or even paying attention to me. I felt my body moving very slowly, kind of like the Bionic Woman when she would run fast. I'm not sure if you remember the Bionic Woman, but you can look her up on the internet. The Bionic Woman had supernatural strength and could run extremely fast. She ran so fast that the naked eye could not see her while she was running, so when they showed her running on television, they would show her in slow motion. It felt like I was walking in slow motion, just like I saw the Bionic Woman do on television.

The song of the Bionic Woman played in my head (look it up), with the sound of little eighth notes as I slid my way past the people on the pew: "Dun, dun, dun; (rest) (now two sixteenth notes) dun, dun, (back to eighth notes) dun, dun, dun, dun." The song sounds a lot better if you put the notes altogether. Anyway, as I slowly put one foot in front of the other, I saw people's heads turning toward me. *What are they looking at?* I thought because as I walked, it felt as if all the eyes in the church were on me. Everyone was looking at me and turning their heads toward me in slow motion. Everything and everyone, including me, seemed to be moving in slow motion. *This is the weirdest feeling*, was the thought that floated through my clouded head as I tried to make it to the end of the pew.

After what seemed to be about fifteen minutes, I finally made it to the end of my pew. As I looked down the aisle, *wow!* was the only thing I could think since it felt like I was entering the Boston Marathon. The usher and the door appeared to be so far away, and I didn't know how I would make it that far. As fear began to enter my heart, I thought, *Help me, Lord. Please, help me to make it down the aisle. I just need to get to the lobby for prayer.* I began to walk down the aisle to the back of the church, and it took everything I ever thought I had in me to move. My legs and my feet felt unusually heavy; they just didn't want to move. As I looked around, I thought *I must look like I am struggling* because the people in the church were still watching me, and they had funny looks on their faces. When I got closer to Sister Karen, the usher at the end of the aisle, she reached out her hands toward me, also in slow motion, and said, "Arrrrrre yoooooou oooooooookaaaayyyy?"

"Wham!" was all I heard as my body hit the floor like dead weight.

Myyyyyyyyyyy shooooooooooes? I thought, as I fell down on the ground and my shoe went flying across the church floor, not my new shooooooes.

"Oooooooh myyyyyyyyyyyy God!" Sister Karen screamed in slow motion once again as she watched me hit the floor.

After I hit the floor, I realized I could still hear Sister Karen talking, which meant I wasn't unconscious at all.

13

Why can I hear her talking? I thought while I was lying on the floor at the end of the aisle in the house of the Lord, unable to move my legs or my arms. Suddenly, I realized I couldn't open my eyes. *What is going on?* I thought to myself, this is really crazy. The fear was overwhelming as I began to panic. *Why am I laying on the floor if I didn't pass out? People don't just fall down, lose their super-cute shoes, and then can't move their arms and/or legs for no reason.* After thinking for a while, I began to cry out, Help me, Lord! Help me, Lord! Help me, Lord! Help me, Lord! Help me, Lord! Help me, Lord! Weights, heaviness, and deadness are all my body felt. *What is wrong with me?* I continued to think. I just couldn't figure this thing out.

"Cover her up," he said.

"Grab her shoes," another person mentioned.

"Pull her dress down," another one ranted.

"Grab her under her arms; you'll get a better grip," he said.

These were the cries I heard being called out around me as my body hung lifeless, my legs dragging behind me, and the soles of my feet facing toward the ceiling as I was carried out of the church in the arms of men I didn't even recognize.

"You'll be okay, Sis; just don't worry," Elder Sharp said in a calm and pleasant voice. He and another brother carried me to a room and sat me down in a little, red, hard, rubber, stackable chair. And then the questions began:

"Are you a diabetic?"

"Are you anemic?"

"Have you eaten?"

"Are you this?"

"Are you that?"

Questions, questions, questions. They were throwing so many questions at me so fast, I didn't even know who was talking, nor did I have time to answer or fully understand what they were asking me. I finally regained control over my arms, and I began to wipe my tears. The tears were running down my face, as if some child had left the faucet on while brushing his/her teeth, and then, hearing his/her mother's voice scream out from the other room, "Turn off that water; money doesn't grow on trees!" That is exactly how it was; the tears flowed profusely.

"Don't cry, Sister Leeta. It'll be alright," a warm voice spoke out from the small group that huddled around me.

"Are your legs okay?"[5] Bishop asked.

"They are, are, are ha ha heavy," I replied as I continued to weep. While breathing hard with short, quick breaths, with my shoulders hunching up and down, I spoke, sounding like a five-year-old that couldn't stop crying after a real good whipping.

"Can you feel them?" asked Sister Diana. Sister Diana is very soft-spoken, has a slender build, and is maybe about five feet, seven inches, but only about a size 8. She seems timid and doesn't say much at all. If you don't look, you may never know she is there. She has dark eyebrows and long dark hair; a pretty lady who kind of reminds me of a school teacher. When she smiles, she just makes you want to smile back at her. She is very sweet—just very sweet.

"I know my legs are there," I said. "But... but... I just can't make them move," I sighed as I exhaled a deep breath. They felt like little pins and needles, like little prickly things were crawl-

---

5 Overseer, one having spiritual or ecclesiastical supervision.

ing all over my legs. I just couldn't explain it to them. My head felt funny too.

"I don't want to be inappropriate, so will someone rub her legs for her, please?" Bishop requested.

Sister Diana began working on my legs, rubbing and massaging them, "is this okay?"

"Yes," I said as I sighed again, but this time with a small amount of relief.

"They are going to move you into my office where you can be more comfortable—if that's okay?" Bishop asked.

"That's fine," I replied with a shaky, teary voice.

Elder Sharp and, who I found out later to be, Minister Roads, not Elder Roads, grabbed my arms and escorted me into the bishop's office. By this time, I was able to kind of slide my feet along the floor, but I was unable to bend my knees. It felt like I had no control over my body at all. Why won't my body do what I want it to do? I was aware of my surroundings, but I just couldn't make my brain do what I wanted it to do. We finally made it to Bishop's office after about a five- or ten-minute slow stroll down the hall. Bishop has one of those big recliners in his office; it's a soft leather material, kind of reddish, and it has all the bells and whistles.

"Here, Sis, sit down here, and you should feel much better," Elder Sharp said as he directed me toward the big red, comfy chair.

"Thank you," I said as I sat down slowly in the chair.

"Here you go, Sister Leeta," Bishop said as he went out of his way to turn on the chair to show me how fancy it was. The chair started to vibrate.

"Whoaaaaaaaa!" I said, as my head felt like it was going to shake right off my shoulders. I turned my head sideways and looked at him like a mother looks at her son when he runs in from outside with the biggest worm he could find. "My head," I said, as my head started shaking uncontrollably.

"Her head, her head," someone repeated. Bishop opened his eyes extremely wide as if he had just gotten into big trouble; he quickly reached for the switch and turned the chair off.

By this time, other saints had come into Bishop's office to assist, and some probably came just to be spectators. Bishop's wife, Sister Susie, was there, along with Sister June, Sister Carletta, my sister Sharon, and my mother. There were a bunch of brothers there, but I don't recall who they were. There could have been others there to assist, but I can't recall them either.

"I better go back in so I can preach," Bishop said as he looked down at his watch and noticed the time. And just like that, he was gone to go feed the people their soul food. Bishop always said church is not a smorgasbord; you can't just eat any and everywhere. When you think about feeding the natural man, you examine people and say things such as, "I can't eat after them; they didn't wash their hands. Their house is messy. They have roaches!" You should also examine the man of God that is trying to feed you through the Word of God. You shouldn't just sit down at everyone's table (church) and just start eating and gobbling up everything that is dished out. Ask some questions first, such as, "Have they been washed in the blood of the Lamb? Are they preaching, teaching, and living for truth and righteousness?" It is true you can't testify to someone else's salvation. However, in Mark 16:17, it says, "these signs shall follow them that believe," and if you don't see signs, then maybe they don't believe.

Anyway, as my head stopped pounding for that moment, I focused on Sharon and my mom, as they were telling Sister Diane about all the things that could've made me black out. I hadn't actually blacked out, but they were unaware of that fact. I was aware of everything that was going on around me, and I could hear everyone talking; I was just unable to tell them. I could see them with their fingers up in the air as they started counting out the things that were wrong. "Well, she has migraine headaches to the point where she can't drive, and I've had to drive her home, and she can't do anything but go to bed," Sharon said.

Then they started with the female stuff. "She has endometriosis, and that is a painful condition, and I know because I had it," Sharon says, remembering back to when she had the very same disease. "She has interstitial cystitis, and she said it is exceptionally painful."

They began saying so much I lost track of who was doing the talking. "She has degenerative disk disease, and it causes her to have severe pain in her neck, lower back, and through her pelvic area."

"She has multiple tumors in her pelvic area, not to mention all of the scar tissue from the four or five surgeries they performed to remove the tumors and the endometriosis," which, of course, they both returned.

"Similarly, she has about six or seven cysts on her ovaries, I think, and she has about seven tumors inside of her uterus. The doctors were going to do surgery comparable to a cesarean section, and take the uterus out, cut the tumors out of the uterus, the ones that were located on the outside of the uterine wall, which could be accessed easily. The uterine wall has several layers; if some of the tumors were in between the wall, they would have to stay inside the uterus, and she would have to endure the pain," Mom said as she began to tell my success story.

"However, Sis Rochelle at church and I interceded for Leeta in prayer and fasting, and the doctor decided to do a minor outpatient surgery the week before to check the size of the tumors. God had shrunk the tumors, and the major surgery was no longer necessary. However, now she still has a tumor behind her uterus that is almost bigger than the uterus."

"In addition, she has low blood sugar," my mom said. "She has passed out from low blood sugar on several occasions. Just recently, I checked her sugar, and it was at twenty-six, but it has gotten as low at nine," Mom continued to explain.

"She gave blood on her job and passed out and was unable to move any of her limbs. It was like she was paralyzed or something, and the ambulance picked her up from work and rushed her to the emergency room, but that was about a year ago. She still complains about that 300 dollars ambulance ride," Sharon said jokingly. "I still tease her about being paralyzed; that wasn't funny then, but it is kind of funny now. She could not move for hours. I don't know what in the heck was wrong with her," Sharon ended.

While they continued to talk, Sister June was feeding me some of Bishop's peanut butter and some of his mandarin oranges. He had a whole cabinet full of food. I couldn't wait to get back there and eat because he had so much stuff in the cabi-

THIS IS THE LORD'S DOING

net. I saw crackers and boxes and boxes of goodies. The peanut butter was in a tube; it reminded me of when I was in the army, and we had to eat those MREs (Meal Ready to Eat). MREs came in little hard brown plastic bags, and most of the food was dehydrated. The thing I remember most about the MREs was the fruit cocktail. It was a little yellow square, like those yellow sponges that, once they got wet, they dried out and became extremely hard and stiff. That's exactly how the fruit cocktail in an MRE looked. People would just bite the fruit cocktail and suck it instead of adding water to it until it turned into fruit, but I didn't like them. Nor did I like the eggs—they were green and wet!

I am not sure what part of Bishop's peanut butter reminded me of MREs, but it sure was nasty. It came in a long tube, and Sister June and Sharon took turns sliding their hands from the bottom of the tube up to the top. Peanut butter was all on their fingers, and I had to eat it like that right out of the tube. I was just sure it belonged in one of the MRE packets. When they put it in my mouth, my mouth started to pucker up. I felt like all those years of making mud pies in the backyard had finally caught up with me. I could not believe Bishop actually ate that stuff. "You don't like it?" Sister June said as she watched the expression on my face. Sharon just laughed and shook her head. I guess my brain couldn't send the signal to make any of my limbs move, but just use that peanut butter, and it was sure to get the job done.

"Okay, let's try the mandarin oranges." I'm confessing now. After that peanut butter, I was kind of skeptical about trying anything else in Bishop's cabinet. "No, that's okay; I'm not hungry," I said, with my face still twisted up from trying to get that peanut butter off the roof of my mouth and from in between my lips and teeth. "Come on, Sis, you need to eat. You want to go home and rest, don't you? You need to get your strength up, so you can take care of those boys." I thought about what they were saying, and they were right because every time I thought about that hospital and ambulance bill, I knew I needed to go home and not end up in another ambulance.

Okay, here we go, I thought, as I opened my mouth, and in pops this big, fat, wet, juicy thing. It reminded me of those bugs that you step on, and all that gooey stuff comes gushing out. As soon as I bit into that orange thing, that is exactly what happened; all this stuff (juice) came shooting out. It was so wet and gooey, and it made me gag! I felt so sick I could have just puked right there in Bishop's office. *How in the heck did he eat this stuff?* I thought to myself. *Next time I get sick, I need to be better prepared because Bishop has some of the nastiest food I have ever tasted!*

They continued to talk to Sister Diana while I continued to eat the MREs and bugs. "Also, she has these bone spurs in her upper spine, and the spurs are pushing on the nerves in her neck. The spurs caused major pain in her arms, neck, and head; she was unable to move her right arm for months, and she was unable to write, or use the typewriter or the computer. Before all of this started, she was typing about eighty-five to ninety words per minute. The pain was so excruciating that she had rubbed the skin off her arm from rubbing so hard. I loaned her my heating pad, and she was taking all kinds of pain pills.

"The pills would stop the signal from reaching the brain, and the brain would not send the signal to the nerve to let it know there was pain present. Therefore, the nerve would never let the brain know there was pain. The pain was still there, but her brain just didn't know it. The pills made her gain weight, so she went to the doctor, and they told her that the medicine made her crave food, especially sweets, and she has always been worried about her weight, so she quit taking the pills. After the medicine completely filtered from her system, the pain came back, so she allowed them to give her injections in her neck and spine.

"They injected her in the neck first, and she said instantly, within about ten minutes, she got a headache, and the doctor told her it wasn't possible. But she said she always did the low percentage (speaking negatively). If you told her the low percentage, like only ten percent of the people in the world do such-and-such, then she was the one who did it. The doctor gave her the next shot in the spine. He did not put her to sleep with the first shot. Since they were injecting her in her nerve, they had to use dye to inject it into her nerves. They didn't want to accidentally inject the wrong nerve. For her last shot, the doctor had to put her head under an ultrasound; that way, he could see inside her head and look at the dye while it went into her head to guarantee they had the right nerve in order not to shoot any of the steroids into her brain.

"Leeta said it was excruciating, so the next time they did the shot, she requested she is put to sleep. The injections gave her massive headaches that the doctors told her they could not control. She was unable to drive at times and unable to go to work. She also was unable to take care of her children at times, so she refused to have any additional injections."

Your family will tell all your business, I thought, as they wrapped up their conversation about all my medical issues.

Then Sister Diana, who happened to be a nurse, spoke up and said, "Well, I think you all should take her to the emergency room."

Almost instantly, I protested and said, "I'm not going to the emergency room. That last ambulance ride cost me 296 dollars, and they made me sit for hours in the emergency room just to tell me they didn't find anything. I could have told them I was okay without the charge. I am not going to an emergency room just to sit all day and then give them 300 dollars just to tell me, 'We don't know,' and then still pay the hundred dollars co-pay for the emergency room visit, yadda, yadda, yadda."

My mother looked at me with tears of frustration in her eyes. "I won't let them keep you sitting in the emergency room for hours and hours," she said. There I sat shaking my head, insistent on not going.

By this time, Sister Carletta came back from her mother's house from down the street. Carletta went to get an AccuCheck tester to check my blood sugar level. When tested, my blood sugar was 106; it wasn't bad at all. The elders had gone to find a drugstore to buy a blood pressure cuff. The members of the church suddenly realized all these things they needed and didn't have in case of an emergency like this one.

"Would you like some water?" Sister June said to break the monotony.

"Yes, please," I said. She brought the glass of water to me and held it out so I could grab it. I just hung my head and cried.

"What's wrong?" Sharon and several others in the room questioned.

"I can't take the glass," I said with embarrassment. "I can't move my arms; I can't make them move," I ranted.

"Don't cry. It'll be alright; don't get yourself upset," they said.

Sister Diana said, in such a sweet, comforting voice, "Would you like for me to rub your legs again?"

"Please," I said. "Sharon, would you please turn my head for me?" My head was hanging down to the left on my shoulder, and I was unable to move it. *What was happening to me? I thought, I just don't understand what is going on!* I was getting so frustrated. I didn't want to go see another doctor. Every time I went to see a specialist, they tried to give me whatever it was they specialized in.

"Yes," she said as she gently turned my head forward.

While I sat in that chair, God had already started to humble me. I was no longer all cute and high-class. I had lost the ability to move my own limbs. My head was leaning over to the side, and I could not straighten it up for myself. Someone had brought me a glass of water, and I couldn't even hold the glass for myself. They brought me fruit and peanut butter to eat, and I couldn't hold my own spoon. When the tears fell from my eyes, I could not even wipe my own tears away.

What's really going on? I thought. I am falling apart all in one day. I'm not sitting here all day, I thought. I began to use all the brain power I had to try and move my hands, and they would shake without ceasing until someone would grab my hand and hold it down. If, by chance, I was able to lift my hand, it would snap to my face with great force, hitting me in the face.

Finally, I thought, *I can wipe my own tears.* However, when I did, I smacked myself in the face, and it hurt. *I wonder what ev-*

eryone is thinking about me now, I thought. *I bet they think I'm faking.* Every time I thought about it, I would try with all my might to move my hands and arms. When I was able to move my arms, I smacked myself in the face every single time. *What an idiot*, I thought to myself, as I felt very insignificant and helpless.

The people who had gathered around me had started talking to me, trying to comfort me and to take my mind off what was happening. We all talked about several different things. I talked about the women's retreat that the church held. I began to relax, and I started to regain some mobility in my right arm and hand. I could move them freely. Then my left hand started to move a little bit more, but not as freely. I don't use the word *feeling* because I could always feel my limbs; I was just unable to tell my brain to make them move. I was not paralyzed; I could feel every part of my body. I knew my limbs were there; I just could not make them move. I never regained mobility in my legs, feet, or toes. Once I started to feel more relaxed, it seemed like God said, "Not so." Or, maybe it was Satan attacking my body. I couldn't tell the difference.

I looked at Sister June, and I could hear her voice start to fade away. Then, I could hear all the other voices start to fade away. I saw Sister June while she was still sitting in her chair, and she looked as if she and the chair were jumping around the room. Then I noticed the others began to jump around the room while still sitting in their chairs also. What is going on? I thought as my head started doing something I couldn't explain. It felt kind of fuzzy, and I started holding it to the side to try to focus better on them. Then I felt hands everywhere, and they are all over me.

GET YOUR HANDS OFF OF ME! STOP SHAKING ME! THAT HURTS! OUCH, MY HEAD! WHAT ARE YOU SAYING! STOP SHAKING ME! YOU ARE MAKING MY HEAD HURT WHEN YOU SHAKE ME LIKE THAT! TAKE YOUR HANDS OFF OF ME! PLEASE, DON'T DO THAT TO ME! TAKE YOUR HANDS OFF OF ME RIGHT NOOOOOOOOW! I thought.

"Can—"

"Name—"

"ta—"

"Me—"

"Can—"

"Are—"

"Hey—"

"What—"

"Can—"

"Can you—"

"Can you hear me?"

"What is your name?"

"Can you hear me?"

After a few moments, I was finally able to make out what they were saying to me. I also noticed I was no longer in the chair but could feel the floor against my body. Soon after, I was able to open my eyes, but I still didn't have control over my limbs. I managed to just nod my head. I could hear everything they were saying to me, but for some reason, I was not able to respond. I just wanted to let them know that I could hear them. So, I just nodded my head up and down very slowly, as if in slow motion.

"Do you know your name?" Sister Diana asked in a very meek and quiet voice.

"Leeeeeeetttaa," I said, with what seemed to be the last ounce of breath I had left in my body.

"She has slurred speech," Sister Diana said as she turned her head quickly to the side to inform the others. "Do you smell anything? Do you smell anything?" she said as she looked deep into my eyes.

I wondered why the heck she was asking me whether I could smell anything after they just shook the living daylights out of me. They should be apologizing to me; they gave me the worse headache of my life!

No, I don't smell anything! I thought to myself. *Are you crazy? Do you smell anything?*

I slowly moved my head from side to side to tell her no. I didn't want to actually say anything because the last word took just too much of my energy. *I didn't smell anything. Why was she asking me such silly questions, anyway? And why did they just shake me up like that? They knew I didn't feel well; they needed to quit playing, just silly, just silly, I thought to myself. If they ask me if I smell something again, I am just going to muster up enough energy to knock the devil out of one of them! I thought. They better be so glad I can't get off this floor; you let them put their hands back on me again and see what I will do to them.*

They better be so glad I can't talk, or I would really tell them a thing or two, and they really better be glad I am saved because when I wasn't saved, I would have given them a piece of my mind! Thank you, Jesus, for salvation, and please, God, don't let them touch me or shake me again.

These are the thoughts that went through my head as I lay on the floor, trying to regain focus. *Hey, what are they talk-*

ing about over there? I thought as my eyes squinted. I cocked my head to the side, so I could hear them a little better. It seemed as if the people had gotten together like in a football huddle, trying to determine their next play. By this time, the room is filled with people, and they were all talking at the same time, which, for the most part, sounded like gibberish to me. I heard someone talking about going to the hospital, and I even heard Sister June say how her daughter had seizures, but they were nothing like that.

My brain seemed to be moving a thousand miles a minute: *Who had a seizure? Me? Are they thinking I had a seizure? I know they don't think I had a seizure. They just shook the mess out of me. So how could they think I had a seizure? I don't have seizures.* At that time, I wasn't sure what had just happened, but I knew it wasn't a seizure. One thing I could say for certain was I didn't have 300 dollars for an ambulance ride. I also knew my head hurt badly from all those psycho church folk shaking me up and down. All I know is they better not put their hands back on me again, and if they do, boy, you don't know what I will do to them.

OH, NO, NOT AGAIN, NO PLEASE, NO, NO, MY HEAD, HELP MY HEAD LORD, OH MY HEAD, HELP ME, LORD. The hands are back. What are they saying? Are they helping me? They are praying. Thank you, Jesus. I'm sorry, God, please let them touch me; lay your hands on me. Pray, people, pray! Help me, Lord, pray, people, please, I thought.

"The blood of Jesus. The blood of Jesus."

Okay, okay, now I can hear them, but I am still shaking. Why am I still shaking if they are saying the blood of Jesus? Jeeeeeeeeeeeeeeeeeesus, Jeeeeeeeeeeeeeeeeeeeeesus.

"Okay, okay, okay, okay, okay, now it is okay, okay, o, o, o, o, okay, okay, okay."

"Me—"

"I—"

"She—"

"Time—"

"Really—"

"Name—"

"Who—"

"Hello—"

"Can—"

"Where—"

"Ta—"

"Can—"

"Can—"

"Can—"

"Can—"

"Can you—"

"Can you—"

"Can you hear me?"

"Can you hear me?"

"Yeeeeeeeeeeeeeeeeeeeeeeeeeeeeeeeeeeeeeeeeeeeeeeeeee eeeeeeee!."

"Sister Leeta, can you smell anything?" Sister Diana said.

My head moved very slowly from side to side. When it got to the left side, Sister Susie was there to wipe my tears, and I said, "I, I, I, I, I." I felt as if I was stuttering. I could hear myself talking, and I just couldn't believe how I sounded. I just wanted to kick myself back into reality.

"It's okay, Sister Leeta; don't try to talk," Sister Susie said as she cut me off. She cradled my head in her arms. I started up again. "I, I, I, I neeeeeeeeed an ammmmmbbbu—ammmmmbbbu—"

Sister Susie screamed out with urgency, "She needs an ambulance; she is saying she needs an ambulance." Sister June grabbed the phone and began pushing buttons. I guess she only pushed three numbers since 911 only has three numbers, but it seemed like she was over there pushing numbers forever. I could hear my mother and Sharon praying and crying all at the same time. The saints helped me back up into my chair. The elders of the church had made it back with the blood pressure cuff and started to take my blood pressure, but it was fine.

I could hear Sister June talking again. I had forgotten she was even on the phone.

"I told them that she was shaking. I didn't tell them she had a seizure, but they said to turn her on her side if she starts to shake again," she said as she continued her conversation with the 911 operator.

"I caaaaaaaaaaaaan feeeeeeeeeeeeeeeel it." *Why are you talking like that? Why are you slurring your words?* I thought to myself. *Why don't you just spit it out, cut it out, and just say what you mean? What is really going on here? You sound ridiculous! Just open your mouth and speak, Leeta! Stop acting like that.* The frustrating thoughts filled my head as I tried to reason with myself.

"What are you saying, Sister Leeta?" Sister Diane questioned.

"I caaaaaaaaaaaaaaaaaan feeeeeeeeeeeeel it."

"You can feel it getting ready to happen again?" she asked with an anxious voice.

Before, I couldn't shake my head or do anything at all, and before Sister June had a chance to hang up the phone from 911, it started again. They flipped me on my side, and it was on. I was shaking and jerking so hard that my body jumped out of the chair and onto the floor. My dress was above my waist and real close to my neck. So much for modesty because I had on a thong, and all my blessings were hanging out for everyone to see. Not to mention, I had no idea where my shoes were. "Here, take my robe to cover her," Sister Diane said as she slipped her choir robe off.

While my head was flopping around during the seizure, I noticed the ambulance had arrived. I am not sure how long the seizures lasted. However, I do remember the paramedic dropping the oxygen tank on my head. I must have been out of it because it didn't even hurt. "Hold her down," he directed the other medic. "I need to get this IV in her arm; she is having a stroke. What is her name?" he screamed out.

"Leeta," someone answered.

"Hi, ma'am, my name is Allen. I'll be taking care of you. I'm going to do my best to help you."

"I caaaaaaaaaaaaan feeeeeeeeeeeeeeeeeeeeeeel it."

"She is letting you know that she can feel a seizure coming on," Sister Diane said.

"Well, that is probably just the smell of the oxygen coming through the mask," Allen said. Allen knew everything. As soon as he walked in the door, he took charge and started telling the elders and ministers what to do and telling the other people not to touch me. He instructed them to take the robe off me. "We will cover her up when we get her stable," he said. Now that everyone in the room had seen my entire backside, modesty was definitely out the window. Allen really did know everything.

No, really, he did know everything; just ask him, and he'll tell you.

"She doesn't smell anything when she has a seizure," Sister Diane said.

"Has she had seizures before?" he questioned.

"No," she answered in her soft-spoken voice.

"Then she can't tell if she is having a seizure," he said because, of course, he already knew everything.

And wouldn't you know it, to his surprise; there I go again, shaking all over the place like crazy. This thing was beginning to get on my nerves. I was really getting scared. My dress is around my neck; my shoes and my matching purse are missing in action; my hair is a mess; my head hurts, and he just came in and said I had a stroke, so this thing was getting old—fast. It was wild. Even though I was going through these things, I was aware of my surroundings. I knew what everyone was saying, and I could tell what was going on.

I felt like I had just been dropped into the Twilight Zone. This was the craziest thing I had ever experienced in my life, and I was not happy about it. I was too cute to be going through this kind of thing. I could hear what was being said. I may not have gotten the entire sentence, and I may not have been able to put the sentence with the right person, but I heard the sentences.

Thoughts of all the things I had recently done wrong started to pop into my head. I know people said everything they had ever done wrong in their life, but since my brain had been shaken up so much, maybe I could not remember everything I had ever done wrong in life. I could only remember the stuff I had recently done.

I was Christian, baptized in Jesus's name, filled with the Holy Ghost, and speaking in tongues as the spirit of God gave utterance, but at that moment, I was scared. I already know what y'all are thinking: Second Timothy chapter 1 verse 7, "For God hath not given us the spirit of fear; but of power and of love, and of a sound mind." I am confessing right now—I was afraid. I did not have any power. I had people whom I did not love, and I did not have a sound mind—so I was scared!

Allen and his crew packed me up, put me in the ambulance, and gave Sister Diane back her choir robe. They lifted me into the ambulance, and Sharon rode in the front of the ambulance. Bob kissed me on the forehead. "Get my shoes," I whispered. He nodded as if to say yes. Hey, that was the first time I had worn those shoes, and I really did want to wear them for at least one full day.

Allen started asking me all kinds of questions, and I don't remember all the questions; I just remember feeling horrible. "I need to go to Methodist hospital," I said as I gasped for air.

"We will be taking you to St. Vincent because you are in serious condition, and it is closer," he replied.

"I need to go to Methodist. That is what my insurance covers, and that is where I want to go. I am not paying for another ambulance visit from St. Vincent to take me back over to Methodist after they run my insurance," I ranted in a very frustrated voice.

"Hey, looks like we are going to Methodist!" he yelled out to the driver. Little did I know the decision to go to Methodist would later be a great factor in my spiritual walk.

"I caaaaan feeeeel it," I mumbled as I reached my fingers through the side of the bed and grabbed Allen's pants.

"Take it easy, Ms. Bigbee. I've got you. I'm going to have to sedate you if you keep having seizures. Just relax," he said.

Okay, Allen, I'll quit with all this seizure stuff. Really, Allen? I thought. I managed to make it safely to the hospital without being medicated, even though I had a couple more seizures on the way to the hospital.

"This is Leeta Bigbee, black female, thirty-six years old; seven or eight seizures at the church. I believe she may have had a stroke, and she had two seizures in the ambulance that I witnessed myself," Allen rambled as we entered the emergency room. All the questions started again soon as we entered.

I thought, *can't you just get all the answers from Allen? He already knows everything.* Allen would later realize that he surely did not know everything. "She is normally in good health, but all of a sudden, she passed out in church and then started having seizures. She is able to tell when she is having a seizure," he explained to the nurses, "and they were coming pretty fast."

"I caaaaan feeeeel it," I said in total exhaustion.

"There she goes. She is telling you she is ready to have a seizure; it is just the weirdest thing," he said. "I've never seen anything like it."

"Hon, can you hear me?" one of the nurses asked in a soft voice. I shook my head yes. "Do you smell anything?" I shook my head no, *and all the same questions I had answered not only to the people at the church but to Allen and now to the nurse. I was getting frustrated with this 'Can you smell anything' question. Why in the heck are they asking me whether I can smell anything, anyway? Can they smell anything? Maybe the next time they ask me, 'Can I smell anything?' I should just turn around and ask them can they smell any-*

thing? If they say yes, I can ask them what it smells like, so when the next person asks me, 'Do I smell anything?' I can say it smells like such and such! I ranted in my head with frustration.

"I can't move my legs," I said to the nurse.

"Don't worry; we'll get you some medicine to make you feel better." Every time I tried to move my legs, I would get fearful. I would try to grab hold of the sides of the bed to pull myself up, and my arms and hands would shake. After what seemed to have been a lifetime, my mom and Sharon were allowed in the room. My aunts Lois (Lo) and Darla (Luv) came in the emergency room just a few seconds after Sharon and my mom. "Girl, you are just too stressed out; that's all that's wrong with you," Aunt Lo said.

"How do you feel, Lukes?" Aunt Luv asked, as she frequently called me by my nickname.

"I'm okay, just tired," I said.

The two of them started telling me what they thought was wrong with me—you know how family is. I didn't let it bother me; I know it was all out of love. Aunt Luv walked out of the room, worried, with tears in her eyes.

"Here it comes again," I said quickly, as I could feel another seizure sneaking up on me. Sharon and Mom grabbed my arms and tried to turn me on my side, and once again, the prayers started. Aunt Lo just kind of stood back and watched, but I believe she was praying.

"Aunt Lo, help us pull her back up in the bed," Sharon said. They grabbed me and struggled to pull me back toward the head of the bed. The nurse had adjusted the bed to where I was tilted up a little, so when I had a seizure, I started to slide out of the bed.

"I'm going to find the nurse. They need to do something about this," Sharon said as she walked out of the room.

Aunt Starla (Stay) came to visit in the emergency room, but I don't remember her visit very well. Sharon said I talked to her for a long time and told her how cute her outfit was. Her picture is very blurry (you will understand that comment in chapter 2). The nurses came in and filled me with so much medicine, "I feel sick to my stomach. I don't want any more medicine," I said.

"The medicine is the only way to stop the seizures, Ms. Bigbee," one of the nurses said as she continued to shoot that stuff in my IV. As they rolled the bed down the hall and ran what seemed to be hundreds of tests, they continued to give me more medication. I was so drugged that I faded in and out of consciousness while they were doing the tests. I would wake up and find myself in a different hallway waiting for another test, and then I would doze off again. I don't remember what kind of tests they took, nor do I remember where I was the majority of the time. When I got back into the room where my family was, they were still there waiting for me. I felt special that they were still waiting. I also felt nervous because it made me feel like it must be serious if they were still there waiting. They were such a blessing to me the whole day.

The day was going by so fast; it seemed like I had just left church, but morning service was over and night service was soon to start. "Look who's here," Sharon said as she came around the corner.

"Praise the Lord, Sister Leeta," Bishop said as he and Sister Susie followed behind Sharon from around the corner. Bishop and Sister Susie walked in to visit about an hour or so before night service started.

"Praise the Lord, Bishop," I said, with a big smile that no ruler could measure. I was finally done with the slurred speech thing, and I felt pretty good about it. He kissed me on the forehead and smiled back. My dad passed away in May of this year. He was not my biological dad, but he was the only dad I ever knew. So, when Bishop walked into that hospital room and kissed me on my forehead, it was like a dad coming to see about one of his children. Not that he could take the place of my dad, but when someone leaves your life, you often find comfort on similar grounds. Not that anyone could ever fill his space, but Bishop is just sitting in my dad's seat until we meet again. What I mean by that is, have you ever asked anyone to hold your seat when you got up to go do something when you were sitting somewhere? Well, that is what Bishop is doing for my dad. I love my dad, and we will meet again; but until we do, Bishop can hold his seat.

Bishop is a brown-skinned man, about maybe five feet, ten inches or so, and not a heavy man at all. He is soft-spoken but can get loud if he needs to. He reminds me of a teddy bear, real squeezable. He likes to give hugs, and he makes you feel welcome. The yard sign in the front of the church reads THIS IS THE CHURCH THAT WILL LOVE YOU TO LIFE, and it truly is. His hair is thinning on top but not in the front. He is a clean-cut man with smooth skin, and you can tell he smells nice even before you reach him.

When I mentioned Sister Susie earlier, it really wasn't a good time to tell you about who she is. But I can tell you about her now. Sister Susie is the bishop's wife, and yet she is humble—she doesn't let that go to her head. People can talk to her, and she is a down-to-earth type of person. She realizes that she is the bishop's wife and not the bishop. What I mean by that is, if you have a question about rules of the church, biblical questions, or questions that she feels should be directed toward Bishop, she won't give you an answer.

She will say, "I'll ask the pastor, and I'll get back with you." Then she'll give you that smile that she does, and she will squint those eyes like she does, nod her head one time down at you, and walk away. No matter how urgent you think your question is, or no matter how small you think your question might be, she will get guidance from the pastor. She will see what his answer is, and then she will get back with you. She talks very fast, but I think she does that so she can squeeze a word in while Bishop is talking. He talks all the time, and he always has a story to tell. He rarely lets you talk. So, I think that's why she talks so fast.

She has a very pleasant face; she looks like the type that bakes cookies all the time. Her hair is smooth and silky looking, salt-and-pepper gray, and it shines. It isn't that dusty, dirty color that people try to cover up with a purple crayon-colored hair dye. Where did they get that color from anyway? Does it come in a box of several other giant hair coloring crayons? I mean, just how many hair coloring crayons can you buy anyway? Do they have a sharpener in the back of the hair color crayon box also?

Anyway, back to Sister Susie. Her hair is a pretty gray, and it is light and moves when the wind blows when she is outside.

Most people walk outside and grab their hair because they just got it done the day before, and they are trying to save that hairdo for at least a week. Oh no, not Sister Susie; she lets it blow in the wind, and it still looks pretty when she comes back for Sunday night service.

Now, about those cookies I was talking about. Imagine her in the kitchen with an apron on, baking iced oatmeal raisin cookies on one sheet and white chocolate macadamia nut cookies on another. While the windows are open, on a cool spring day, imagine you are a kid playing kickball outside, running past the window. Your ball rolls by the window, and you run past the window to retrieve it. You arrive just in time to smell the aroma coming out of the window. You bend down and pick up the ball and, on your way back up, the smell grabs you by the nostrils, and wow, what a rush. You run back home and ask your mom if you can ask the neighbor if their kids can have any company just so you can get inside to ask for one of those cookies. I know I would. Okay, back to the hospital room.

Almost everything else that happened in the emergency room and the majority of the hospital stay that I write about will be to the best of my knowledge and from what I have gotten from my sister Sharon, Bishop, and others because I was so drugged up, so I don't remember.

I was enjoying my time talking with Bishop and my family, and he was teasing Aunt Luv and Aunt Lo about not coming to Family and Friends Day at church. The nurse came into the room and grabbed my little portable bed, "You have to get ready for your LP," Nurse Hatchet said. That wasn't her name, but it should have been. She was a short lady about five feet tall, with curly short blond hair, broad football-like shoulders, a flat face, round eyes, wide nose, square chin, saggy jaws, dark circles under her eyes, glasses, and a mouth that sank down at both corners like she was always frowning.

"What?" I said.

All eyes turned toward Nurse Hatchet. "Your lumbar puncture surgical procedure," Hatchet said.

"I'm not having that," I said in a stern voice.

"Ma'am, they need to find out what is wrong with you. It isn't a big deal; it is where they go in and drain the fluid off your spine and test it to see if you have any type of infection. Your spine is able to pick up infection deeper than what your blood can, so we need to do the spinal tap," Hatchet said in a nonchalant tone. So, I started freaking out when she told me all of this.

"No, I am not having it! I am not having any procedure."

"Calm down, Leeta. Calm down," Bishop said.

Hatchet said sternly, "She needs to know what is going on."

"She does know what is going on, and she said she isn't going to have it done," Bishop said with authority.

"I can feel it. Pray now, Bishop. Pray now, Bishop. Pray now!" I screamed with insistence in my voice. Bishop began praying a fervent prayer, and Nurse Hatchet (of all people) ran and joined hands in between Bishop and Sister Susie. My eyes were only open long enough to see Nurse Hatchet run out of the room after the prayer was over. I don't recall anything else that happened that night. I believe that Family and Friends day was the longest day of my life, and the only way I knew that I had been admitted to the hospital was because I woke up there the next morning.

CHAPTER 2

Video Tapes, Pictures, and Voice Mail Messages

"This is a spiritual war. I'm protecting your gates, Sister Leeta. I'm protecting your gates!" She ranted as my eyes slowly opened. "I'm protecting your gates, Sister Leeta. I'm protecting your gates!"

"Hey, Sister Shelley, I didn't know you worked here. How are you?"

"For we wrestle not against flesh and blood, but against principalities, against powers, against the rulers of the darkness of this world, against spiritual wickedness in high places." [6]

OUCH! I thought to myself. *Why is she screaming in my ear? Her screaming really hurt my head. What is she talking about? She sounds extremely radical.*

"I am helping you, Sister Leeta. This is a spiritual war, and this doesn't have anything to do with me or you. You be a good soldier, and you fight the good fight of faith!" she instructed as I faded off into unconsciousness.

---

6 Ephesians, Chapter 6, Verse 12.

Now Sister Shelley was a hyped individual, if I can use that word. She was always talking. I didn't care for her when I first met her. She is kind of light-skinned with full lips and two big front teeth, kind of like Chiclets chewing gum, but she is really cute. She is really small; at the most, I would guess about a hundred pounds and about five feet tall. Don't get me wrong; she is grown—in her twenties. She has a lot of hair, big hair, and it is brown with some reddish-tan color highlights. She reminds me of one of the Bratz dolls, with full lips and big hair.

When I first saw her, her hair was in a natural style, tightly curled. I think I didn't care for her because I had already made up in my mind that she had an attitude problem. More often than not, we allow the enemy to put thoughts in our heads that someone doesn't like us or is looking at us funny, and we will hold a grudge against those people. They don't even know we are mad at them or that we don't like them. I hadn't actually spoken to Sister Shelley at that time, but the enemy had me believing she didn't like me, so I didn't like her either.

Most of the time, the young people of the church would go skating on Friday nights. Usually, I was doing all I could just to stay on my feet and off my behind. It was a struggle to skate well enough to make it from one side of the floor to the other. One day, I went skating by myself, and I hoped I would see Ivory there. I had skated with Ivory several times before, and I was waiting at the door for her to arrive. When I saw her pull up, I rushed outside to meet her. I had on this little bitty blue jean skirt and a pair of tights. My legs were numb due to the cold air. I was literally shaking as I walked to Ivory's car. When I got to the car, I discovered Sister Shelley and a lady from Ivory's job had ridden with her. "Praise the Lord, everyone," I said as I walked up to the car window.

"Praise the Lord, Sister Leeta. Are there a lot of people in there?" Ivory said.

"Not many," I said. "I sure am glad you came," I replied.

"I may not stay; I'm not feeling it today," she said.

"Come on in. I have a coupon, and we all can get in for only four dollars. Come on now; please come in. I don't want to stand out here too much longer. I am freezing."

Right about that time, Sister Shelley looked at me, interrupted our conversation, and said, "You're cold because you got on that little short skirt; it's too cold for all that."

I pulled my head back out of the car window where they were sitting, turned up my nose, looked her up and down, and said, "Whatever, it is a lot easier to get up off the floor after falling in a short skirt than it is in a long skirt." I sighed, "I was really waiting for Ivory (she is Elder Sharp's daughter) to come in so she can use my coupon," as if to say, "You don't have anything to do with this, so mind your business." I didn't say that, but I must confess, I did think it. Ivory and I seemed kind of close, and we would always skate together when we would see each other out. After what seemed to be a lifetime, they finally got out of the car, and we all walked in together so we could use the coupons.

Ivory and I would always skate in the middle of the skating rink where the slower, inexperienced skaters skated. The middle was like the safety zone with big blue barriers in a circle to give us leverage as we were skating or falling, whatever the case may have been. We would practice going forward without falling for a while, and then we would try to skate backward without falling. If we were able to stay standing long enough to gain some confidence, we would then go outside of the safety zone to skate with the big kids. Anyway, as I carefully turn around on my skates, who do you think I saw skating all cute to the music? Yes, you guessed it, Sister Shelley. I mean, she was getting it: backward skating, crisscross skating, going to the music, just doing all the cute stuff on skates that I couldn't do and wished I could. I could have knocked her right off those skates. I already had a bad attitude that day because I had fallen about twenty times, so you know I didn't want to see her skating well and cute.

I really didn't know why I didn't care for Sister Shelley; I just knew I didn't. I know, we as women do that all the time. People will ask us, "Why don't you like her?" and we give a little shoulder shrug and say, "I just don't." Maybe I'm not speaking for all women when I say we do that, but I know I have done it more than once.

At any rate, one day, my Holy Ghost began to deal with me about the way I felt about Sister Shelley. You see, I like to buy clothes and most times I shop online. I have had four surgeries on my feet, so I would much rather shop from a book or a computer than cause my feet to feel any more pain by walking around the mall. So, getting back to the Holy Ghost dealing with me, I was supposed to pack up some of my clothes and take them to church to give to Sister Shelley. I thought to myself, *Uhhhhh, no, I'm not doing that.* So, the Holy Ghost continued to deal with me, telling me to give her the clothes. I will not say that I did what the Holy Ghost told me to do the first time, or even the second time, for that matter. The funny thing is if you don't listen to the Holy Ghost, it will stop talking to you and just leave you alone.

Eventually, I went into the closet and picked out a bag of shirts that might fit Sister Shelley; most of the shirts still had the tags on them. The sad part about me not wanting to give the shirts away was that I couldn't even fit them. When I put those shirts on, I felt like Baby Huey bursting out of the clothes. But that wasn't the point; the point was that I had bought them, and I wasn't going to give them to just anybody.

When I saw Sister Shelley in church, I said, "I have some clothes for you. Is it okay if I bring them to church to give them to you? Some of the clothes I have worn and some I have not." The reason I told her I had worn some of the clothes is because I knew she was the type that didn't want to wear hand-me-downs. She said, "Okay, that sounds great."

"Now, if you don't like them, just give them back. Don't throw them away, okay?" I said with a big fake smile on my face. I had already made up my mind she would just trash them once I gave them to her. She nodded as she walked away, as if to say okay.

"Huh? What? Now, why did she even say that? She knows she is not going to wear those clothes. People get on my nerves accepting clothes and don't even wear them," I mumbled under my breath and shook my head as I walked out the door to my car after Sunday night service.

"Tommy, go find Sister Shelley and tell her I have a bag for her after Bible class," I said as we walked in the door about ten minutes late for Bible study. We were always running late for something. We were really a busy family. Tommy was in a musical at the local theater, and he had rehearsal every day from 4:00 p.m. to 6:00 p.m. I would get off work at 3:30 p.m., and my niece Stephanie would bring him to my job. I would leave work, take him to rehearsal, leave there, run back out east, and pick up Timmy. This was about a twenty-five to thirty-minute drive from where I dropped off Tommy. I'd pick up dinner at a drive-through, and by that time I got the food, it was time to pick up Tommy from rehearsal. Then we would sit in the parking lot at church and eat our meal. Therefore, by the time we actually walked into the sanctuary, it would be about 7:10 p.m. or 7:15 p.m. Bishop made sure Bible class always started promptly at 7:00 p.m. That's the reason we were always late. So, I guess it was kind of his fault.

Tommy wasn't able to catch Sister Shelley after Bible class that Tuesday night. I had to take the bag back home and try again on Sunday. Sunday passed, and we didn't catch her that time either. When we came back to Sunday night service, she was there, and I asked her to meet me after church for the bag. Seems like I had to do a whole lot of running around to give away some clothes to somebody I didn't want to give them to anyway. When I gave her the bag, it appeared as though the clothes were trying to jump out of the bag; there were so many of them.

I had stuffed the clothes in a thin, white grocery bag. I guess I could have found a better bag, but it was Monday night when we were looking for the bag, we had a busy schedule, and I just didn't have time to find a better bag. Tommy still had his practice, and I still had to pick up Timmy, and we would meet at the church for young people's service on Monday nights. So, at that point, any old bag would do because she wasn't going to wear the clothes anyway. The tags from the new shirts were hanging outside of the bag. "Here you go," I said as I slung the bag her way. "Sorry, I didn't have a bigger bag."

"That's okay, thanks," she said as she hurried out the door with her son.

Thanks? Thanks? I knew it, I knew it, and she didn't even appreciate the clothes. Whatever! I thought to myself. "Let's go, guys," I said in total frustration.

"What's the matter, Mommy?" one of the boys asked.

"Nothing. Let's just go," I say in a brash voice as I brush past the remaining people in the church lobby. I pushed the door open and began to search for my car in the parking lot.

I can't believe we are late again, I thought, as we walked in the church doors for Bible class about ten minutes late. I did all I had to do and walked to the third row of church, so I could sit down. Offering time slowly came, and the officials announced, "Take your monies into your right hand," and they began to pray. After the prayer, we always turned to the side, preparing to walk out of the pew to take our offering around to the front of the church, where the offering baskets awaited us. While I was standing, I haphazardly looked a few rows back, and who do you think I saw? Sister Shelley was standing in church, wearing my favorite color, and it just happened to be one of the shirts that I had given her. "I can't believe she actually wore one of those shirts," I said to myself, as I felt joy and sorrow all at the same time. I felt joy because I was wrong about her, and then I felt sorrow because I was wrong about myself. *I can't believe I prejudged her and acted in such a manner,* I thought. After church, I tried to stay away from her because I was a little embarrassed about how I had judged her. I felt I didn't have to try too hard to stay away because it was so hard tracking her down all the other times when I tried to give the clothes to her, so that day shouldn't have been any different.

Soon as church was over, I proceeded to move quickly so I could exit the church.

"Sister Leeta, Sister Leeta!" she screamed out as she came running in my direction. I was trying to look the other way, as if I didn't see her coming, and I walked just a little bit faster. "Sister Leeta, hey Sister Leeta, hold on a minute," she said again in a loud voice. "Mommy, Sis Shelley is calling you," screamed out Timmy. *Leave it to kids,* I thought. I turned around with kind of a half-cocked smile on my face as if I just got caught doing something wrong. "Praise the Lord, Sister Shelley."

"God is," she said. She always would say "God is"; she says it that way, so it leaves it open for God to be whatever you need Him to be. "I'd like to talk to you. Will you step over here for a minute?" she whispered as she took me by my forearm. We walked over to the coat racks in the lobby. "I just wanted you to know that you were such a blessing to me the other day when you gave me that bag of clothes. I was having such a hard time getting rid of some of my worldly clothes. You just don't know how you blessed my soul. God is going to bless you, sister." She hugged me and kissed me on the cheek as she rushed off, just as she had the day I gave her the bag. *Thank you, Jesus,* I thought to myself, *you never know what people are going through.* "Please, Lord, help me to love like I am supposed to love, and please don't let me prejudge people," I prayed softly as I walked out the door.

"Mwah" was the first thing I felt on my forehead as I awoke to the gentle strokes of Sharon's hand as she rubbed my hair. "How do you feel, honey, honey?" she said in that baby voice that she often spoke in. She was the caring, nurturing one in the family out of all my mom's children. My little sister Mia would always say, "If I feel down and I need to be babied, I'm going over to Sharon's house. Don't get me wrong," she says, "Leeta cares about people, too, and she is just a little bit harder. If you felt bad, Leeta would say, 'Sorry you feel bad,' and she would mean it, but that is about all you would get from her. She just isn't the hugging, babying type." I guess I am that way because I pretty much had to do things for myself. I have worked since I was in the fifth grade. I learned not to whine and complain about a lot of things and also learned how to hide my feelings.

For example, like when my dad died, Mia took it really hard. At the funeral, Mia was crying a lot, and I could tell she was hurting. She was leaning all over the church pews and crying. She was driving me crazy. I knew she needed comforting; I just didn't know how to comfort her. I was sitting the closest to her, and Sharon was way down at the other end of the pew. "Tap, tap, tap," is all my brother felt as I interrupted his grieving period. "Tell them to get Sharon," I whispered as I pointed to the person sitting next to him.

Whenever the next person to him on the pew would look at me, I would point toward Sharon and whisper the same command over and over, "Get Sharon." Finally, the person who was sitting next to Sharon looked at me. "Get Sharon," I said as I pointed several times at a fast pace. When Sharon looked at me, I stuck my thumb up, similar to that of a hitchhiker, and used it to point toward Mia. I didn't even have to say anything; Sharon immediately got up from her seat and started right on the job of patting up Mia. *Phew*, I thought. I felt so much better because I knew Mia would be all right once Sharon started that hugging, rubbing, and all that comforting stuff. Sharon and I didn't always get along, but God had to work some things out just like He works out everything else.

"I don't feel so good," I said as I looked at Sharon. "I am a little sore, and this catheter is bothering my legs. Look at the rash and blisters the catheter gave me. You know I am allergic to everything. Why did you let them put this thing in me, anyway?" I asked while I whined like the helpless baby I felt like.

"You aren't able to get up and walk around right now, sweetie, so this is the only way you can go to the bathroom. You said you didn't want to use the bedpan. Did you change your mind?" she said with a smirk on her face.

"You know I am not using that thing," I snarled with pride in my heart and all over my face.

"Then you have to leave it in," she said while speaking in a baby voice.

Fading in and out of consciousness is how I spent the rest of that week. Sharon was there the next morning again to greet me with her warm and loving smile. She had taken off from work to stay and sit by my side for the next three days, and she didn't even get paid. I was so out of it from the medication I didn't even remember her being there, but I am grateful that she was. When I woke up, another day had passed. The prayers of the people are one of the things that stuck out to me most. I remember praying in my heart because, more often than not, I could not open my mouth to pray. I recall people grabbing my hands and saying, "Let's pray."

I would then start to pray in my heart, "Lord, please, keep me safe from whatever they are praying." I know you are probably thinking, "What is this girl saying? Protect her from whatever they are praying?" Well, I told you that I don't recall all who came to visit. Everyone does not pray for God's will, and that is all I want for my life. I did not know what they were saying when they were in the room alone with me because I would fade in and out of consciousness. I just figured everyone that came to see me wasn't looking out for my best interests, even though they may feel like they were. The safest place is in the will of God, and that's the prayers that I wanted going forth on my behalf. Life and death are in the power of the tongue. I felt so paranoid half the time, and I just didn't know what the heck was going on. Therefore, I would pray to God, the only wise God, to keep me safe, to protect and watch over me and allow His will to be done in this situation and in my life. "Lord, if I ask for something that is detrimental to my soul, please, Lord, no matter how much I kick and scream, please don't give it to me," I prayed.

When I woke up one time, Kevin was visiting with me. Kevin had been unaware that I was in the hospital. Because when he left my house Saturday night after dinner, everything was fine. Kevin and I talked on the phone all the time, but when I arrived at the hospital, I couldn't remember his telephone number to call him to let him know what was going on the Sunday I ended up in the hospital. We were supposed to have study group at five o'clock pm. I knew I would not make it to study group after ending up in the hospital. By the time five o'clock rolled around, I was still laid up in the emergency room, unable to feel my legs.

So, when Kevin came to visit me, he told me he was very upset with me for not calling him and telling him I was in the hospital. He had to find out when he made it to study group later on Sunday night when I ended up in the hospital. He said he was unable to concentrate the entire time during study group because he was so concerned about me. After I got out of the hospital, he told me later that during his hospital visit, we talked in-depth, and I told him about the struggles I had while in the hospital.

"Kevin, the nurses aren't very attentive, nor are they very sympathetic," I began to tell him. "I am able to feel when I am getting ready to have a seizure," I said. "The objects in the room start to move really fast, and they seem to start jumping around the room. As I lay in the bed, minding my own business, the clock on the wall started jumping around. When I looked at the clock, I saw that the time was 12:50 p.m. I reached over and grabbed the call button to call for the nurse because I had that seizure feeling. My hands began to shake as I pushed the button several times. I could feel my body start to shake. I had to start talking to myself," I told him.

I thought to myself, *Okay, brace yourself, Leeta. Here we go; you can do this.* I grabbed the nurse's call button and pushed it a few more times to let them know that I urgently needed them, but they never came. They had been giving me some type of medicine to stop the seizures, and I needed it right away. Right after I pushed the call button, my entire body began to shake. My head was shaking and hurting; I realized I was having another seizure. I thought to myself as I began to shake, *where are they? I pushed the button a year ago. Don't they know I need help?* After a few moments, my body slowly began to loosen up and relax.

"As my eyes slowly began to focus, I looked around the room to see if there was anyone in the room with me. I could not believe my eyes; not one nurse was in the room with me. *I could have died,* I thought to myself. I grabbed the button and began to push it several times to get the nurses' attention. I was determined that they were not going to ignore me. In a matter of seconds, my body starts to shake, rattle, and roll yet another time. I can't believe this; I am having another seizure and no one ever came to check on me during the last seizure. You better believe I was upset," I ranted to Kevin.

"It seemed like my body must have shaken for about an hour. I was so tired, and I could barely move my arms to pull myself back up in the bed. I was still unable to move my legs on my own, and it felt as if my whole body was going through spasms. It took me a while to focus again, but when I did, there still wasn't anyone in the room to help me. Kevin, I was so angry at them; you can't imagine all the things that went through my head about suing them. Anyway, Kevin, while I was having the third seizure, someone from housekeeping came in and saw me shaking in the bed.

"'Somebody, somebody, this girl is in here having a seizure. Can anyone hear me?' she said as she pushed the call button several times. *Thank you, Jesus,* I thought to myself, *I am finally going to get some relief.* When I looked at the clock, it was 1:25 p.m. I had three seizures, back-to-back to back, while I waited for a nurse to come in the room. I had been in that room seizing for thirty-five minutes, and no one ever came to help me."

"'Where were you?' I screamed as the nurse walked into the room. 'I was tending to another patient, ma'am,' she said as she walked over to my IV and started shooting medicine into it. I'm telling you, Kevin, you don't ever want to end up in Methodist, and it isn't the best for customer service, either," I said.

Then, Kevin, I continued with disbelief, I was lying in bed asleep, and when I came to, I focused on a doctor sitting in a chair at the foot of the bed, looking just like the devil's advocate. He said, 'We did several tests on you and the MRI, EKG, EEG, and so forth, and they all came back normal.'"

"Wow, they did all those tests on you?" Kevin asked with amazement.

"Hold on; you haven't heard anything yet. He said, 'You had some blood work done in October, and your ANA was over 600.' I interrupted to say it was not. 'Yes, it was, and it is still over 600, and you have lupus,' he continued. 'We will be sending in a specialist to look at you,' he said, and then he got up and walked out of my room. That was one of the rudest doctors I had ever talked to. When I was afraid to get the spinal tap, the same doctor sent word by the nurse that he would have me discharged from the hospital if I didn't get the spinal tap. He never once tried to calm my fears or even tell me anything about the procedure. He was just rude," I continued to tell Kevin as I felt tears well up in my eyes. "I was supposed to get the spinal tap today, but something went wrong, and I couldn't get it. But they did test for West Nile virus and all other kinds of viruses," I said.

"Well, that was really rude," Kevin said.

"I told you, that doctor has a horrible bedside manner," I continued. "I asked for another doctor since that doctor was so rude, and he sent word with the supervisor over patient advocate services to tell me that if I wanted another doctor, I would have to check out of the hospital and then get a second opinion. I didn't even ask for a second opinion; I just said I wanted a different doctor. Kevin, I was really scared, and I didn't know what to think because I didn't even get a chance to ask him any questions about lupus or any other conditions or tests that he told me about."

"Try not to worry about it, Leeta. God will work it out," he said with his mouth, but it sure didn't sound like he meant it in his heart. Kevin told me that the day he visited, I was supposed to get the lumbar puncture, and they had given me some medicine to keep me sedated so I wouldn't have a seizure during the procedure. But I didn't have the LP that day because of some scheduling conflicts. As I rested in the bed talking to Kevin, I began to drift in and out of consciousness and began thinking back, and it is amazing Kevin and I are even friends. Kevin used to get on my nerves so bad in the past.

For instance, last year, my sons' school was taking a trip to Florida, and I decided to take them. The school trip was a great deal financially. The cost was 600 dollars per person, and that price included the price for our bus ride, entrance into Universal Studios One, Universal Studios Two, Disney World, Sea World, a luau, the hotel room, and breakfast with the Disney characters.

There was also another part to the price: if the children or the parents were willing to participate in a fundraiser, the price of the trip would be lowered according to how much each family sold. Normally, I don't participate in the fundraisers because the boys usually take the order forms for the products and pass them around to people and worry about collecting the money later. I would then have to come out of my pocket to pay the difference between the amount that was due and the amount that they had actually collected. I told myself, *This fundraiser will be different.* I decided to sell the items myself, and the items would not include any candy. I picked calendars to sell. The boys weren't interested in selling calendars, so I did the majority of the selling for our family.

Tommy would ask people at church whether they wanted to buy a calendar and if they said yes, he would direct them to me. I believe we only sold about ten or twenty calendars between the three of us. The small amount that we sold allowed us each to a hundred dollars from the price of our trip, so the boys and I ended up going to Florida for 500 dollars per person. I believe Kevin still had to pay the whole 600 dollars since he wasn't allowed to participate in the fundraiser because he didn't have any children at the school, and the trip was sponsored by the school. Many people from school thought Kevin and I were dating when they found out we were going to Florida together. But the truth is when I told the people in my class about the trip and what a great deal it was, he just wanted to go.

Anyway, the bus ride was about eighteen hours long. At first, Kevin and I were sitting side by side, but when the bus was ready to take off, we noticed that there were enough seats for us to have our own set of seats. Kevin was totally prepared for the trip; he had a cooler packed with food. He had a cheese ball thing stuffed with meat and onions with crackers. "I can't believe you brought all that food with you; we won't be on the bus that long," I fussed at Kevin as he reached in his bag for more goodies. I hadn't really traveled long distances before, so all I had in my cooler was juice and a few bags of chips for the boys. *Wow, that food sure looks good,* I thought to myself while I tried to figure out a way to ask Kevin for some. I really didn't want to ask for a piece because I had given him such a hard time about it just a few hours earlier. "Hey, what is it that you are eating over there?" I whispered.

"A cheese ball," he said while he licked his lips and fingers.

"Who made it?" I said as if I still didn't understand why he brought it on the trip.

"I did," he said, short and sweet, as he continued to eat.

I thought to myself, *Here is my chance to ask for some.* "Yeah, right, sure, you made it," I said as if to say, "I can't believe you can make anything."

"Yep, sure did," he said, with a mouth full of cheese ball and crackers. I know he knew I wanted to taste it. My stomach was growling, and I was hungry. I tried to get an attitude with him for not telling me before we took the trip that I needed to pack some food with me. "Well, let me taste it and see if it is any good," I said as if I really didn't want any. "Wow, this is really good!" my taste buds scream out. Then it was all over; I was eating that cheese ball the rest of the night. Kevin didn't let my attitude bother him most of the time. He just kind of overlooked me and my smart comments, and this time I was really glad he ignored me because I sure was hungry.

I had taken my digital camera on the trip to Florida, and my batteries were dead. The was a shop where I could buy batteries, but the battery I needed was a lithium battery. I don't remember exactly how much the battery was, but it was between fifteen and twenty dollars. So, I decided to just get some AA batteries instead until I got home. Chris and Tasha had kids at the school, and they were there also, and they agreed that this would be the best thing to do. Kevin stood there and just argued with me about this battery for about twenty minutes. I finally said, "Just don't talk to me, Kevin! I am sick of arguing with you! You want to argue in school, at home, just everywhere we go! You will no longer get a rise out of me!" After screaming at him, I stormed away. The rest of the day was pretty quiet; I didn't talk to Kevin for the remainder of the day. Kevin said he enjoyed getting a rise out of people, but I don't think he enjoyed the one he got out of me that day because he stayed away from me the remainder of the day. The Lord had to send someone to help me that night because I carried that anger with me all day and into the night.

"Sorry for going off on you yesterday. But you like to argue too much," I said as I delivered Kevin a backhanded apology.

"No problem," Kevin said as he continued to tolerate me. We began talking again after that, and I was no longer mad at him, or should I say, he was no longer mad at me.

At the amusement parks, we were taking turns renting baby strollers because we had so much stuff to carry. I don't ride roller coasters, so while the others went to ride, I took the stroller that had Tasha's purse, my purse, Chris's digital camera, Kevin's digital camera, my digital camera, Kevin's video camera, my video camera, all the snacks, and all the water bottles. I saw some other people from the bus, so I spoke to them. I took a couple of pictures with some characters and then sat down to rest. I tried to keep the stroller close by while I sat at the table because I knew I had thousands of dollars worth of equipment and money in the purses that were in the stroller, not to mention our IDs, credit cards, and whatever else could have been in the purses.

Ouch, my neck hurts, I thought as I rubbed the back of my neck. Right about then, I realized my eyes were closed, and my head was lying down on the table. As I slowly opened my eyes, I saw a huge shadow standing in front of me. Since we were at an amusement park, I thought maybe it was the Jolly Green Giant. The shadow stood tall with his hands on his hips, and he seemed to have big muscles. As my eyes began to focus, I noticed the shadow wasn't green, and it wasn't a giant—it was Kevin! He was giving me the meanest look he could muster up. I sat up in my chair as swiftly as I could. I felt like a sleeping student in an algebra class that had just been discovered by the teacher. "Hey," I said as I wiped that little bit of slobber off the side of my face.

"What are you doing?" he screamed.

"Where y'all been? Y'all left me here for hours," I screamed, coming to my defense. I swiftly glanced over at the stroller, which had rolled a few feet away from me. I was truly thankful all the items appeared to still be in the stroller. "We've only been gone for about two hours," he said as if to say we were only gone for a minute.

"Well, I was tired. I can't believe y'all have been gone that long," I continued to rant.

"You could have gotten all of our stuff stolen. Come on, girl, let's go," he said as he shook his head and began walking away.

I grabbed hold of the stroller and began to follow slowly behind Kevin. I was still groggy.

"Hey, Mom, we had a great time. We rode the Hulk and the..." the boys exclaimed as we continued walking.

Its day four of our trip, and we were notably tired and weary. "Y'all up?" Kevin yelled as he knocked on the door.

"Yeah, we're up. Give us a few minutes, and we'll meet you in the lobby!" I yelled back through the door. After getting dressed, the boys and I headed to the hotel lobby.

Once we arrived at the park, Tasha and I took Timmy and Little Chris to Dr. Seuss Land, and it was extremely cute. It looked exactly like the pictures we had seen in the Dr. Seuss books. Kevin and Chris didn't want to go to Dr. Seuss Land, so they told us they would catch up with us later on the bus. We allowed the boys to ride as many rides as they wanted. We rode the Cat in the Hat last because the park was going to close in about an hour, and it was the closest to the entrance/exit of the park.

When we sat in the car inside the Cat in the Hat ride, they told us, "Buckle up, keep your arms inside the car, and don't get out while the car is moving for any reason." The car started moving, and I thought, *no big deal; this thing moves super slow.* I had my sun visor and my digital camera sitting on my lap, and I saw no need to hold on to them because we were barely moving. Tasha and I sat in the front seat of the little car-like thing, and the boys sat in the back. The ride had a little silver bar that snapped down over our laps to secure us in. Our knees were bent while we were sitting on the seats as we road the little cars down through the streets where Sally from the Cat in the Hat and her brother Conrad lived.

The car moved slowly through the tunnel. As we approached a corner, the car made a quick, jerking spin and zoomed off around the corner. "Whoa!" I said as I reached toward my sun visor as it flew off my lap and onto the floor of the car. "Whew, I grabbed it just in time," I told Tasha as I sat back up. "Good thing you grabbed it," she said. Right about then, my digital camera slid off my lap and onto the floor of the car. I tried to wiggle my way free from that silver bar, and before I had a chance, we hit another corner, and the camera slipped right between my fingers and flew out of the car, landed on the ground, and slid over in a corner in a dark part of the tunnel. Even though I was told not to get out of the car, I did everything I could possibly do to get out of the moving car to get my camera. However, I was locked in so tight with the silver bar that I could not get out of the car or move. I turned my head around, looking backward in the car as I looked behind me for as long as I could until the camera disappeared out of sight.

Tasha tried to comfort me, but I could not enjoy the remainder of the ride because I was too concerned about the 300 dollars I paid for that camera and the seventy dollars I paid for the memory chip that was inside the camera. Literally, as soon as we could see the light at the end of the tunnel, my demeanor began to improve. Once the car came to a halt (which seemed to take forever), I sprinted to the attendant and explained my dilemma. "You need to speak to the manager, ma'am, and he won't be back for about twelve minutes," she said in a pleasant voice.

"Twelve minutes, twelve minutes!" I screamed. "Look, lady, I do not have twelve minutes; we have to leave. We are not from here, and we are leaving tomorrow. I dropped my digital camera back there on that ride, and yadda, yadda, yadda," I continued to explain.

"Yes, ma'am, I understand. You told me, but you still have to wait for the manager. There are other people who have dropped things too; they are waiting for the manager also. The manager has to wait until the last car has come in from the ride. Then he and another crew member will have to physically walk through the ride with flashlights and go looking for everyone's belongings. One person starts at the front of the ride, and another starts at the end of the ride, and they cross in the middle. Hopefully, they will be able to find and restore unto everyone everything that was lost."

Tasha waited with me; we were instructed to wait for the manager in a little, tiny room. "Ma'am, that's the manager," the attendant said as she pointed in the direction of the ride.

"Excuse me, sir," I said as I began to tell my story all over again.

"I'm really sorry, ma'am; another lady lost a diamond tennis bracelet. However, to us, there is no greater item. I can't close down the ride until the park closes, and the park doesn't close until 7:00 p.m. But don't worry about a thing. Just wait until closing time, and hopefully, we will find it."

"Hey, Tasha, Ms. Jones said the bus can only wait for you guys for about ten more minutes, and then they will have to leave you, so you guys better hurry up," Chris said as he walked over to the ride.

"What do you mean they will have to leave us?" I asked with a puzzled look on my face. "We weren't supposed to leave the park until 9:00 p.m., and it's just now a quarter to seven."

"Ms. Jones said they want to hurry up and make it to the thrift store to buy souvenirs before the store closes," he replied.

"Tell her I am waiting for my camera. I dropped it on the ride. Kevin, please take Timmy with you and put him on the bus. I'm going to wait for my camera, and you tell Ms. Jones not to leave me," I said, looking at Kevin as if to say, "and you know I mean it, too." He just shook his head. Most times, it seemed as if Kevin just kind of let me talk but didn't really listen.

"Chris, take Little C. with you to the bus. I'll wait with Leeta," Tasha said.

"Okay," he replied, "but you guys better hurry before she leaves you."

We continue to wait until closing time. After a few minutes, Chris and Kevin came back, "she said you guys have about three minutes, and the bus will be pulling out without you."

"Did you tell her what I said about the camera?" I questioned.

"Yeah, she said leave it," Kevin said while smiling and shrugging his shoulders.

"Is she crazy? I paid almost 400 dollars for the camera. You tell her she better make sure the bus is there when I get there!" I screamed. Kevin wasn't really saying anything; he just shook his head.

"All right," Chris said as he and Kevin faded away in between the rides.

Tasha looked at me with a sad face, "Don't worry; hopefully, we'll make it in time," she said.

"We better make it in time. I am not playing with her. She better make sure the driver doesn't leave us. We are eighteen-plus hours away from home. I slept most of the way here, and I have no idea how to get back home; she is talking about packing up and leaving us to go and get some souvenirs. She sounds like Job's wife, a straight-up foolish woman. I can understand if she said she was going to leave us at the mall back home. But she is talking about leaving us in Florida. Oh no, oh no. Like I said, she better not leave me. And I am not playing!" I screamed.

Pretty soon, the manager gave the okay that they could start looking for the lost items. Right about that time, Chris and Kevin came back again and said, "I told Ms. Jones what you said, and she said she is sorry, but she is leaving without you." Tasha looked at her husband, and he looked at her and he said, "You coming?" She looked at me with puppy dog eyes, and I just turned my head without saying anything. "I'm going to stay with Leeta," she said. "See you later, baby," he said. And once again, he faded away. By this time, I was rehearsing in my head all the things I was going to say to Mrs. Jones when I saw her. You must realize this was a time way before Uber and Lift drivers, so I couldn't just have someone come get me and take me back to the hotel. Not to mention, I didn't even remember what hotel we were staying in.

After about ten minutes, the manager came back, and he began to ask questions about the camera. I answered all the questions correctly to assure him it was mine, so he handed me the camera, and we left.

Tasha and I rushed off to try and catch the bus before it left. While we were walking, we saw the bus driver's daughter casually, and I do mean super lackadaisically, taking her time buying a Cinnabon at a food stand. When I saw her standing there, I felt like my head was going to explode; I was so angry. I could not believe Ms. Jones was harassing me like that, and she knew the bus driver was not going anywhere without his daughter being on the bus. And I know she knew his daughter wasn't on the bus because, for the duration of our trip, she sat at the front end of the bus, right across from the bus driver and right in front of his daughter. She and the bus driver talked almost the entire drive to Florida. Ms. Jones knew that girl was not on the bus.

"I'm still going to say something to her, even though she didn't leave us," I said as I walked even faster.

"You should just let it go, Leeta. Please let it go," Tasha pleaded, "You said you would say something if she left us."

"No, I will not just let it go; I am going to tell her about herself as soon as I get on the bus because she was going to leave us. Like I said, I can understand her leaving us at the mall at home. I would have been able to find someone to pick me up from there. But who in the world is going to drive all the way out here to Egypt and pick me up from Florida?" Tasha didn't answer me. "That's what I thought, no one. I'm going to tell her as soon as I get on the bus," I said in a feisty voice.

As we approached the bus, I could see people standing on the outside of the bus just talking. I could see Amber, Tasha's older child, Kevin, Chris Sr., and lots of other people. At that point, I didn't care; I just kept walking. As we got closer to the bus, I could hear Chris say, "Is Little C. with you?"

"No, Chris, I was with Leeta. I told you to take him with you!" Tasha screamed frantically. "What happened?"

"Well, he was walking with me, Tommy, and Timmy, and he kept walking away from me and closer to Amber, and then he just disappeared," Kevin explained.

I just shook my head and kept walking. *First, the daughter runs away from the hotel, and now the son,* I thought to myself, *Little C. is probably somewhere hiding since he is always doing stuff to get his parents' attention.*

"Come on, Tommy and Timmy," I yelled. They quickly ran and caught up behind me because I wasn't going to help look for Little C. I was still on a mission, and I had something that needed to be said. Kevin ran and caught up as he said, "I don't want to be around when they find that little boy because he is going to be in big trouble!"

When I got to the bus door, everyone was talking about how Little C. should get a whooping when they find him. I just tuned all that noise out and walked up the stairs of the bus to complete my mission. As I walked up the stairs on the bus, I walked around that little plastic wall that was immediately to the left. Once I passed the wall, I saw Ms. Jones. She was sitting to my left in the first set of seats as I entered the bus. She was sitting down, but when she saw me come up that last stair, I saw her stand up. She must have known I was upset. She didn't say anything; she just looked at me with those big bug eyes. Her mouth was closed tight, and her lips kind of reminded me of a monkey. Remember when we were kids, and we used to put our tongue under our top lip and pull our ears out and pretend we were monkeys? Well, that is how her lips looked.

"I cannot believe you had the audacity to think you were about to leave me out in the middle of Egypt," I ranted while pointing my finger about a millimeter away from her nose.

"I was only doing what the driver wanted me to do," she whimpered.

"The driver, the driver, who is he?" I questioned as I pointed to the driver as he sat in his seat and listened. "We don't work for the driver; the driver works for us! Last time I checked, he didn't pay us any money; we paid him! And you knew good and darn well he wasn't about to move this piece of junk until his daughter got on here."

"I didn't know his daughter wasn't on the bus," she said, coming to her defense.

"Now you know you just stood up there and told a bald-faced lie!" I screamed.

"Come on, Leeta. Now you know it ain't even worth all this," said Donna, one of the passengers on the bus, as she tried to calm me down.

I began to calm down a little once I listened to what Donna was saying. As I turned around to walk to my seat, I noticed Ms. Jones' goddaughter sitting a couple of seats back. She was about twenty-four years old, and she was a little thicker than me and taller too. But when I saw the look on her face, it made me angry all over again, and I wasn't a bit concerned about her size.

"What? What? You feeling froggy? Leap! Leap! If you think you're bad enough to get in the middle of this, then you go right ahead and say something. This doesn't have anything to do with you," I said, feeling as if I were about ten feet tall. That girl had me by at least forty or fifty pounds, and I know at least six inches, but I didn't even care because normally, the maddest person is the one that wins the fight. At least, that is how I had it all figured out in my mind. I had also planned to hit first in case I didn't get another lick in.

"I didn't even say anything," she said as she turned her head and looked out the window.

"I'm sorry, Ms. Bigbee," said Ms. Jones in a really sincere and heartfelt voice.

"Yeah, you are sorry!" I said, and by this time, I was so close to her face that if I stuck out my tongue, I could have probably touched her on her nose with it. My fists were clenched as tight as they could be without breaking a nail. I wanted to hit her so very badly.

"Come on, Leeta. Just sit down. It's not worth it," Donna continued to say as she grabbed me by my shoulders. By this time, Tasha, Chris, and Little C. finally got on the bus. The sad part was after Tasha waited with me all that time for the camera, I wasn't even concerned about Little C. Everyone just looked at them because they were expecting the big whooping any minute. Chris took Little C. to the bathroom on the bus, but we didn't hear any screaming. People could hardly sit still in their seats. They were trying to watch me in the front of the bus and listen to Little C in the back of the bus. But we never heard any sounds coming from the back. Everyone on the bus was completely silent as we rode for the next twenty minutes to the souvenir shop. Kevin acted as if he was scared to say anything to me as if I might bite his head off too.

After the bus stopped and I had time to think about what I had done, I searched for Mrs. Jones. "Mrs. Jones," I called out. She turned around to see who was calling her. "Hold on a minute, I'd like to talk to you," I said as I walked over to where she was standing.

"I apologize for my behavior; I was totally out of line," I said.

"It's okay, don't worry about it," she said as she walked away. Mrs. Jones went on as if nothing was wrong, but I didn't feel any better. "Soon as I get home, I am going to confess what I did. Lord, please spare my life long enough for me to confess," I said as I pleaded with God.

You are probably thinking, *But you didn't hit her, so why are you confessing?* I had to examine myself after our interaction, and no, I didn't hit her, but when my fists were clenched, they sinned. When my mouth spit horrible words, it sinned also, and my body parts are members of my body, so I sinned because in Romans 6:16, the Scripture is basically saying, "Didn't you know that whomever you allow to use you is your real master?" In other words, I was not being used by God. I was allowing Satan to use me in every way, and it showed. I felt I had to go and get it right with Mrs. Jones and with my pastor.

As I lay in the hospital bed, I continued to drift in and out of consciousness. I thought about the day Kevin came to the hospital, I do remember seeing him, but I don't actually remember the conversation we had. He sat to the left of the hospital bed and had on tan shorts and a tan-and-orange, checkered short-sleeved shirt. His hair was well-groomed with deep waves, and he sat up straight with his hands on his lap. I don't recall him actually talking or anything like that. It was just a snapshot in my mind, and I can see him sitting there like a picture. The only thing is, I just can't seem to find the picture anywhere. He visited another time, and on the second visit, he brought his little brother with him. Kevin is twenty-five years old, and his brother is only one year old. There is no one in between the two of them, and yes, they have the same mother.

The second visit from Kevin was also like a picture, except Kevin sat at the foot of the bed this time. He wore dark clothes, and his hair seemed to be longer and appeared to be kind of messy. Kevin sat slouched in a chair instead of with correct posture like the first time. His hands were busy with his brother, trying to calm him down. His brother had on dark clothes also; I guess that was so the candy and snack stains would not show up on his clothes. I have children, so I understand those types of things, like wearing blue jeans over and over until you can actually see the dirt on them. Well, maybe I should rephrase that—until the dirt no longer wipes off with a wet washcloth.

Anyway, his brother's hair looked kind of fuzzy, and his back faced me, but he leaned forward toward Kevin. The upper part of his body was hanging over Kevin's left thigh, reaching for something that I'm sure he had no business touching. And those are the details of that picture that I can't seem to find.

During my hospital stay, they kept me heavily sedated, which is why I don't recall all of the conversations I had with the people that visited me. Mostly, while people visited, I would drift off and then just dream about how I knew them or times that we may have shared together. One time I recall when Redd came to visit just seconds after I had the three seizures back-to-back. Redd must be special in my life; he had a picture and a video. As I lay in the bed with my eyes closed, Redd walked into the room. "She may not be able to talk to you; she just had three seizures, and we gave her some medicine to help her rest," the nurse said as she walked out of the room.

"Hey, Leeta. It's me, Redd. Do you know who I am?" he whispered.

As the tears rolled down my face and my eyes remained closed, I just nodded my head yes. I knew who Redd was; I just couldn't get it together long enough to talk to him. As I lay there in the bed, my head felt cloudy. I slowly opened my eyes, and I saw Redd sitting in the chair next to my bed. He was talking to me, and maybe I was talking back; I just can't remember. That is when I took the picture in my mind of Redd. He was real cool. He had on a canary yellow polo shirt, faded jeans, a fisherman's hat, and of course, his forever famous sunglasses. He just sat in that chair with his feet apart and his huge hands resting on the arms of the chair. He wasn't smiling at all; it was as if he didn't want to have his picture taken.

The video of his visit is like a silent movie that plays over and over in my head. Redd is a big guy. He kind of reminds me of Fat Albert because of the way he sways when he walks, and he is shaped like him a little bit too. He walked over to my bed and handed me a stuffed Snoopy dog with sunglasses, beach shorts, and the words Surfer Dude written on his tank. I reached up slowly and grabbed the dog. Redd sat back down in the chair, and that was the end of his video. I didn't understand why I had a video and a picture of Redd until Tommy told me, "Redd must be special to get both a video and a picture." Then I started to think about what Tommy said, and he was right— Redd was special.

Redd worked for GSA (General Services Administration) as an electrician way before I was hired there. However, by the time of his visit to the hospital, he was retired. While at work, he treated me like I was his little sister. He frequently bailed me out of trouble when I had done something wrong. I recall this one time I had made about 900 dollars in international calls on the company's phone. I had been dating a guy named Chief (his rank was actually chief warrant officer, so we called him Chief) when I was in the army, and he had been transferred to Germany. We often would talk on the phone. Before he transferred, he was stationed in Kentucky, and I would call him all the time from the office phone, and no one ever noticed.

I talked quite a bit with Laura from next door, and she told me, "You can call long distance at work for free; everyone does it."

Wow, I thought. *That is right up my alley.* I could talk to Chief all day long and not pay for any of the calls. Back then, we had to pay for long-distance and roaming charges on our cellphones and home phones.

"Just dial 8 when you make a long-distance call, instead of 9 as we did for local calls, and no one will ever know the difference," she instructed. No big deal; everything was working fine as long as I called him while he was stationed in Kentucky. But as soon as he moved to Germany, I couldn't dial the phone number like I had been dialing before. Germany didn't use the standard 1–999–999–9999 numbers like we do in the States. They had a sixteen-digit number that had to be dialed direct without using a one, and I had to dial 9 to get out instead of 8.

I was pregnant with Tommy at the time when I was making the calls to Germany. I knew that the calls were starting to mount up because I had seen a telephone bill when it came in to the office, and it was about 300 dollars. I was getting nervous about the bills, and I feared that someone would say something to me about the bills, but they never did. I went on maternity leave, and everything was fine; no one ever mentioned those bills to me. I knew I had gotten away scot-free. I talked to Chief at home the entire time I was on maternity leave, and my long-distance bills at home had started to pile up. I couldn't wait to return to work to make those calls for free.

I returned to work, and it was business as usual. I continued to call and talk to Chief as if it were no big deal. After I had been back to work for about two months, I saw the telephone bill back on my supervisor's desk with several notes on it. *Oh, my God,* I thought. *What am I going to do about that bill?* I couldn't believe the bill still hadn't been paid, and now it was almost 900 dollars. *I should take the bill and hide it. I'll just lie about the bill. I'm going to get fired,* I thought as I stood by my supervisor's desk, literally sweating while looking at the bill. "Redd, you have to help me," I cried as I ran towards Redd.

"What's up, Leeta?" he said in a calm, cool voice.

"Here is what happened," I said as I began to explain my situation. "I'll just say I didn't do it. They can't prove it was me!" I ranted as I carefully planned all the lies I would tell about the phone bill.

"Now, that isn't the way to handle it," Redd calmly stated.

"What do you mean? I could get fired!" I screamed.

"Just go in there and tell the truth," he suggested.

"Are you crazy? I'm not going to tell them I made those calls!" I continued to scream.

"I'm telling you, it will work. They can prove it was you. The calls stopped when you went on maternity leave, and they started back when you returned to work. They are all ready to drag you over the coals and fire you over this bill. When they ask if you did it, just say yes. Believe me, they won't be expecting that, and they won't know how to respond to it. After you admit to making the charges, ask them is there a problem. They won't know what hit them. Then explain to them how you were told that we could make long-distance calls whenever we needed to and how everyone else was doing it," he instructed.

"Okay, Redd, if you say it will work, I'll try it," I said as I walked away.

"Leeta, Jay and I need to see you in his office now," said Sue, my supervisor, as she walked away from my desk.

"Okay, this is it. Brace yourself and get your story straight," I mumbled to myself as I walked behind my supervisor, heading into her boss Jay's office. The situation went just as Redd said it would go. They didn't know what hit them; they couldn't believe I told the truth. "Redd, they didn't fire me," I exclaimed as I ran down the hall to tell him the good news.

"I told you it would work; just trust me. I'll get you through this if it kills you." And he did just that. "They said I have to pay the money back. But they said I could make thirty dollars payments every month. Thanks, Redd," I said as I hugged him around his neck. He called me his little pit bull because he said I was always going off on someone (all bark but no bite). I did go off on people all the time, but they deserved it.

While working at GSA, I couldn't stand my supervisor Sue, and it was clear that she didn't like me either. One day she called me in the conference room and started to tell me how she was going to write me up about something I had done. "Let me tell you something, lady," I said as I pointed my finger in her face. "If you don't stop harassing me, I am going to put my foot up your behind," I screamed as I walked out the room and slammed the door. Well, as soon as I calmed down, I realized I probably shouldn't have said that, and I probably really would be written up or, even worse, maybe fired. So, of course, I ran to Redd and told him the story. "When you get called in Jay's office with Sue, just say you didn't say it," he said.

"What do you mean to say I didn't say it? Sue knows I said it; we were the only two in the room," I explained to Redd.

"I know you were the only two in the room, and it is your word against hers, so just say you didn't say it," Redd instructed. When I got called in the office, I did just what I was instructed to do. "I didn't say that," I said with confidence.

"I know you said it because you were the only two in the room," Jay said.

"And that is how I know I didn't say it because we were the only two in the room, and it is my word against hers," I said as I looked at him as if to let him know he wasn't in the room. He knew I had him then. He just looked at Sue and said, "Let's just try to work together. Okay?" After that, I knew I could count on Redd to get me out of every jam I got myself into. He was brilliant! Redd and I became close friends after that.

When Redd got promoted to a Planner Estimator, he was relocated from the basement into the office I was in, and he was excited. "From now on, I want to be called by my first name. I am no longer an electrician, and you need to show me some respect and use my first name instead of my last name," he said as he made his demands. All of the custodians, electricians, and mechanics were called by their last names back then. In order to be hired, you had to be a veteran, and all of those guys were. So, they all called each other by their last names as they did when they were in the military. The office staff also called them by their last names because that is the way it was always done. But now that Redd was no longer an electrician, he felt he was just like everyone else in the office, and we should call him by his first name. Everyone in the office agreed to call him Donatello, which was his first name.

"Whatever, man, I am going to call you Redd; you aren't anyone special just because you moved up here in the office. You are going to keep calling me Leeta, aren't you?" I asked.

"Yeah, but that is different... " he said.

"Well, then," I said as I cut him off. "You keep calling me by the same name you did before you came up here, and I'm going to keep calling you by the same name, too." And that is exactly what I did. Redd has been retired for years, and we still talk on the phone and have lunch together. And I still call him Redd; he wasn't able to make me call him by his first name. So, every time I see him, his name is still Redd, and now my boys even call him Redd.

Now, in the picture of my grandparents' visit, they too sat at the foot of the bed. I believe they sat with their backs toward me for most of their visit; at least, that is how the picture is in my mind. But my grandmother turned her head several times, kind of counterclockwise, to see what I was doing. She looked concerned about me. Their picture looks like one of those sports cards when you turn it from side to side; it looks like the figure on the card is moving. That is exactly what my grandmother does in the picture of her that I have in my head. Her head turns from front to back every time the card is slightly moved from side to side.

If you knew my grandmother, you would really enjoy her. She would have you laughing for days. It is the kind of laugh that, when you keep thinking about what she said, cracks you up laughing all over again. It would make you want to go back over to her house just to see what else she was going to say. I have a big family; my mother has seven sisters and four brothers, three of whom are deceased. So, when we get together for holidays, birthdays, and special occasions, between my grandmother's children, the number that normally shows up is about eighty-plus people in and out of the house at one time or another.

Okay, I started all of that to tell you a little bit about my grandmother. My grandmother looks very good for her age. She would not tell us how old she was for a long time because she said we didn't need to know. She is from Mississippi, and she kind of has a southern accent. She let us know that she is too young for us to call her grandmother. So, instead of calling her Grandma, Nana, Grandmother, or any of those kinds of names, she told us to call her Mama just like her kids call her. So, that is what we still call her to this day. I am thirty-six years old, and I, along with any of the grandchildren close to my age, still call her Mama. However, my children and all of the younger grandchildren call her Grandmother.

My grandfather used to do a lot of videotaping for the holidays, and I remember one Christmas, my Aunt Stay had gotten mama a pair of tan suede pumps that were very cute. Mama held those shoes right up in front of the camera and said, "These shoes *showl* (sure) are nice." Then with her head kind of tilted to the side, looking at some of the other siblings, as if to say, now pay attention, "but it ain't what I ask you fo'." The whole room just turned beet red, trying to keep from falling on the floor laughing. If you could have seen the look on Aunt Stay's face, it was really funny.

When my grandmother had a headache, she would tie a cloth diaper around her head, and I guess the headache would go away. Maybe the diaper had some sort of powers or something. My Aunt Slim told me my grandmother would put salt on the top of her head to get rid of a headache also. In order to stop a baby from crying, my grandmother said she used to have to blow smoke up the baby's behind. Now that is one I have never heard of before. My grandmother had an odd way of doing things, but I guess that kind of stuff worked back in those days. My grandmother once told me, "If you ever get one of those bumps on your butt from sitting on a public toilet, just remember—Vaseline is a healer, and just put a little down there, and it will get rid of it."

When I was a child, my grandmother would give us fifty cents to sit in a chair to part her hair and scratch her scalp. No, I am serious; we would have to part her hair with a comb and scratch real hard until we got the entire dry scalp to flake up. It wasn't fun, but there was this candy store up the street, and it had the best penny candy and the best Faygo Red Pop that I had ever tasted, and we could get them both for fifty cents. Looking back on that stuff just makes me laugh; those were fun times back then, but that's just the way mama was and still is.

There was one time when one of the family members started to pick up weight, Mama told them to turn around. And when Mama looked at them from the back, she said (I know this is going to be hard to imagine saying, but she is saying "child." Just think southern), "Chow, if you don't stop eating, you gonna end up with titties on the back side." Can you imagine someone having titties on his/her back? She is so funny; you just have to get to know her. I believe she says those things out of love. One time we were all at a birthday party, and she said, "Leeta, you have those boys looking just like the big boys, just as sloppy as they want to be." When I told my Aunt Slim what she said, Slim said, "You know that was a compliment; Mama just has a different way of saying things." We both laughed; I knew what Mama meant, but it was still funny.

Now, my granddad is really mild-mannered, unlike my grandmother. I call him daddy, and he calls me Lunky. Everyone else in the family calls me Lukes. Don't ask me why, but our family has the weirdest nicknames. Normally, when we have a get-together, Daddy is the one that greets us at the door. "Hey, Lunky Lunk," he would say. With a big, gigantic smile on his face, he always gives me a big hug and a kiss when I walk into the house. He really is a cheerful man. When he opens the door, he usually has on a white V-neck undershirt. It looks like it has been washed a bunch of times because it is kind of see-through. He normally has on a pair of tan shorts and a pair of house slippers that cover your entire foot, and he always has on a pair of knee socks. Daddy looks like he has a Native American heritage or something. His skin is the color of coffee that has had cream added to it. His hair is like that of a Native American real straight, and it is mostly black, with streaks of gray. It is completely gone on the top and only remains on the sides. You are able to see his ears through his hair, and it is perfectly shaped with sideburns. It rounds around the back of his neck without touching his collar.

There was a time when I was having surgery for something, and I was over at my grandparents' house sleeping over, so they could take me to surgery in the morning. I have had several surgeries, so I don't recall which surgery this one was for. But anyway, I was fasting because the doctor's office instructed me not to eat after midnight the night before surgery. I believe I had to be there about six o'clock in the morning, but I wasn't sleepy that night. So, I went to the back room in the den with my grandparents to watch the stories (soap operas) that they had recorded earlier. "Hey, chow, cum' mone' in here and sit-down wit'cho daddy and me," Mama said. So, I did. I normally work during the day, so I wasn't interested in watching soap operas. I wasn't really watching the soap operas; I was just basking in my own boredom. My grandmother could see that I was getting restless. "Wats' a matta', chow, you hurtin'?"

"No, Mama. I think I'm just going to go to bed."

"You tired?" she asked.

"Not really," I replied.

"Then why don't you go in there and get that comb so you can scratch yo' mama's head?"

Why couldn't I just keep my mouth shut? I believe I ended up scratching her head for about forty-five minutes. Daddy looked over at me with a sigh of relief and said, "Lunky, I sure am glad you are here. She makes me scratch her head every night, and I hate it." Then he flashed a gigantic smile and just continued to watch the soaps as I began to scratch Mama's head.

Now, the picture I can't find of Sister Jeanie and Sister Susie's visit is not as clear in my head as the other pictures. I guess

I just didn't get to look at it as long. I can't even remember where Sister Jeanie was sitting. I don't recall what they were wearing or what they talked about. I do recall them being there, and I did see them smile. But that is all I recall about that picture.

Sister Jeanie is the pastor's secretary; she is a really soft-spoken, very well-groomed, brown-skinned lady with bright white teeth. She is a very pretty lady. Her hair is a brownish color with a few strands of gray. She also has very smooth skin. All that is fine and good, but when the quickening power of the Lord hits her, and she gets to shouting, that hair is all over her head. She does not mind getting ugly for the Lord; that is what I love about her. She is really down to earth.

Sister Rochelle is the pastor's sister, and she came to visit with Sister Joni. Sister Joni doesn't go to our church anymore; she started her own church, so I was really surprised to see her. I believe Rochelle sat on the right side of the bed, and Joni sat on the left side of the bed. It seems like they both had on white sweaters in their picture, but it is kind of blurry and out of focus, so that is all I remember. However, I do have a small videotape in my head of them. Sister Rochelle stood up and said, "Let's pray," and they both grabbed my hands. That is all I have on the video from that visit. Sister Rochelle is the one that God gave the vision about the women's retreat. Sister Rochelle is kind of tall. She has a darker complexion; dark chocolate is the color that comes to mind. Sister Rochelle talks really fast and has a semi-deep voice. Her voice reminds me of Mahalia Jackson or someone like that. My sister Mia said she sounds like a hustler. When Mia said she sounds like a hustler, I just fell out laughing because she hit the nail right on the head. Sister

Rochelle is really fun to be around, but she can kid with you and not even crack a smile. She sounds like an auctioneer when she starts telling a story or something. Sister Rochelle and my mom were in kindergarten together, so they are good friends.

Sister Joni has been one of my favorite people since I was a little girl. I used to babysit for her sister Barb many years ago. Sister Joni has always been pretty; she has long hair and dark facial features. If I could be honest for a minute, she kind of favors bin Laden's kin people. When I was a kid, I always wanted her to notice me. You know how when you are a kid, you think it is cool if the popular people pay attention to you. Well, maybe I should change that. I thought it was cool if they paid attention to me, to tell me how cute my outfit was or how nice my hair looked. When I started attending Love, and I saw her, I felt pretty good, like I was a part of the in-crowd. I know that is silly, but that is the way I felt at that time.

I didn't remember some people's visit at all. Hector came to visit twice and seems like I have a videotape of him pointing to the board, showing me the date he wrote on the board of his visit. I saw the date on the board, but I didn't remember what it was supposed to symbolize. Hector is my uncle, well, not really; he and my Aunt Slim actually divorced many years ago but seems like he is still in the family. He is a pretty boy; he has that wavy black hair like the Hispanics and the same skin color too. He is a helper to those that need help; he is kind of like a handyman. What I mean by helper is he is an all-around, fix-it kind of guy; you know, a jack-of-all-trades, master of none. If you need your car detailed, call Hector. If you need your carpet cleaned, call Hector. You can call Hector for just about anything, and he will see to it that it gets done.

Of course, my room was flooded daily with family members and people from church. Sister Shelley also spent lots of time in my room since she worked at the hospital. Concerning my family members, I just have small video clips. Mostly I just see them walking in and out of my room, kind of pacing back and forth. Aunt Cynthia and Aunt Angela really stuck out to me for some reason.

Slim's daughter Bee Bee came, and her video was a silent one. In her video, she just walked around the right side of my bed and hugged me. There were others in the room, but they weren't as clear on the video as she was. My boys had almost the exact same video as Bee Bee. They walked around to the right side of my bed, hugged me, and then faded off as they walked out the door. Thinking back on it, it was the weirdest thing.

Several other people came to visit, and some I have pictures of and some I don't recall seeing at all. There were three people from church—Marcie, Alex, and Gwen—who came to visit, and I do recall their pictures. Gwen sat in a chair, and Marcie and Alex were married, and they sat on the windowsill. Their picture is one of the ones where the figures move when you turn it from side to side. When their picture is turned, I can see the three of them holding their heads back, kicking up their feet, holding their hands over their mouths and stomachs, and just laughing. I don't know what was so funny during their visit, but I sure am glad they made me laugh. There were other people from church who came, some I remember and some I don't. Minister Black and Elder Sharp came and prayed, but I don't have a picture, video, or message to remember them by. I don't remember them visiting at all; I was just told by Sharon that they visited. I tried to figure out why some get videos, some get pictures, some get messages, and some get nothing. But I couldn't figure it out, and I've just learned to accept it.

Now, Brother Ron came to visit, and I was semi-alert when he came. Sharon was there also, and we were all talking in the room. "I'm here to take her for her MRI," the nurse said as he walked over to my bed. I don't actually remember riding through the halls of the hospital; it was as if I was bewitched or something, and all of a sudden, I, Sharon, Ron, and the bed just appeared in the room for the MRI.

Sharon stood at the right side of the bed, and Ron stood on the left. I can recall looking up at them, and suddenly they began to bounce around. "Don't focus on it, Leeta," Sharon said as she grabbed my hand. "The devil is a liar; you won't have another seizure," she said as if she could stop me. I could feel my body begin to shake, and there was nothing I could do about it. "I can't do the test; she's having a seizure," the technician said as he walked over and looked at me on the bed. By this time, Sharon had already begun to pray. I'm not sure Ron was even aware of what was going on, but when he saw Sharon praying, he immediately started praying too.

The next thing I knew, the same way I got to the testing site was the same way I ended up back in my hospital room. I felt like such a mess: I couldn't remember anything; I was losing consciousness frequently; and they had me so drugged up that I didn't know if I was coming or going. As a matter of fact, I didn't know if anyone else was coming or going either. I was really tired of it all. During that visit, Sharon and Ron shared a video, and it also had sound. I do recall Ron visiting another time, but he had a silent video the next visit. He walked into the room, handed me a bag with a grape soda and some chips, and left. And that is the end of that video. Ron later told me he stayed and talked with me for a while, but I just don't remember it.

I talked to several people on the phone during my hospital stay, and that is where most of the telephone messages came from. I ended up staying in the hospital for seven days, and I had left the dog outside in the backyard. So, I called Rebecca from class and said, "Hello, Rebecca, I left the dog outside. Will you get some dog food and feed him?" I asked.

"I don't have any dog food, Leeta, but I can feed him some cat food," she replied.

"Okay, cool," I answered. But I guess I wasn't happy with the fact that Rebecca wanted to feed my dog cat food. Because I was later told I called a guy from work and asked him to go buy the dog some food, and I would pay him back. Then I'm not sure if I thought he wasn't going to buy the food or what, but I later told Sharon the dog didn't have any food and asked her to go and buy some also. Maybe I wasn't satisfied that they would buy the food; I don't know why I asked some many people. But I later called Auntie Ruthie, and I guess I told her she could have the dog. The conversation with Auntie Ruthie seemed to be just a very short message on the machine, and it said, "I'll take care of him, baby," and that is all I remember from the conversation with Auntie Ruthie. So, needless to say, by the time everyone had picked up their portion of the dog food to drop it off for the dog, he was gone. Auntie Ruthie had rescued him from the heat and took him home to live with her and her other two dogs.

On the day I had the lumbar puncture, I recall a message that kept playing in my head. At first, I couldn't remember who had left the message in my head, and the more I heard it playing in my head, I realized it was me. I was so afraid to have the lumbar puncture (LP) done. I had seen it performed on television, and they made it look as if it was intensely painful. Before my dad died, he had to have an LP, and my mom said he cried through the whole procedure. I just didn't want to have it done, but the doctor told the nurse to tell me that if I didn't have the procedure, he would discharge me from the hospital. I didn't want to go home still having seizures, especially with my children and me in the house alone.

Therefore, I agreed to have the procedure done in order to allow them to try and find some answers about what was going on with me. The message that kept coming to mind said, "Bishop, I know God didn't give us the spirit of fear, but I am afraid." Evidently, I had called Bishop an hour or so before I was supposed to have the procedure done. The weird part about that answering machine message in my head is that the only words are from me, and I am already talking to Bishop. When someone calls the church for Bishop, they usually have to go through his secretary Sister Jeanie. I am sure I had to talk to Sister Jeanie before I spoke to Bishop, but I don't remember a conversation with her. I actually don't remember Bishop talking back to me either.

However, I know I was actually talking to Bishop and didn't imagine it; because when I came back from the procedure, Bishop was waiting for me in my room. I have a picture in my head of Bishop. He had on a brown jacket, and he sat in a chair by my hospital bed. His arms were folded and lying in his lap, and he leaned a little to the side. He didn't look like he felt well. I don't recall talking to him or even seeing him for more than a couple of seconds before I dozed off. The tripped-out part about it is Bishop said he and my uncle Hector stayed, prayed, and talked with me for over an hour. I don't recall seeing or talking to my uncle at all during Bishop's visit. That was another really weird picture because two people came to visit, but only one person got in the picture.

When Mariah and Linda came to visit, they brought Ms. Denise. They were talking to me, and I remember talking back to them. I'm not sure what we were talking about, but I felt pretty good in my body during their visit. I remember looking at them, and then, all of a sudden, I started having seizures. They had a videotape with sounds because I can recall Linda cursing and trying to get the nurses in the room as they were holding me down, so I would not shake myself out of the bed. "Grab her legs, Linda," Mariah said as she continued to hold me down.

"Where are all the nurses?" Linda screamed. Ms. Denise didn't move; she seemed extremely scared. I remember opening my eyes, and when I did, I saw the nurse enter the room. She headed over to the right side of my bed with a needle in her hand and injected some medicine into my IV, and that is all I have on that videotape. Mariah and Linda are sisters, and I have known them all of my adult life and part of my teenage years. I met Mariah through my friend Shelia. Shelia dated my older brother in high school, and I guess in order to get closer to him, she started being my friend. Normally that is how high school girls operate. When they find a guy they like, they start being friends with the sister in order to get closer to the brother. Shelia and my brother didn't date long, but Shelia and

I continued to be friends throughout high school, but we don't talk at all now.

It was kinda strange that Shelia introduced me to Maria because Shelia didn't like me hanging out with white people because, she said, that is all I dated in high school. It wasn't that I only liked white guys, but they were the only guys who ever asked me out back then. Shelia wrote in my school yearbook, "Watch out for the guys in college because you know you like them light, bright, and most times white." Then she drew a picture of a preppy white boy next to it. Little did Shelia know I had no intentions of even going to college, even though I had received an acceptance letter from two well-known colleges. I just wasn't feeling college at that time.

One day while we were in high school, I was at home doing the dishes, and I heard a knock at the door. When I opened the door, I saw Shelia standing there, and I said, "Who is that?" As I looked out the door and saw the white girl sitting in a car parked in front of my house. I became very puzzled. She was bouncing her head up and down to the beat of some rap song, and she had the music cranked up as loud as it could go.

"That's Mariah. She lives down the street from me," she calmly answered.

"What are you doing with that white girl?" I questioned. "You don't even like white people," I reminded her.

"She's got a car, so throw on some clothes, and let's go!" Sheila exclaimed.

"Go where?" I asked as I was still confused about Mariah being white.

"Who cares? Did you hear what I said? She's got a car! Now hurry up, and let's go!" she yelled. Now, what in the world did she say that for? "Oh, a car!" I acknowledged as I shook my head and ran off to get dressed. Shelia's parents died when she was younger, and my mother was a single mom, so neither one of us had a car or any money for a car. We were thrilled to find a friend who had a car. Mariah was only sixteen years old, and she was allowed to take the car all by herself. That was all Shelia had to say, and Mariah was our new best friend. After high school, we remained friends. I also lived with Mariah and her family for about a year while I was pregnant with Tommy. Mariah and Linda are the youngest out of the five children, and Linda is younger than Mariah.

Mariah, Shelia, and I hung out every day from that day forward. Shelia and Mariah lived across the street from each other; they would drive over to my house and pick me up. Mariah would beg me to take little Mia with us, and we would go to all the carnivals that were in town. One day after one of the carnivals, Mariah decided that we would all spend the night at her house, and that was fine with me. All I had to do was ask my mother. "You guys come in the house with me so I can ask my mom," I said, thinking that my mother wouldn't say no and embarrass me in front of my friends. We all came into the house and hung out for a few minutes before I decided to ask my mother the big question. I hadn't slept over many peoples' houses before, but I hadn't really asked either, so I didn't think it would be a big deal.

We hung out in my bedroom for a while until my mother came in to check on us. "Hi, girls," my mom said as she walked into my room.

"Hi, Mrs. Thompson," they said in unison.

"Ummmm, Mom, is it okay if I sleep over at Mariah's to-night?" I said as I looked at Shelia and Mariah, nodding my head as if I had it in the bag.

"No," she answered quickly.

"No?" I yelled in confusion.

"That's what I said," she replied.

"Why not?" I questioned.

"Because I said so; now sit down and shut up," she said in a stern voice.

By this time, Shelia and Mariah are sitting on the bed, look-ing terrified.

"Why do I have to sit down? I'm just asking you why I can't go," I said as I continued to talk.

"Wham!" before I could even finish saying the word go, she reached over and punched me dead in my arm.

"What did you hit me for?" I screamed.

"Because I told you to sit down and shut up," she said as she punched me again. "Now, do it!" she screamed.

"I didn't even do anything wrong, and you are hitting on me!" I yelled as I refused to sit down. What did I say that for? She reached over and punched me another time. I mean, she hit me extremely hard that time. By the time she hit me the last time, Shelia and Mariah were sitting so close together that they could be mistaken for one person. They are clinching the edge of the mattress, bracing themselves as if they were about to be punched too.

"You can punch me all you want! I'm still not sitting down because I didn't do anything wrong!" I screamed once again as I stood there and braced myself for the next punch. I had taken three punches so far, and I was not about to back down in front of my friends now.

"I think it is time for you girls to leave," Mom said as she pointed to the door. After Mariah and Shelia tore themselves away from the mattress and off the bed, they raced for the bedroom door, ran down the hall, and all I heard was the back door slam behind them. "Wham!" before I even turned around to look at my mom, she laid one more good punch right on my arm. This time, I went flying off my feet and landed on the bed.

"Now, next time I tell you to do something, you better do it!" she said as she walked out of the room, looking and feeling like Mike Tyson.

I was so angry I could have just screamed, but I didn't dare to because Mike would have come back into the room and laid another knockout punch on me. Needless to say, I didn't get to spend the night at Mariah's house that night.

The next day, when I hooked up with Shelia and Mariah, all they talked about was how my mom knocked the snot out of me. I didn't think I would ever live that one down. "Why didn't you just sit down?" Mariah said in a puzzled voice.

"Because I wasn't wrong," I insisted.

"I don't care; I would have just sat down," Mariah said while she shook her head in disbelief. The truth is, I don't know what made me think I could stand up to my mom and not get beat down. My mom didn't take any mess from any of us. I remember a time when Sharon and I got in a fight while Sharon was pregnant, and my mom whooped all of us. That's right; she whooped me, Sharon, and Stephanie, while she was still in Sharon's stomach. I can also recall a time when Sharon tried to stand up to Mom, and all we heard from the kitchen was Sharon's body hit the hallway floor. Mom had picked Sharon up and slammed her on the floor. I usually just keep my mouth shut because my mom really didn't take any mess. My mom was more lenient on me the next day, and I was allowed to spend the night over at Mariah's house. I guess it was just the principle of the thing for her.

When I walked into Mariah's house, her dad looked like he was about fifty years old; he was sitting in his office. He had an earring in his ear, a ponytail, and he had the rap song *Dear Yvette* by LL Cool J playing on the radio while he was bobbing his head up and down to the beat. All of a sudden, it clicked; I could see where Mariah got it from. Shelia, Mariah, and I really had some good times back then.

Mariah and I don't hang out anymore now, even though I got her a job at GSA. Seems like after I got her hired, she really changed. She is very difficult to work with, and she doesn't always tell the whole truth, if you know what I mean. For instance, there was this one time she had been transferred to the building I was located in, and my boss was giving me a hard time at work. And believe me, this was only one of those times because he was always giving me a hard time. He came over to my desk and started screaming at me, being rude, disrespectful, and degrading. The situation had gotten so disruptive that Mariah went down to the union office to complain to the union representative. My boss had me very upset this particular time, so much so that I went to the Equal Employment Opportunity (EEO) officer, which was Redd at the time, and I filed a complaint against him.

Redd agreed I had a case and went forward with the suit. I had spoken to Mariah to let her know I filed suit with the EEO about the incident that occurred. When it was time to collect a deposition from Mariah, she told the representative that she didn't even remember the event happening or ever going to the union office. I couldn't believe what I heard. The incident was so disturbing to Mariah that she took it upon herself to go to the union office and tell the union representative, but when it came time to give a sworn statement, she couldn't remember any of it.

Well, I don't know why I let that situation surprise me; Mariah was always doing things like that. When I would arrive at work, she would scream out, "Oh, you finally made it to work, or you've been to lunch all this time!" She would say little phrases like that, just loud enough so the boss could hear. I guess she thought it would score brownie points. You know what? I guess she was right because she did go from being a contract employee to a federal employee. So, it looks like it did pay off.

My boss's boss (the big boss) told me to my face, "You are very intelligent, and I know you know what you are doing; no one doubts that. But since you don't like it here, I will never promote you." My boss sat right beside her and listened and nodded his head in agreement. I said, "So what you are saying is, if you were a teacher and if I were in your class, and if I were an 'A' student, the fact that I didn't like your class, you would give me a 'D'?"

She said, "Yes." And you know what? I haven't been promoted since. If she announced a job, and I applied for it and was qualified, she canceled the job announcement.

Now Linda, Mariah's little sister, can curse like a sailor; she and Ms. Denise from work really could be related if that were all there was to go by. Linda was, and still is, totally spoiled. She is the one that really let me know there is a difference between white and black parents. Linda could go off on her mother and curse at her, and her mom would just let her do it. Mariah would often jump in the middle and try to shut Linda up. My mom would have slapped me in my mouth so many times that I would have lost count and some of my teeth.

Anyway, Ms. Denise and I worked together for about four years. We had become pretty good friends. Denise left and went to work for the Marion County Sheriff because they grew up together and went to school together. Ms. Denise told the sheriff that I was in the hospital, and he came to visit me too. I also had a video of the sheriff: I remember him sitting in the chair to my left in his sheriff's uniform. I felt badly the day he came, and I dozed off several times during his visit. However, I do recall him asking me whether I wanted him to arrest the doctors who were being mean to me. I just laughed and dozed off. He and I were cool. Well, I guess we would have to be if I call the sheriff by his first name when everyone else calls him Sheriff or Chief. I worked with him for about ten years when he worked in the office next door to GSA. When the sheriff became a US Marshal for the second time, I also worked in the US Courthouse with him for the eight years that he held that position. When he was the marshal, I still called him by his first name; I must admit it felt pretty good to be that close to someone of power that everyone else looked up to and respected because of his position.

Even though Ms. Denise left and started a new job, she and I would still go to lunch together on occasion, and we kept a steady line of email conversations back and forth. She seemed scared when she visited me in the hospital. She sat in the chair to my left for the entire visit and didn't move. I talked to Ms. Denise several times after I got out of the hospital, and she was sincerely concerned about me.

I do remember Ms. Denise's picture, though; she had on a gold shirt with her hair pulled to the back in a ponytail, with a curl on each side of her head. The weird thing about Ms. Denise getting a picture is because she came with Mariah and Linda, and they got videos, but she only got a picture. On the day the three of them visited, Tasha from one of my classes in the bachelor's program came also. Tasha and I had gotten very close during our accounting class. The students in my class would say Tasha is a short, little, white version of me. I noticed we did have a lot in common after we started talking and studying together. We are both perfectionists, and we wanted to earn an "A" in every class. All thanks to God, I got an "A" or "A–" in every class in my bachelor's program and also in the associate's, except for one B; and believe me, I was extremely upset about that B. Tasha and I worked closely throughout many of the classes in the bachelor's program; we were both dedicated and wanted the best grades, so we could achieve a high-grade point average (GPA). My GPA turned out to be 3.89 on a 4.0 scale. We both had our own study groups in college, but it felt as if most of the people in class only wanted the degree and weren't concerned about the grades they received. Many of the people in my class already worked in the field they were getting the degree in; they just needed that piece of paper (diploma) so they could advance and be promoted at their current job.

Tasha's visit was a picture. She sat at the foot of my bed with her legs crossed and just observed. She wore a white sweater; at least, that is the way I see it in the picture. When I spoke with Tasha after I got out of the hospital, she told me that I asked her to bring me some pajamas because my back side was hanging out in the hospital gown. Needless to say, I didn't recall asking for the pajamas, so I left them in the closet in the hospital room when I checked out. I really should have replaced those pajamas. I just wasn't aware of the things I was saying or doing while I was in the hospital because of all the medications they had me on.

The week I was in the hospital was a week that I can't seem to remember, but it is also one I will never forget. As I began to wake up, I heard the nurse say, "You're going home today, Ms. Bigbee," as she walked over and started taking my IV out of my arm.

"Great, did they find out what was wrong with me?" I asked.

"Your test results came back normal; everything is fine," she said as she continued to disconnect me from the hospital equipment and machines.

"Hi, Leeta. How are you?" Olivia said as she walked into the room.

"I'm feeling great! Can you take me home?" I asked.

"Take you home? Are they letting you go today?" she questioned.

"They're letting me go right now. I just need to wait on my discharge papers," I answered.

"What did they say was wrong?" she continued to question.

"Nothing, I'm fine, and I'm ready to go. So, will you take me?" I asked again.

"Sure," she said as she reached for the ringing phone. "Hey, Sharon, it's Olivia. No, they are letting her go. Right now." I could only hear Olivia's side of the conversation, but from the way she was talking, I gathered that Sharon was surprised that I was being discharged. "Here, Leeta, Sharon wants to talk to you," Olivia said as she handed me the phone. I explained everything to Sharon and told her I would call her when I got home. "Is it okay if I take a shower first, Olivia? I've been laid up in that bed for a whole week, and I really need one," I said.

"Sure, Leeta, I'll wait," she answered. That water felt so good to my body. My body was so sore and achy that I just wanted to stay in the shower forever. I had to sit in the chair that was in the shower for support. As I sat in the shower, I began to reminisce about some of the good old times Olivia, and I had when we were younger.

Olivia and I met at church over twenty-five years ago. I was in the second grade, and she was in kindergarten. Olivia and I hung out for years. I stood by her side when her mom died when she was in the seventh grade. I even rode in the limousine with the family on the day of the funeral so that I could be there for Olivia. Through the years, we have become very close. Both of our mothers were saved, and so they wouldn't allow us to do certain things. For instance, my mother wouldn't allow me or my sister to wear pants or go to parties and stuff like that.

Olivia and I had it all figured out, "Ask your mom to pick me up and drop us off at the bowling alley," I said to Olivia.

"Then we can catch a cab from the bowling alley to the skating rink," she replied.

"Sounds like a plan. I'll see you when you get here," I said and then hung up the phone. We would sneak to the skating rink almost every weekend. We were really a couple of regulars there, especially when we weren't even supposed to be there at all. It did get kind of ugly after her mother died. Olivia would tell me we had a ride home and that so-and-so's mother was going to take us home, but after the skating rink closed, we would be stranded with no ride home. So, we would call a cab and tell the cab driver to let us out a few houses from Olivia's house and then tell the driver our mother had the money. We would go through someone's backyard, jump the fence, and then run home and never pay the cab driver. Wow, I just can't believe all the things we did.

The one thing that really had me scared was when Olivia had us stranded at the rink; and she went to a guy and asked him for a ride home, and when he told her yes, we all jumped in the car. He just thought he was taking her home, so the rest of the crew was a surprise to him. Well, he stopped at White Castle to grab a bite to eat. He left the car running with us in the car. Olivia sat in the front seat. "Let's take his car, y'all," Olivia offered with a devilish grin on her face. I was so afraid. I just kept praying to God. "Lord, if You get me out of this, I swear I will never do this again." You know how we do. We make vows to the Lord and oftentimes never keep them. Well, I did. I stopped doing stuff like that, and God did not allow us to steal that man's car. He came out of White Castle a few minutes after Olivia's comment.

When Olivia's mom died, she was thirteen years old, and she was driving. She was also allowed to wear pants, so when we would go skating, to a party, or an under-twenty-one club, she would pick me up or have someone else pick me up and have a change of clothes for me to change into in the car. At first, I felt a little embarrassed about changing in front of guys, but after a while, it didn't bother me anymore. As a matter of fact, I got so good at it, that I would go across the street to my uncle's yard, which was a wooded area, and I would change into my pants before and after I went to school.

Once I figured out the trick, as long as I came back into the house the same way I left, everything was fine. One day I just got fed up with it all and went out and bought my very first pair of blue jeans. They were dark blue in the back and light blue in the front—my very own two-tone pair of jeans. "What are you doing?" my mother asked.

"I'm ironing my clothes," I replied as I starched my jeans before heading out for skating.

"You will not be wearing those in my house," she demanded.

"I'm not going to be in your house. I'm leaving," I said as I closed up the ironing board and walked out of the kitchen, headed to my bedroom to put my jeans on. I couldn't believe it; I finally told my mom that I would be wearing pants. From that day forward, no more changing clothes in the bushes or in cars. I walked out of the house fully dressed in what I would be wearing for the day. Of course, I didn't live with my mother much longer after that. I moved out when I was about eighteen years old.

Things had gotten pretty rough for Olivia after her mother died. She was only thirteen and was allowed to drive the Volvo her mother had left her. We were hanging out and doing just about whatever we felt like. All I had to do was tell my mother I was going to spend the night over at Olivia's house, and it was on after that. Olivia's dad basically let her do whatever she wanted to do. She would take his credit cards, and we would go shopping and just live the good life. We had even started to smoke weed. We were headed nowhere fast. Olivia's dad had a girlfriend, Starla, who would give us weed for free. She would even get high with us; we thought she was the coolest adult in the world.

One day while we were waiting to hang out with Starla and her friends, Olivia brought me a blunt to hit. I took a hit, then another, then another. My head started spinning, and so did the room. "What the heck is this?" I asked as I passed the blunt back to Olivia.

"Ah, don't worry about it; it's laced," Olivia said as she and Starla pointed and laughed at me.

"What the heck is laced?" I asked.

"You know, we put a little cocaine in it," Starla said as she took a couple of pulls off the joint.

"I can't believe you gave me that mess, Olivia. What is wrong with you?" I screamed.

"Ahh, it's no big deal, Leeta; just enjoy it," she said in a calm, dopehead voice.

"Take me home. Take me home right now!" I demanded.

"Come on; just hang out with us for a moment," she insisted. We went back and forth for a while until they finally took me home. I just couldn't believe how out of control things had gotten. I don't think I had ever really gotten high before that night. I wasn't really a smoker, and I guess I just wasn't doing it right, but that night, I felt like my head was going to float off my shoulders.

Olivia and I drifted apart after that night. When we met up again a few years later, she had a son about three or four years old. She was no longer getting high and had calmed down a lot. Olivia was dating a guy named Jay Jay, and they all lived with her father in her mother's old house. Jay Jay and Olivia had been dating since high school. I just didn't know it had continued because we hadn't kept in touch after the laced-joint incident, which was about my freshman year in high school. We jumped right back in where we started and began hanging out again.

As a matter of fact, she is the one who talked me into getting back with Tommy's dad, Roman. Most times, people called him Ro for short. Tommy's dad and I hadn't really been boyfriend and girlfriend. I had known him from school and thought he was kind of cute. I didn't actually hook up with him until years later when I saw him dancing at the nightclub and decided I liked the way he danced. Olivia and I had gone our separate ways by the time Ro and I started hanging out.

Anyway, when Olivia found out that I had dated him, she thought we would make a cute couple since we were both so short. He is about five feet, six inches, and I am five feet one inch, so we did look really cute together. I gave him a call, and we started hanging out again. We weren't really the boyfriend-girlfriend type, and we didn't really spend a lot of time together. I could count on one hand the number of times we had been together. Now, one of Ro's friends named Lamont and I had become pretty close. I'm not sure how we actually started hanging out together, but we became good friends. Lamont would hang out over at my house and teach me all the latest dance moves. One day Lamont was over, and he just happened to mention that the "fellas" were going on an overnight trip to Kings Island, and they were all taking their girlfriends. "Did Ro tell you about it?" he asked.

"As a matter of fact, he didn't," I answered. Ro wasn't my boyfriend, but since he was the one I was kickin' it with, I felt worthy of a free trip to Kings Island. During our fantabulous trip to Kings Island in the middle of arguing, we happened to do what sinners do, and God blessed us to create Tommy.

Since Ro and I weren't really good friends, he didn't take the whole pregnancy thing well. He told me he wouldn't be a good dad, and that is about the only honest thing he said to me during my entire pregnancy. I've raised Tommy by myself and didn't expect much from Ro. I asked Olivia to be Tommy's godmother. She accepted.

Olivia was at the church while Tommy was blessed, and she did a great job at being his godmother. She spent time with Tommy, and she was always buying him the latest sneakers and other cool stuff. I had Tommy's first birthday party at Olivia's house in her backyard. Looking back over things, time has really helped us to grow up. Olivia and I did frequent the clubs, but it was nothing like we did when we were younger. Olivia and Jay Jay were dating seriously, and she didn't do much without him.

A few weeks before Tommy's second Christmas, Jay Jay came over to my apartment to talk to me. He asked me several questions about things that happened while he and Olivia had broken up. To tell the truth, they were always breaking up and getting back together. I tried to stay out of it. I wasn't the boyfriend-girlfriend type. What I mean is, I didn't keep a boyfriend long; they seemed to get on my nerves quickly. One time, my brother asked me why I broke up with someone, and I told him because I could hear the guy breathing. My brother thought that was the funniest thing. "You are just petty," he told me. I didn't care; I wasn't going to be bothered with someone whom I could hear breathing when I sat close to him.

Anyway, Jay Jay continued to question me about people and events in Olivia's life. Jay Jay was cool, but I didn't talk much to him. He was a gangster type, and drama always seemed to follow him. Olivia and I were always following him somewhere and sneaking around and checking up on him to see what girl he was cheating with at that time. I wasn't aware if Jay Jay knew that Olivia dated someone else while they weren't together, but I wasn't about to tell him anything that she had done. She never cheated on him, and he had cheated on her several times, and she knew it. But it was just different when it came to guys. Actually, they just thought it was different when it came to their "woman." Most guys felt like once you had a baby by them, you were theirs forever.

"Did Olivia date anyone while we were broken up?" he asked.

"Nope, she never dated anyone," I replied.

"Come on, Leeta. You can tell me; I won't get mad. We weren't even dating back then," he reminded me. "Just tell me; I'll pay you for the information."

"No, she never dated anyone," I insisted. I knew not to tell Jay Jay anything because he was a very violent person. I can remember working at Taco Bell, and I could see the kids walking home from school. People thought that Olivia and I were cousins since we were always together. Well, I guess they also thought we were cousins because we told them we were. But anyway, people would run into Taco Bell and tell me Olivia and Jay Jay were over in the parking lot fighting. I don't think I ever said anything to Olivia about it. I tried when we were younger about other guys that used to hit on her, but she wasn't trying to hear it. She liked gangster-thug types. So, I was very careful when I answered Jay Jay's questions that day. "No, Jay Jay, she never dated anyone else. I think the most she ever did was go to the movies with some guy named Rick. And that is it, Jay Jay; she never cheated on you," I said.

"Okay, Leeta, thanks," he said as he laid sixty dollars on the entertainment stand and walked out of the house. I didn't speak to Olivia that day, so I didn't get to tell her about the conversation with Jay Jay. I didn't rush to tell her about the conversation because Jay Jay seemed fine when he left my house, and I didn't tell him anything that would make him upset. I took the sixty dollars and bought Tommy a huge train that went around the bottom of the Christmas tree. My mom came over, and I put the train together around the tree while she kept an eye on Tommy. While she was over, the phone rang, and from looking at the caller ID, I saw that it was Olivia. "Hey, what's up?" I asked as I answered the phone.

"What in the heck did you tell Jay Jay?" Olivia screamed from the other end of the phone.

"Nothing," I said.

"You did tell him something because when I came out of the mall from buying your son the new Jordan's, he was outside by my car. When I walked up to Jay Jay like nothing had happened, he smacked me with a gun and then shot up my car," she said.

"What?" I said in amazement.

"I can't believe you would betray me like this," she said.

"Betray you? What are you talking about? I didn't tell him anything, I promise," I said.

"Soon as I find a way home, I'll be over to tear up your car just like he did mine. I know you told him something because he said you told him I slept with Rick, and how else would he know Rick's name!" she screamed.

"Olivia, I swear I didn't tell him you slept with Rick. I only told him you watched a movie with him. I swear I didn't tell him that," I said, trying to convince Olivia. She was not listening to one thing I said to her. Olivia slammed the phone down, and the next thing I knew I was listening to a dial tone.

"Who was that?" my mom asked.

"Olivia," I said as I filled her in on everything that had happened. Olivia and I talked much more about the situation, and she still believed that I told Jay Jay that she had slept with Rick. "Okay, Olivia, just answer me this. Why would I tell Jay Jay about you sleeping with someone over a year ago, and I hadn't told him about the other guys you have been with this year?" I questioned.

"I don't know why you would do it. Maybe you said it because you want him," she said.

"What? Are you crazy, Olivia? How could you say something like that? I don't want him," I said. "He isn't faithful to you, so what would I want with him? Just think about it, Olivia. I have known you for twenty years, and I have never lied to you. He, on the other hand, has known you for ten years and has done nothing but lie to you about all the women he has had. You have to believe what I am telling you," I said.

"Don't let me catch you on the street!" she screamed as she slammed the phone in my ear. I couldn't believe it. How did we end up here? Olivia was the closest friend I ever had, and now she was willing to fight me and tear my car up over some lie her boyfriend told her. I sat there for a while and thought about all the times I rode with Olivia to harass the women that Jay Jay messed around with. I also thought about how the police were searching their apartment one time, and Olivia went to a pay phone and called me and asked me to meet her. Once I arrived at the pay phone, Olivia said, "Take this home with you," as she tried to hand me a large plastic-wrapped brick of cocaine.

"What? I'm not taking that home!" I screamed.

"Be quiet. Someone may hear you. The police are at our apartment right now, trying to find drugs, so they can lock Jay Jay up. Please, Leeta, just take it. I will never ask you for anything else. Just do it, please," she begged. And you know what, like an idiot, I took it home and hid it in my closet just to keep him safe. I didn't like Jay Jay much because he beat Olivia and just made her miserable in general.

I recall one time I went skating with her. Well, I told my mother I was going bowling because I wasn't allowed to go skating. Olivia was driving, and she would not take me home after we left skating. "I'm meeting someone at this hotel. I'll be back in a few minutes," she said.

"You are going to leave me in the car while you go meet someone?" I questioned.

"It won't take long, I promise," she said. Like an idiot, I slept outside of the hotel all night long in the car while she did whatever she felt like doing on the inside of the hotel room with someone that wasn't Jay Jay. I was so scared because it was a Saturday night, and my mother did not play about coming home. I had to be in the house at a certain time. Well, needless to say, I did not get home until about 8:00 a.m. Sunday morning. When I walked into the house, my mother was coming out of the bathroom from taking a shower and getting ready for Sunday school. I felt like I had just swallowed a frog. The bathroom door opened, "Oh, you are already up for church; that's good," she said as she walked past me and went into her room to finish getting dressed.

"Yes, I've been up for a while," I said as I closed my eyes and began to pray and thank God for covering me one more time. Believe me, all the idiotic stuff I had ever done for and with Olivia ran through my head that day. I vowed never to be that type of friend again. I just wanted her to like me, and to be honest, I needed her to have clothes to change into and to have a ride to the clubs.

When I look back over my life as Olivia's friend, I begin to think about something that recently happened to me. I attended the church reunion at my former church, and a few of us were sitting in my car listening to some songs that we were going to sing for the reunion choir concert. One of my childhood friends, Toni, was in the car also, sitting in the back seat. When I spoke to Toni, she reminded me of how awful I was as a child toward Tee-Tee. Well, of course, I didn't want to hear that because the truth hurts. "You were my first friend at church, Leeta," Toni said. "You were so nice and sweet to me and Tee-Tee at first," she continued. "Yeah, I was mean to Tee-Tee sometimes, wasn't I?"

"All the time," she chimed in quickly. "What happened to you?" she asked.

I said, "Well, when Olivia and I became friends, she didn't like Tee-Tee, that's all; and I just wanted to be Olivia's friend. Everyone liked me, and I just wanted you guys to do what I wanted. You know how it is when you are poor, and Olivia kind of took care of me and let me wear her clothes, and I just didn't want to lose that." The more I talked, the shallower I sounded and the worse I felt. "You know what I mean? I just liked her so much, and she didn't like Tee-Tee, so I just kind of acted mean to Tee-Tee because she wanted me to." Toni just sat there with that pleasant smile on her face, just as she did when we were children when she tried to get us to stop fighting.

As I look back on it, I started almost all of those fights. I wanted everyone to know my hair was longer than Tee-Tee's, and you know what, everyone said my hair was longer. But I don't even know that it was. I was just such a bully to Tee-Tee because, truthfully, Olivia was a bully to me, and they would have done what I said just so I would leave them alone or so I wouldn't get Olivia mad at them. "Why did she let me beat her up all the time anyway? She was way bigger than me!" I screamed out in a defensive voice.

"I guess she couldn't fight that well," Toni replied, as she bounced her head to the music still with that annoyingly pleasant smile on her face, just enough to make me feel like dirt. I just sat there in the car, listening to music, letting my Holy Ghost minister to my soul and whip me. Toni really put some thoughts in my head that day. Please, people, don't ever let someone else dictate to you who you should and should not be friends with. I saw Tee-Tee later that day, and it brought tears to my eyes, and my heart began to literally ache as I looked at her face. Tee-Tee was one of my best friends, and she has never caused me any hurt. I loved her, and she loved me, and I deeply apologized for all the hurt that I caused her. I pray that she can forgive everything I have ever done toward her.

After the discussion where she threatened to fight me and tear up my car, Olivia and I didn't see each other again until I was pregnant with Timmy. Which was about two years later. Mariah and I were still good friends, and I had stopped over at her house after work, and Olivia was already there. When Olivia saw my car pull up, she came running out of the house and tried to start a fight with me. Mariah had to grab her and hold her back. I wasn't even aware of what was going on. Not only was I pregnant, so was Olivia. After I had Timmy, things kind of died down, and Olivia was no longer angry with me. Olivia and I don't spend much time together, nor do we talk regularly. She did come to my dad's wake, and of course, she came to the hospital to see me; cause she's waiting on me now. I spoke with her in great detail about the situation that caused the fallout after I got saved, and I believe she knows now I never told Jay Jay the things he said I did. Maybe there was some remorse for her behavior at that time; I don't know. But I was glad to see her at the hospital.

I guess all that thinking must have gone to my head because I started feeling horrible in my body and decided to get out of the shower. "Will you close the door for me, please, Olivia?" I asked as I peeked around the wall with the towel wrapped around me. "No problem," she said as she walked over and closed the door to the hospital room. I sat on the bed and began to dry off. After I dried off from the shower, I began to put my clothes on. I must have been looking funny or something because when I came out to sit down, Olivia said, "Are you okay, Leeta?" Before I could even answer her, I was sprawled out on my back on the bed as I went into another seizure. Olivia pushed the button for the nurse to get me some assistance. "May I help you?" said the voice through the call box on the wall.

"Uhhh, she's having a seizure; someone needs to come in here," Olivia explained.

"I'll be right there," she said. Within seconds, the nurse was in my room, injecting me in my upper arm with more medicine. Once again, I was sedated, laid up in bed, and tired. "Sharon, she just had another seizure, and I don't think they are going to let her go today," Olivia said as she talked to Sharon on the phone. She had called Sharon while the nurse was injecting me with the medicine. She felt that I would be staying in the hospital because of the seizures and wanted Sharon to know what was going on. After Olivia hung up the phone from Sharon, she told me she would talk to me later, and she walked out of the room. Once again, I dozed off into unconsciousness. Years later, Olivia accused me again of wanting Jay Jay and having a relationship with him while they were married. However, this time I just said, "No, I never wanted him; I never lied to you; and I never had any type of inappropriate relationship with him." Then I shut off all contact. It really hurts me because I don't think I have ever loved a friend like I loved Olivia. I realized the loyalty and love I had for her was unhealthy and wasn't worth my peace.

"Hi, baby, how do you feel?" Auntie Ruthie said as she walked into my room and kissed me on my forehead. "I feel okay, but I just had another seizure," I managed to say.

"We're going to take her down for an EEG since she just had a seizure. You can wait for her if you want or go with us," the nurse said as she helped me into the wheelchair.

"I'm going with her," Auntie Ruthie insisted. I recall sitting in a small room and lying on a medical table. "I'm going to glue these electrons on your head to measure your brain waves. Here, ma'am, put on this blindfold. I am going to flash a series of bright lights at your eyes to try to induce a seizure. The electrons will then measure the seizure and record the brain activity. Well, maybe it will record it. Sometimes the seizures show up, and sometimes they don't. But since we aren't having any luck with anything else, we will try this," the nurse explained.

"Okay, I'm ready," I said. I just wanted it over. I was sick and tired of getting poked and prodded. I just wanted to go home. The lights began to flash, and the test seemed to last forever. I braced myself and endured the bright lights. "Are you okay, baby?" Auntie Ruthie said from the other side of the room.

"I'm fine; I just have a headache," I replied.

"Just hold on; everything will be just fine," she said as she tried to comfort me. To my surprise, and to the nurse's surprise, I didn't have a seizure.

"You did great, Ms. Bigbee, and I'm all done," the nurse said as she removed the blindfold and cleaned all of the electrons off my head. "I'll help you off the table and back into the wheelchair. You can just wait in your room until I show these to the doctor, and he will come in and talk to you when he is finished reading the results of the test." She grabbed my arm to help me off the table. Auntie Ruthie stood up and helped assist me to the wheelchair. She pushed me down the hall and back into my hospital room, where we packed up my belongings, just in case the doctor said I could leave.

"Here you go, ma'am. These are your discharge papers. You need to make the following follow-up appointments in the next couple of days. The doctor said everything was fine, and he will see you in a couple of days. Oh yeah, don't drive or operate any machinery," the nurse said as she handed me the discharge papers.

"Is that it?" Auntie Ruthie asked.

"That's it. The test didn't show any brain abnormalities, so she is free to leave. Take care." The nurse said over her shoulder as she walked out of the room.

"Come on, Auntie Ruthie, let's go," I said with great anticipation.

"Okay, baby, I'll drive you home, but you need to be very careful," said Auntie Ruthie.

"I will; let's just go. I'm ready to go home. I'm tired of this hospital," I said as I hobbled to the wheelchair.

Auntie Ruthie pushed me into the wheelchair while the nurse followed. "Is anyone going to stay with you, baby?" Auntie Ruthie asked as she looked at me in the passenger seat of the car. "I'll call Sharon and tell her to meet me there. She gets off work in thirty minutes. She'll come over," I said as I picked up the cellphone to call Sharon. "This is Sharon. May I help you?" Sharon said when she answered the phone.

"Sharon, will you come over and stay with me when you get off work?" I asked.

"Where are you? I thought Olivia said they weren't letting you go home," she asked in a surprised voice.

"I'm in the car. Auntie Ruthie is driving me home now. Can you come over after work?" I asked.

"Sure, I'll be there; just let me call Mom. Love you, sweetie, and I'll see you in a minute," she said.

"Love you, too. Bye," I said as I hung up the phone. "She'll be there," I said to Auntie Ruthie.

Soon after, we pulled up to my house; Auntie Ruthie helped me gather my belongings and helped me to the door. As I walked into the house, I turned around to say goodbye. "Take care," she said as she placed my things on the floor directly inside the door. Gave me a big hug, turned around, walked away, and left.

CHAPTER 3

Home Visits and Back to School

Within minutes, Sharon was knocking at the door. "How are you, honey, honey?" she asked when I opened the door.

"I'm fine, just tired," I answered.

"Hi, Mommy," said Tommy as he walked in and hugged me around my waist.

"Hi, hon, where is your brother?" I asked as I hugged him back and laid a big fat kiss on his cheek.

"He's over at Stephanie's house. I didn't want to go," Tommy answered.

"Well, I'm just going to stay here until Mom gets here, and then I am going to go home with Bob. I haven't spent much time with him since I've had the boys and since I've been at the hospital with you. I just want to spend some quality time with him. Okay?" Sharon asked.

"Yeah, that's fine, I understand. Thanks for helping me with the boys and staying with me up there," I said.

"No problem, hon. You just go sit down and take it easy," she said as she helped me walk through the house and into the family room. I was still a little weak, and I couldn't walk very well. I didn't eat much while I was in the hospital because I spent most of my time unconscious.

"Do you want me to fix you something to eat before Mom comes?" Sharon offered.

"No, I'm not hungry. Maybe I will eat later," I said.

"Okay, well, you just sit here, and I'll get the door," she said as she walked toward the front of the house to answer the door.

"It's Mom," she yelled.

"Hi, honey," Mom said as she walked over and kissed me on my forehead.

"Hi, Mom," I said.

"Okay, I'm leaving. Take care, and I'll see you tomorrow after church," Sharon said as she came over and hugged me and gave me a kiss goodbye.

"Bye," I said as I hugged her back.

Things seemed to be going well. I sat in the family room and began watching television with Mom and Tommy.

"I have to go to work tonight," Mom said, "so Angela is on her way over to stay the night with you."

"That's fine, Mom. Thanks for coming," I said as I continued to watch television. "Tommy, come in here, please!" I yelled out.

"Yes, Mommy," he said as he came around the corner.

"Mom is going to leave, and I just wanted you to know what to do in case I have a seizure," I said. "If I start to have a seizure, you need to call 911 and tell them what is going on and ask them what to do. Okay?"

"Okay, Mommy, I'm not scared." All was well while Tommy, Mom, and I sat and watched television in the family room. "The phone is ringing, Mommy. Can I get it?" Tommy asked.

"Sure, Tommy," I answered.

"Hello… Who's calling? Hold on. It's for you, Mommy. It's Sam," Tommy said.

"Bring it here, Tommy," I said as I stretched my hand out to reach for the phone.

Sam is Shelia's husband. They moved out of town about eleven years ago, but during this time, we managed to still keep in touch and remain friends.

"Hey, Leeta, what's up?" Sam asked.

"Nothing much, just got out of the hospital," I answered.

"We will be in town in about an hour. Is it okay if we come by?" he asked.

"Who? You and Shelia?" I asked.

"We have the kids with us, too—is that okay?" he asked.

"Yeah, that should be okay. My mom is here with me," I said.

"We are pulling up to White Castle. Do you want us to bring you something?" he asked.

"Sure, get me a number one," I said.

"Do you want cheese?" he asked.

"No, I don't really like cheese on my White Caaaaaaaaaaa—" I tried to finish as I began to shake out of my chair, right onto the floor, in another seizure.

"Jesus, Jesus!" my mom screamed out. "Tommy, grab the phone and tell them she has to go."

"My mom is having a seizure. Bye," Tommy said as he grabbed the phone. "Hello 911, my mom is having a seizure," he told the 911 operator.

"Tommy, why did you call them?" my mom asked. "Hand me the phone!"

"My mom said I should call 911 if she had any seizures," Tommy cried out to his defense.

"She meant if you were here alone with her," she said as she grabbed the phone. "Hello... No, I am here with her, and she is going to be fine. No, ma'am, she just got out of the hospital today from having seizures. I'm here with her, and everything will be fine. Her address is 9339 East 36th place, but I don't need you to come out. She doesn't have a home phone; I'm talking to you on her cellphone. Really, ma'am, everything is fine. Okay, I will call you back if we need you. Thank you. Everything is going to be fine, Leeta. Get her medicine, Tommy," my mom directed.

"Don't get the medicine, Tommy; get the blessed oil," I mumbled as my mom helped me sit up on the floor. Tommy ran into my bedroom and grabbed the blessed oil, ran back into the family room, and handed it to my mom.

"The blood of Jesus, the blood of Jesus," chanted my mom as I sat on the floor with my arms wrapped around my mom's legs; she rubbed the oil on my forehead. "Do you want to sit here or get back up in the chair?" my mom asked.

"I'll get back in the chair," I answered. Mom grabbed me by the hands, helped me off the floor, and guided me backward into the theater chair. I stayed in the chair for the remainder of the day until Aunt Angela arrived. Aunt Angela really babied me. She offered to cook and clean. She didn't want me to move the entire time she was there.

Shelia, Sam, and the kids finally arrived. We watched a movie and talked about my stay in the hospital. They stayed a few hours, and then they left to head back home. Aunt Angela stayed the night and watched over me as I slept. I was seizure free for the remained of the night.

"Good morning, little Leeta," Aunt Angela said as she entered my room. "Are you going to church this morning?"

"I don't think so. I don't feel so well," I said.

"You hungry?" she asked.

"No, I'm not hungry. Maybe I'll eat later," I answered.

"Okay, don't worry about it; I'll fix you some bacon and eggs, French toast, fried potatoes and onions, and some orange juice. Is that okay?" she asked.

"That's okay, Aunt Angela, you don't have to do that. I'm not hungry," I answered again.

"Okay, I'll just let you sleep," she said as she walked out of the room.

"Close my door, please," I said as she walked away. I threw the covers over my head and rolled over on my side, crunched up in the fetal position, and just laid in the bed. I was so tired. Those seizures had taken a toll on my body. My muscles felt like I had been on a nonstop workout. I just wanted to lie in bed and not move a muscle. As I laid there, I kept trying to recall the last week of my life. The more I thought about it, the more my head hurt. I couldn't remember anything that had happened the previous week. *Wow,* I thought, *I spent an entire week in the hospital and can't remember any details from the last week.* I lay there a little while longer and tried to remember, but I couldn't. I eventually dozed off to sleep.

"Here you go, hon," Aunt Angela said. I snatched the covers off my head and looked up, and there was Aunt Angela with a full tray of food.

"I said I didn't want anything, Aunt Angela," I said as I expressed my frustration by throwing the covers back over my head.

"Just eat a little bit, Little Leeta, and I'll let you go back to sleep. Okay?" she asked.

"Okay," I said as I slowly pulled the covers from over my face and pushed myself up in the bed.

"Here, try some," she said as she pushed the fork into my mouth.

"It's really good, Aunt Angela. I'll feed myself," I said.

"Okay, but I am going to stay in here and talk to you just to make sure you eat it all," she said.

"Morning, Mommy," Tommy yelled out as he walked past my bedroom.

"Morning, Tommy. Don't talk so loud, okay? My head hurts," I said as I gripped the sides of my head and massaged my temples.

"Sorry," he said as he yelled out again. After finishing my food, I went back to sleep. I stayed in the bed the majority of the day until it was time for night service to begin. Aunt Angela volunteered to take me to church. On the first Sunday night of the month, we always have prayer at church. I felt like I really needed some prayer. My body was falling apart, and I didn't know why. God was the only one who could help me.

Aunt Angela drove up to the front door of the church to let me out. I must admit, it was difficult getting in and out of her SUV. I was annoyed with the fact that I was at a stage in my life where I needed the help of others to do everyday activities. Bro and Sis Miller was walking up to the church and saw me trying to get out of the truck. They walked over to my side of the truck to assist me. They held my hands as I slid out of the front seat onto the ground. They held on to my forearms and escorted me into the church. "Are you sure you should be out already? You should have stayed home," Sister Miller said as she and her husband helped me walk into the sanctuary.

"Tonight is prayer, and I need all the prayer I can get," I humbly replied. I was slowly escorted into the back of the sanctuary, where I kneeled down to pray. When prayer was over, I was not even sure who it was, but someone reached over and helped me off the floor. When I sat down in my seat, the room was spinning. All the people in the church seemed to blend together. I couldn't make out the faces. I felt like crying because I felt sorry for myself. I wasn't able to walk into the church on my own, and it seemed like my brain was quitting on me. *Why me, God?* I questioned several times within myself, *I just don't understand.*

"Is there anyone that has a praise for the Lord?" Gerald said before he began singing songs of praise. The saints began to stand up and prepared to testify. It took everything within me, but I stood up too. Gwen was an usher, and she stood next to the pew where I was sitting. She reached over to help me stand, "Are you okay?" she asked.

"I'm fine," I answered. I didn't care for Gwen. She seemed nice enough to other people. But there was this one time when we were all going out to dinner after church. Gwen had the largest car/SUV out of all of us, and mostly everyone wanted to ride together. I would have rather driven my own car, but I didn't want to ride alone. "Come on, Sister Leeta," Gerald said. "Ride with us."

"Okay, I will if there is enough room," I answered.

"Gwen's Explorer holds seven people, and there are seven of us, so there is enough room," he added. So, we all began to pile into Gwen's SUV. "Okay," she said. "All the smaller people need to sit in the back of the truck because it has the smallest seats." I was okay with sitting in the back of the truck, but as I started to walk to the truck, Gwen yelled out, "Are you too good to get in the back of the car with those Coach shoes on?"

"No," I said surprisingly. "I can get in the back; I'm okay," I answered. *No, she didn't just try to call me out. The nerve of her,* I thought. After Minister Black, his daughter, and I got in the back seat, Sister Black, Phil, and his wife climbed in and sat in the middle row. Phil and his wife have a two-year-old, and she sat on Sister Black's lap. That was all good with me, but then I looked at the front seat and saw Gwen in the passenger seat, and Gerald was driving. I almost flipped my lid. *Gerald was in the front seat? What the heck was Gerald doing in the front seat? I know I have about twenty-five pounds on Gerald. He couldn't have weighed more than 115 pounds soaking wet,* I began to think to myself. From that point on, I really didn't care for Gwen. *She made me sit all scrunched up in the back of the truck and talked about my shoes,* I thought to myself. I could have grabbed Gerald by the collar and snatched him into that back seat. He was small enough, so I felt as if I could have done it.

So, when Gwen asked me whether I was okay, I didn't have two words to say to her. I felt she didn't care for me. So, why was she asking me if I was okay? *Just fake,* I thought, *just fake!*

When I stood up to testify, I was doing all that I could do just to stand. When Gerald saw me standing, he immediately called on me to give my testimony. "I'm free; praise the Lord! I'm free," I began to cry out. My voice was shaking, and I could barely speak. "No longer bound, no more chains holding me," the congregation began to sing along with me. I stood there and cried the whole time I sang that song. I didn't feel free at all. I felt like I was deep in bondage, but like the apostle Paul said in Acts 26:2 to King Agrippa, "I think myself happy." I, too, tried to think myself happy. "For as he thinketh in his heart, so is he" (Proverbs 23:7). I was really feeling that thing; I needed to believe that everything was going to be all right. Every chance I had, I tried to think myself happy.

After I finished my song, I just sat down in my seat. I didn't hear any of the other testimonies. I was so out of it that I could barely see in front of me.

"Excuse me," I said as I tapped Gwen on the arm. "Can you get someone to help me to the bathroom?"

Since Gwen was ushering and she didn't care for me any-way, I figured she would go and find someone to help me to the restroom. Instead, Gwen reached over and held my arm, and started guiding me in the direction of the restroom. *Wow,* I thought as I struggled step by step to walk to the bathroom. I held on very tight to Gwen's arm for fear that I may lose my bal-ance and fall. Once we entered the restroom, I figured I could brace myself on the walls and hold on as I made it to the stall, and I did just that while she opened the bathroom door for me.

"Do you need some help in the stall?" she asked.

"No, I can make it," I said. I did my business and grabbed the walls, and walked to the sink to wash my hands. Gwen waited patiently while I finished and escorted me back to my seat in church. I didn't think much about what she had done until she and Gerald came to my house a couple of weeks later.

Sister Shelley had come over to drive me to my appointments and cook for me. Since I had been having seizures, the doctors said I couldn't drive for six months, and I wasn't able to stand at the stove and cook for myself. While Sister Shelley was at my house, she seemed a little radical to me. When the television was on, she would point at the TV and say, "Sister Leeta, you need to turn the channel; don't let those evil spirits in your house."

"What are you talking about?" I asked.

"That is how the devil sneaks in," she said. "He comes in through the TV while we are watching certain shows. You shouldn't watch all those scary movies and stuff like that. You really need to be careful what type of shows you watch on TV and what type of movies you bring into your house. You need to clean house, Sister Leeta. And what I mean by that is you need to go through your house and get all the evil spirits out."

"What are you talking about? We don't have any evil spirits in our house," I said.

"Come on. I'll show you," she said as she began to walk through my house. "Look at this mess right here," she said as we entered Tommy's room. "You cannot allow your children to read just any old thing. You need to monitor what they read. Books and movies that conjure up spirits don't need to be in the house of a child of God. Then you wonder why your children are misbehaving, and there is no peace in your home. This stuff right here is the reason why, Sister Leeta. You keep inviting spirits into your home through books, movies, and whatever else y'all bring in. You need to get this stuff out of your house and stop bringing more in. You really need to watch what you allow your children to watch and read."

"Okay, Sister Shelley," I said. *She is really out there,* I thought as I shook my head.

We continued to watch television throughout the day, and Sister Shelley continued to scream, "Change the channel!" every time a vampire, demon, or any other type of scary movie came on or was previewed on the television. It was about time for Timmy to go to football practice. Gerald had volunteered to drive the boys to their rehearsals and football practice. When Gerald came over, he was driving Gwen's SUV, and she was with him. I opened the door to greet them. "Hey, Gwen is with Gerald," I told Sister Shelley.

"Yeah, they have been dating for some time now," she said.

"I didn't know that," I said.

"They are supposed to be getting married," she said. It finally started to make sense to me. I couldn't for the life of me understand why I had to ride squashed in the back seat, and Gerald got to ride in comfort. But now, it made a lot of sense, and I felt much better about the whole situation. Once they came into the house, they wanted to take a look around the house. While Gerald waited for Timmy to get ready for football practice, I went into the kitchen. "Gwen, will you come here for a minute, please?" I called out. Gwen came around the corner to the kitchen smiling, as she often does. "I just wanted to say thank you. I wasn't really thinking clearly at church that Sunday when you helped me to the bathroom, so it didn't dawn on me what you had actually offered to do for me. You asked me if I needed any help in the stall. After I thought about that, I was really touched by that. You didn't know if it was my time of the month or if I had to do number two or whatever, but you were willing to assist me in any way you could. I truly appreciate that," I said.

"No problem. That is what we are here for; we are just a big family trying to help each other out," she said, with a big smile on her face. I gave Gwen a great, big hug and thanked her again. I could not believe that this person who didn't even like me was willing to go out of her way to help me. *I guess she does like me*, I thought. That was the third time I had prejudged someone and thought they didn't like me and found it not to be true. I thought that Sister Shelley didn't like me, and she was in my house cooking for me. I thought that Gwen didn't like me, and she helped me to the bathroom. I also thought Sister Trina didn't like me, and she was the person who drove me back and forth to church when I was unable to drive due to the seizures.

The reason I didn't care for Sister Trina or thought she didn't care for me was because she wouldn't buy any Avon from me. Well, not actually because she wouldn't buy any, but the way she told me she wouldn't buy any Avon from me. We were at church practicing for a play we were going to do at the women's retreat. I was not a member of the church yet; I was just going to be in the play. The retreat was for anyone who wanted to go. I had just started selling Avon, and I had brought my Avon books with me to the play rehearsal.

I extended my arm with the book in hand and said, "Sister Trina, would you like to buy some Avon?"

She didn't even look at the book or at me, for that matter. She put her hand out toward me as if to stop the book from getting any closer and said, "No, thanks, we already have a sister at church who sells Avon."

She got up off the pew and walked away from me while she was still talking. "Oh, no, she didn't just walk away from me," I said under my breath as I tucked the book back into my bag and vowed not to ask anyone else at that church to buy from me.

Once I had gotten out of the hospital, I wasn't walking very well, and I believe the majority of the people at church could tell that I wasn't doing well mentally or physically. When Sister Trina came up to me one day in church and said, "Do you need a ride back and forth to church?" I thought to myself, *the nerve of her asking me that when she wouldn't even buy any Avon from me.*

"No, I don't need a ride," I snapped. I had no idea how I would get back and forth to church, but I knew she wouldn't be the one taking me.

"If you do, just call me. Here is my number," she said as she pushed a piece of paper in my hand with her number on it and walked off.

When we first came back from the retreat, she asked me did I want to work out with her. I told her I would. Then she had the nerve to say, "I know you have a car, but I will pick you up anyway to show you where it is." I thought, the nerve of her thinking I didn't know my way around. Little did I know I had it all wrong about Sister Trina. After missing several church sessions, I decided to call her. It took a while for me to muster up *the nerve to call her, especially after I never returned any of her calls about working out.* I tried to think exactly how many times she had called me to pick me up, and I just ignored her calls. I couldn't remember. *Well, here goes,* I thought as I picked up the phone early on a Sunday morning. "Sister Trina?" I said as the person on the other end said hello.

"No, my mother is praying," her son said. "Want me to have her call you back?"

"No, I will try again later. Bye," I said as I quickly hung up the phone. *I guess I won't be going to church today,* I thought as I laid back down in the bed. Even though I said I would call Trina back, I had no intentions of calling her back. I knew she lived closer to the church than I did, and she would have to backtrack to come and pick me up. I hadn't been all that nice to her anyway, and I just didn't feel comfortable asking for a ride. Maybe, her not being able to come to the phone was the best thing that could have happened. About thirty minutes after my phone call to Trina, the phone rang. I looked at the caller ID and saw that it was Trina calling me back. "Hello," I answered.

"Praise the Lord, Sister Leeta. It's Sister Trina," she said in that fast-paced voice she often spoke in. "Did you need a ride to church this morning?" she asked.

"Uhhh, yes, I did, if that is okay with you," I answered.

"No problem. Do you want to go to Sunday school, or is that too much for you right now?" she asked.

"I hadn't started back going to Sunday school yet, but whatever you want to do is fine with me," I said.

"I'll just pick you up around 11:00 a.m., and we will skip Sunday school until we get you back in the swing of things," she said. "I'll see you in a little bit."

"Okay, thanks," I said as we hung up the phone.

As we rode to church, Trina talked to me about the Word of God the entire time. "This test isn't just for you, Sister Leeta," she said. "Other people may need to gain something from this test you are going through."

"Wow, I hadn't really thought of it like that," I said. Trina had a great deal of boldness about her. She seemed to really know the scriptures, and she wasn't afraid to talk about them. "One time when I had jury duty," she began to say. "There was a man on trial for stealing a shirt. They gave us a questionnaire to fill out before we were even selected for jury duty. One of the questions was, 'Do you think you could give a fair judgment against someone?' I wrote, 'As long as it lines up with the Word of God.' I didn't want to be on the jury, anyway. So, I knew when I put that down, they would kick me off. But they didn't. I sat in the jury box with my mouth closed and just listened to all the other jurors talk about how they wanted or didn't want to be a juror. Then they called on me. 'Ms. Greenwell,' the prosecuting attorney said, 'you said you could be fair as long as it is in line with the Word of God. What did you mean by that?' He asked.

"I said, 'The Bible tells us to speak what we do know and to testify to that we have seen. If I do not know it for myself or if I have not seen it for myself, I can't say if that man is innocent or guilty.'

"'You mean to tell me, Ms. Greenwell,' he said, 'if I show you evidence that can put this man in the store at the right time and show you the clothes that he stole, you can't make a judgment on him?'

"'That's correct,' I said. 'I can't tell you if he stole anything because I didn't see him.'

"Then the man's own attorney tried to get me to say the man was guilty. 'Even if we show you a videotape of him taking a shirt, you won't say he is guilty?' His attorney asked. I thought, *I can't believe they are trying to get me to say this man is guilty. Even his own attorney is trying to get me to say he was guilty.* I turned around and started pointing at the judge, the prosecuting attorney, and the defending attorney, and I told them, 'All of you have stolen before. When you go to lunch, and you take an extra five or ten minutes, do you mark that down? Or do you just go on as though nothing has happened? The Bible says there is no greater sin. How much time should each of you get from stealing time or an ink pen from your job? Stealing is stealing, and I am not the one to pass judgment on any man. That is God's job. So, I cannot say if that man is guilty or innocent.' They had heard about enough of me by that time, the judge said 'You are dismissed, Ms. Greenwell.' I have no idea where that boldness came from. God had just allowed me to recall those scriptures back-to-back as if I had them written down. If you read your Bible regularly, God will allow you to remember those scriptures when you need them. Like David said in Psalm 119:11, 'Thy word have I hid in mine heart that I might not sin against thee.' Sister Leeta, you have to hide the Word in your heart, not only so you don't sin, but so that you will be able to help someone else in the time of need."

Sister Trina wasn't anything like I thought she was. But why should that surprise me? I had misjudged two others people, and those are the people who helped me when I needed help.

When I testified at church, I told the saints not to feel sorry for me because they saw me as frail and sick. I would have never gotten my heart right to love my sisters like I was supposed to if I didn't need help from them. I would have been in danger of hell fire. In St. John 13:34, it says, "A new commandment I give unto you, that ye love one another; as I have loved you, that ye also love one another."

I was doing all that I knew how to do to live right, but it still wasn't enough. Because the Bible also says, in Hebrews 10:26, 'For if we sin wilfully after that, we have received the knowledge of truth, there remaineth no more sacrifice for sin.' The apostle Paul said in 1 Corinthians 13:2, and I'm paraphrasing, if he has all these material things but doesn't have charity (love). I am nothing. God started showing me situations in my life where I wasn't loving people the way the Bible said to love. Once I found out the truth about myself, I began to correct the situations. Peter 5:6 says, "Humble yourselves therefore under the mighty hand of God, that he may exalt you in due time." I had not humbled myself previously, so God had done it for me. If I hadn't gotten sick, Sister Shelley wouldn't have been cooking for me and driving me to my appointments; I would have had the strength to stand and cook my own meals and drive myself around. Sister Gwen would have never needed to help me to the bathroom because I would have been strong enough to walk by myself to the bathroom. Sister Trina would not have been driving me to church if I hadn't started having seizures because I would have been able to drive myself. That's why I am grateful that God saw fit to allow me to suffer for Him in order to get myself right in the eyes of the Lord.

Trina continued to drive me back and forth to church. We seemed to always take the scenic route to church. During our drive to church, we always talked about the goodness of the Lord. Trina was a big help to me, and she continued to encourage me through my healing process. When I would feel down about what was going on in my life, Trina would tell me what to pray for and how to pray.

During the time when Trina would drive me to church, we became friends. Sometime later, the church had been on a solemn assembly fast. That is a sacred fast where we distance ourselves from our fleshly pleasures and desires. For instance, no television, no eating or drinking for certain hours, no newspapers, no books (except spiritual books), no carnal pleasures, no social media, and no telephone conversations (except when necessary).

The church had fasted for eight days. Communion was the following Monday. I sat in church day after day and listened to Bishop preach, and I just couldn't keep up with the service. Bishop would direct the congregation to find a scripture, and even if I was following along with my finger while reading, I could not keep up. I would lean over to whoever was sitting next to me and ask, "Where are we reading?" I had done that to Sharon one day, and she gave me the wrong chapter. We were reading in Acts chapter 2, verse 12, but Sharon said Acts chapter 12, verse 2. I just felt like crying; I could not believe I had gotten that lost in the scriptures when I was following along with my finger. I looked over at Sharon and said, "What chapter?"

"Chapter 2, you know what I meant," she said in a nasty tone. I just hung my head as the tears filled my eyes and tried to find the Scripture.

Sharon and I just didn't seem to communicate well at all. We weren't friends growing up, and I don't know her ways, and she doesn't know mine. I am a person that says what I mean and mean what I say. I have heard other people say that but don't really mean it. But if you tell me that, I expect that from you. So, when you have friends, they usually hang out with you enough to get to know your personality and your ways. Sharon and I weren't like that, even though we were sisters. It was like we were butting heads all the time.

She always expected me to know what she meant to say regardless of what she actually said. For some reason, when I talk to people, my tone seems to bother them. I don't actually notice it, but I am told that my tone bothers people. I'm told it isn't what I say but how I say it. People say I talk down to people. Therefore, I've been asking God to help me with my tone and how I speak to people. I have noticed more often than not, people don't like the truth, and when they hear it, no matter how nice you say it—they don't like it, and they get offended. That's how Sharon and I were. She even said I was mean, and I replied, "I'm not mean; I just tell the truth." She replied, "That's the same thing."

Communicating with Sharon is difficult for me because we don't expect the same things when we communicate. During the most difficult time in my life wasn't any different. I just couldn't seem to make her understand that I actually needed help finding the scripture. If she said chapter, then I thought she meant chapter; if she said verse, then I thought she meant verse. I have never been good at deciphering what she meant to say, even when she didn't say it. And during this test, it seemed to intensify. I had gotten so confused since the seizures. I wanted to believe the report of the Lord, but the situation looked grim. I wasn't able to do any of the things I used to be able to do. I couldn't read very well, I was unable to work the computer at all, and I couldn't understand the preaching. I felt unloved and alone. I refused to ask for any more help after that. I just suffered through the confusion and cried about it later.

While Bishop was preaching for the communion service, it seemed that he would just disappear before my eyes. One minute he would be on the right side of the church preaching. Then the next minute, he would be gone, and I would turn my head, and he would appear on the left side of the church. I felt so frustrated, and I didn't understand why God wasn't even allowing me to hear the preaching.

During the communion service, I didn't have the strength to walk around to the communication plate by myself. I sat in my seat and waited until the majority of my section went around for communion. Then, I slowly got up out of my seat and made my way to the end of the aisle. Once I made it to the end of the aisle, a couple of sisters came along and grabbed me by the arms and helped me to the communion plate and cup. My body was deteriorating so quickly; it was unbelievable. After service, I sat at the back of the sanctuary and waited for Sister Trina to finish visiting with the other saints.

While I was sitting on the pew, Bishop came over to me. "Praise the Lord, Leeta," he said as he reached down and gave me a hug. "How are you?"

"I'd like to talk to you, Bishop," I said as tears filled my eyes.

"What's the matter?" he asked as he kneeled down on the floor next to me.

I couldn't say a word because if I did, the tears would fall from my eyes and flood the entire church. "Come on," he said, "you can talk to me in my office," he said as he helped me off the pew. Bishop held me by my arm and walked with me to his office. I walked, taking small steps as I struggled with my balance, and limped to his office. Once we entered Bishop's office, I sat in the chair, and I just cried. "What's going on?" he asked. "How are your finances?"

"I don't want to talk about my finances," I said. "I have been so confused lately," I said. "Sister Cynthia and Sister Beth took me to the doctor on Friday, and I had a card with the address written on it. I told them that they had to go over to the church and the doctor's office was on West 38th Street. Sister Beth lives over by the church anyway, so she had to leave her house and come all the way to the east side of town to pick me up for the appointment. She said she was okay with that. Anyway, once we were in the car, we talked about the goodness of the Lord. When we arrived at the doctor's office, I pulled the card out of my purse to get the suite number. 'That's okay,' I told Beth."

"'That's okay what, Sister Leeta?' she said. With great embarrassment, I said, 'I just noticed that I had you drive me to the wrong place. My appointment is at 9240 N. Jefferson, clear on the other side of town, and my appointment was at 1:00 pm. It is close to that time now. Don't worry about it. I will reschedule my appointment.' 'Call them, Sister Leeta, and tell them you will be a little late. I'll get you there; don't worry.' Then, Bishop, I called the doctor's office and got their voicemail, and it said they were out of the office until 1:30 p.m. Once I heard the recording, I was extremely confused because the card I had said my appointment was for 1:00 p.m. Beth drove me there anyway. We got off the highway and found the doctor's office."

"So, today, just a couple of days after that, Sister Clair had to take me to the exact same location for a doctor's appointment. Sister Jeanie said she would find someone to take me to my appointment since I was unable to drive. I told her to make sure they already knew where they were going and not to listen to me because I was a little confused about the directions. Sister Clair and I were talking, and I told her about the seizure that God had stopped for me, and I started shouting in the car. Every time I moved in the seat, the seatbelt grew tighter and tighter, and that is the reason I'm limping today because the seatbelt bruised my side."

"Well, while we were talking, I told Sister Clair I knew exactly where we were going because I had just been there on Friday. When we exited the highway, Sister Clair made a left turn, and after driving a while, she said, 'I think I went the wrong way.' I said, 'You did because I remember going the other way on Friday.' I told her, 'Don't worry, Beth did the exact same thing when she brought me out here, and we had to turn around and go in the opposite direction.' We laughed, and she turned the car around. Sister Clair drove the car a little further and said, 'I think I need to turn around again. I am going the wrong way.'"

"'No, you aren't,' I said. 'I remember this very well. If you keep straight, you will see 9240 N. Jefferson up here on the right side of the street.' We went back and forth a couple of times with me knowing exactly where I was going, and when we arrived at the light, it read 103rd Street. 'I am so sorry,' I said. 'I can't believe I took you in the wrong direction.'"

"'Don't worry, Sister Leeta; I should have looked at my paper, anyway.' She reached down and pulled her paper out, and eventually, we arrived at the doctor's office. Tears welled up in my eyes because I couldn't grasp how turned around I was. I was as confused as if I had never been in that area before. That was the third time I had gotten someone lost when I wholeheartedly believed I knew where I was going."

"I did the same thing to my little sister last week. I was unable to find a street that was located a couple of streets away from my job. I have worked downtown for over twenty years. Bishop, I don't understand what is going on with me. I can't keep up in church. I was unable to follow the sermons. I get lost while driving or when having someone drive me around. I'm struggling to read and comprehend. While trying to read my emails, I was unable to figure out how to turn on the computer. I have been completely confused about almost everything in my life."

"Whenever you are preaching, I can't seem to keep up with the message, nor am I able to follow along in the Bible. What is going on, Bishop? I don't understand. Today at the doctor's office, they ran some tests, and they brought me out this huge bag of supplies for diabetic testing. They didn't say I had diabetes; they just showed me how to use the supplies and to check my blood sugar before I drive, before meals, and after meals. They told me to do all of that, or I could go into a diabetic coma.."

"Don't take that mess, Leeta," he said.

"Huh, what do you mean don't take it?" I asked.

"Don't take it; there is nothing wrong with you. Isaiah 53:1 says, 'Who has believed our report? And to whom the arm of the Lord revealed?' In Numbers chapter 13:33, God told the children of Israel to go and possess the land. Moses sent two spies to search the land. God had already told Moses that He had given them the land. When the spies returned with the report of the land, the children of Israel were afraid to possess the land. They said the Canaanites were like giants, and we were like grass-hoppers; we cannot overtake the land. After all God had done for them, they would rather go back into Egypt in slavery than have faith in what God was going to do for them. In Numbers 14:12–14, the Lord was ready to kill those people because they chose to believe the evil report. Now, whose report are you going to believe, Sister Leeta?"

"I understand what you are saying, Bishop, but what do I do when I feel myself getting ready to pass out from low blood sugar? What do I do when I can't see in front of me because of the blurred vision? I know I should pra—" That was all that came out of my mouth when I started rejoicing in the Lord because I began to think back on what God had done for me. I thought about the other night in the bedroom when He stopped a seizure that even though the doctors said they could not be stopped. After I finished rejoicing in the Lord, Bishop didn't have to say anything else to me. I went home and trusted in God. I didn't take any of the diabetic medication.

That night, God revealed to me in a dream exactly what was going on in my life. I didn't see the face of God, nor did I actually hear His voice on the outside of my head, but I knew it was Him talking to me. I had several dreams before that gave me a funny feeling, but I didn't know how to explain the feeling to anyone. Sometimes I just knew a dream was going to come true; because of the feeling I had during the dream and the feeling I had after I woke up and thought about the dream. That night, God spoke to me and said, "How can you say that I will not allow you to hear the Word of God? Don't you recall when Bishop preached about collecting on your benefits in Psalm 103:2 and Psalm 116:12–14? When he spoke of the pen of the ready writer in Psalm 45:1, why is it you don't realize how you achieved such a high score on a test or in school in general? Well, it was the pen of the ready writer that helped you through and wrote all of the information in your brain. Don't you remember the dreams you once had about the two sisters and how you knew one would be pregnant from the dream and that she would have a baby boy?"

The dream God reminded me of was a dream that I had right after I received the Holy Ghost. Before salvation, I would party with these two sisters, Tachina and Nikki. I went to high school with Nikki, and she always called me "Lil' Girl." Tachina is Nikki's big sister, and I initially met her while she was on break from college. One day we were all over my house, and I said, "One of you is pregnant." They both were like, "It isn't me. Why would you think one of us is pregnant?"

I said, "Because I had a dream."

"What was your dream?" Tachina asked. I said, "Nikki was sitting on the bar stool, and a little boy tried to climb on the empty bar stool next to her. She pointed at the little boy and said, 'Get down.'" Tachina and Nikki just stared at me, waiting for the rest of the dream. Then Nikki spoke up and said, "What else happened?"

"That was it," I said. Instantly, they became somewhat frustrated and started ranting about if someone dreams about fish, then that means someone is pregnant. Then Nikki asked, "How do you know it was a boy?"

"Because I saw him; he was about four," I replied. They went on to tell me how there is no way that dream means one of them is pregnant. I insisted, "I don't know about dreaming of fish, but I know 100 percent the dream I had means one of you are pregnant with a boy." They laughed and mocked me about the weird dream I had. But their comments didn't bother me at all. I continued to stand by what the dream meant.

The very next night, I dreamed the little boy died. I decided to keep that part to myself since the pregnancy dream didn't seem to make sense. Even though I never told them, I started to question why did I think that dream meant that one of them was pregnant. I didn't understand either dream fully, but I still believed the dream was going to come true.

A couple of months went by, and wouldn't you know it, Tachina found out she was pregnant. A couple more months passed, and Tachina was far enough along in her pregnancy to have an ultrasound to find out the sex of the baby. I hadn't thought much about the dream until Tachina told me she was having a boy. I was excited about the news, but I became a little nervous because my initial dream had come true. I thought about the dream I had when the little boy died, and I felt concerned. But I still didn't tell Tachina about the dream where he died.

When Tachina was about seven months pregnant, she went into preterm labor and delivered a baby boy. The baby was having some complications because he was premature. I asked my mother to pray for the baby. I also told my mother about the dream I had when the baby died. In spite of all our prayers, he only lived for four days. The situation happened exactly like I had dreamed it.

"When I get the feeling that lets me know a dream is going to come true, I call that dream a true dream. I didn't fully understand why I felt the dream meant someone was pregnant. I rehearsed the dream several times in my mind, and I didn't understand how I knew one of them was pregnant. Because truth be told, nothing in the dream was about pregnancy. However, I still believed one of them was pregnant. As I began to ask God how did I know what the dream meant. God spoke to me and told me that He is the one that gave me the interpretation of the dream.

The moral of the story is, no matter how much someone tried to convince me that the dream meant something different. I believed what God told me the dream meant, and I didn't doubt it. God reminded me of the dream because I fully trusted God without a doubt. God allowed me to know that I needed to do the same thing in my own situation. But this time, it was hard to trust God for my own situation.

Throughout the entire duration of me being sick, I had been saying that I was just like Job in the Bible. I felt as if I was like Job because I had gotten extremely sick without notice. I could not work, so I didn't have any money. Because of my lack of income, I lost my house and my car. The night God reminded me about the pregnancy dream, I realized I had no other choice but to trust and believe what God said. I reminded myself daily that God showed me the scripture in Jeremiah 30:17 that allowed me to know he would restore my health.

In Job 1:6–13, Job was going through a test that hit him totally by surprise. In Job 1:6–9, Satan was basically saying, "Why wouldn't Job serve You, God? You take good care of him. When God asked "Hast thou considered my servant Job?" Well, of course, Satan had considered Job; that is how Satan knew

God had a hedge (fence of protection around) about Job. If Satan hadn't considered him, he would not have known that God was protecting him. God watches out for His people and has a hedge around all of us. Satan has to get permission before he can do anything to any of us. God watches out for his people, and I encouraged myself in knowing God was watching out for me, too.

Eight days had passed, and the church had completed their fast, but I decided to continue mine. I wasn't watching television or eating anything before 4:00 p.m. I would drink fluids all during the day so that I could continue to take my medication during the fast. I had gone so long without food that I had trained my body not to be hungry.

Trina would check up on me frequently to see if I needed anything. One day when Trina had called, Brooke from my class was visiting. When Brooke first called, I had been feeling pretty good in my body, and she wanted to come by. I told her, "Ms. Laura from class will also be coming over, but Sharon won't be bringing the boys home until later."

"That's fine. I just want to come by and see you. Is it okay if I bring dinner?" Brooke asked.

"That's okay," I said, "I'm not hungry."

"I would very much like to do this for you and the boys. I know you said people were coming over, but is anyone bringing you something to eat?" she asked. I wasn't hungry at that time. I hadn't been eating for a few days, and I had pretty much lost my appetite.

Brooke insisted on bringing something over for dinner. "Can I bring you a pizza so you won't have to cook?" she asked. She was so sweet, and she just wanted to help.

"Sure, Brooke, pizza is fine," I said.

"Is Pizza Hut okay?" she asked.

"That's fine," I answered. We got off the phone, and I continued to wait for Ms. Laura to arrive. Ms. Laura was in my associate's class a couple of years earlier. When Ms. Laura arrived, I led her to the family room and began to tell her all the things that had been happening in my life.

"Ms. Laura, it is wild. I haven't really been able to read very well since I got out of the hospital. But now, I am able to read and interpret the Bible. God has really opened my understanding of the scriptures," I said. Ms. Laura is Catholic, and we didn't believe in the same things when it came to salvation.

"That's great, Leeta," she said as she continued to listen to me.

"I have to tell you what happened. Before I begin to tell you my story, I am going to warn you that I am going to shout (dance before God) after I tell you how God helped me." I began to tell Ms. Laura how it all started. "I began witnessing to Kelly about homosexuality in Genesis," I said as I told her the entire story about that first Saturday before I ended up in the hospital. "As you see, I don't walk very well, but when I talk about God's goodness, I can dance in the Holy Spirit and run all around. I told God that I wouldn't be afraid to tell of the things that He had done for me and that I would give Him the praise. That's how I know when I tell you what happened; I am going to shout because every time I've told the story—I shout," I said.

Right about that time, I heard a knock at the door. I thought maybe it was the police or something because they were knocking very hard. I opened the door, and it was Tasha; she had been picking the boys up from school and bringing them home for me. "Why are you knocking that hard?" I asked.

"Sorry, that wasn't me; it was Tommy," she replied.

"Why are you knocking like that, Tommy? You know, loud noises hurt my head and could send me into a seizure," I said.

It was as if Tommy started screaming as loud as he could, "They keep lying on me and—"

"Hold on, Tommy; stop talking so loud," I said. "What is going on?"

Then Tasha started explaining, screaming just as loud as Tommy. "Tommy has detention, and he keeps getting into trouble and—"

"Tasha, please stop talking so loud," I asked. "Listen, Sharon will be here in a moment. Please, just wait and tell her about what happened at school with Tommy. I don't feel well, and I am just not able to handle this right now," I added. It was as if I hadn't said anything to Tasha. She continued to tell me about the problems Tommy had in school, and she continued in the same loud voice. The door was still open from when they came in, and I saw Sharon's car pulling up. I walked over to the door and held it open until Sharon came close enough for me to tell her what was happening. When Sharon entered the house, Tasha was still talking and explaining to me the events of the day; it was as if Tasha didn't care. She disregarded every time I asked her to keep it down. I had found Tasha to be very stubborn. She didn't listen to reasoning about most things.

For example, a few weeks back, she had been fervently seeking answers in the Bible. I had been trying to help her, and I invited her to church. I had been having Bible study with her almost daily. She seemed to be understanding what was truly expected of us from God. We talked about the baptism in Jesus' name, and I showed her, in Acts 19, where all of the disciples were baptized a second time in Jesus' name because they had only known the baptism of John and they had not heard of the Holy Ghost. I showed her in Matthew 28:19, where Jesus tells the disciples, "Go ye therefore, and teach all nations, baptizing them in the name of the Father, and of the Son, and of the Holy Ghost." Then I showed her the scriptures (John 10:30, Matthew 1:21, John 14:26) that tell you the name of the Father, the name of Son, and the name of the Holy Ghost, which the name for all three is Jesus. The disciples already knew the name of the Father, the name of the Son, and the name of the Holy Ghost. We are to follow the apostles' doctrine, which is the gospel of Jesus and what he taught the disciples.

After about two weeks of studying the Bible and asking questions, Tasha decided she wanted to go to church with me. She drove us to church, and we went on a Wednesday morning to Bible class. The preacher confirmed just about everything that Tasha and I had been discussing. She became very excited after Bible class. She wanted to meet with the pastor and ask him some questions. Bible class was over at 11:30 am; Tasha went right in to talk to the pastor after it was over. I waited in the lobby and talked with some other sisters from the church. Tasha did not come out of the pastor's office until 3:00 p.m. When she came out of the office, she, the pastor, and Sister Jeanie all headed for the sanctuary. She wanted to be baptized. I was super excited: all the scriptures, reading, and praying had paid off. Tasha was baptized, and almost immediately, I heard her in the changing room speaking in tongues. I waited in the sanctuary while they were in the back of the church, seeking the Lord and tarrying for the Holy Ghost with Tasha.

Bishop's daughter came out and told me I could come back where they were, and I could see Tasha. When I went in the back, Tasha wasn't speaking in tongues anymore. She had her arms stretched out in front of her waving them back and forth, eyes closed, and she just kept repeating, "Oh, I need-oh, need-oh, need-oh, I need." Sister Jeanie kept saying, "Just praise Him, Tasha, just praise Him." Tasha totally ignored what Sister Jeanie said and just kept saying, "Oh, I need-oh, need-oh, need-oh, I need." I thought to myself, *what is she saying? Is she trying to make herself speak in tongues?* Right about that time, Bishop said, "Tasha, Tasha," She finally opened her eyes and looked at him. He said, "God already knows you need Him. You need to start praising Him. Thank Him for the things He has done for you. I know you have felt the power of God today, but you can't do it by yourself. Acts 2:4 says they began to speak as the Spirit of God gave them utterance, so you cannot force the tongues. God has to speak through you. When God comes into your life, you will speak a heavenly language. Do you understand what I am saying?" Tasha shook her head, closed her eyes, stuck her arms out as if she was reaching for something, and started up again, "Oh, I need-oh, need-oh, need-oh, I need." We stayed at the church until about 5:30 p.m.

I didn't understand why Tasha was acting like that, so when we got in the car, I said, "How come you just didn't start praising God like Bishop asked you to do?"

She replied, "Well, I know I was being disobedient, but I am just spoiled. I should have done what they asked; they were just trying to help me."

"I said they can't help you get the Holy Ghost; you have to get it for yourself, and being disobedient isn't the way to allow God to enter into your life. Bishop tried to tell you that God already knows that you need Him. God deserves our praise, and He is pleased with it."

"I know," she said as she cut me off. "I am just spoiled, but I should just wait until I get to heaven to be spoiled."

"I said you're not going to be spoiled in heaven."

"He said He has many mansions for me," she said.

"We were created to worship Him. When we get to heaven, that is exactly what we will be doing—worshiping Christ. Heaven doesn't have anything to do with you or me; it is all about Christ." She didn't say much after that; it was as if it all went over her head. She was only concerned about herself.

So, when she stood in my living room, ignoring everything I had asked her to do, I guess I shouldn't have been surprised. Sharon came into the house and began to take over the situation concerning Tommy getting into trouble at school. I went back into the family room and continued to talk to Ms. Laura. "As I was saying, Ms. Laura, I went to church a couple of Sundays ago, and a lady named Pamela stood up to testify. She spoke about how she was down on her knees praying, and when she finished, she tried to get up and got so dizzy that she fell back down. She said she was in pain and wasn't able to get off the floor. She said she tried to crawl to the phone to call someone to pray for her. She said she couldn't reach the phone, and she started to panic. Then she said while she was lying on the floor, God began to speak to her and told her she had the same Holy Ghost as whoever she was trying to call. She said she thought about that and prayed for herself. When she finished praying, she got up off the floor and went about her day."

"So, that takes me to what happened the very next day, which was Monday," I said. "I put the boys to bed and then went to bed myself. When I lay in the bed, I felt my eyes start to jump around. Instantly I was afraid. I had gone almost a week without having any seizures, and I didn't want to end up back in the hospital. I lay in the bed with my eyes closed tightly. Sharon told me in church one day, after I had fallen out and started to go into a seizure, not to focus on the objects in the room jumping around and stuff like that.

"Therefore, I kept my eyes closed very tight, I explained to Ms. Laura. However, I would open them quickly from time to time, just to see how fast the pictures on the wall in my room were moving. The faster the pictures moved, I knew that meant the more advanced the seizure was. I lay in the bed in the fetal position, with my fists clenched and my eyes closed tight. When I went to the doctor, I asked, "How do I stop a seizure?" The doctor told me, "You don't stop a seizure. When you feel a seizure coming on, you should clear a place on the floor so that you don't hurt yourself and then lay down on the floor.

"I was highly upset with that doctor," I ranted. "I just wanted a miracle pill and to be done with all of this."

As I opened my eyes quickly and closed them again, I noticed the pictures were moving even faster. The thought came to mind that I should call 911. Then I thought, if I call 911, they are going to have to kick my door in when they arrive, which would cost me money to have it repaired. Then they would search my house, see that I have children, and the boys could possibly end up in foster care, so that wouldn't work." Then I thought, *I can just call Sharon since she lives just around the corner. Sharon could come over and help me get the kids, so they wouldn't end up in foster care.* However, she doesn't have a key, so she would still have to call 911, and they would still break down my door, so that won't work.

"Then I thought, *I could call out and wake up Tommy; then he could call Sharon, she could call 911, he could open the door, then I wouldn't have to get a new door, and the kids could go with Sharon instead of foster care. Then I thought, I don't want Tommy to see me like this,* as I opened my eyes and looked at the pictures again. *Okay,* I thought, *I am just going to have to lie on the floor and go through this seizure without any help.* When I tried to get down on the floor, I realized that the seizure was too advanced, and I could not move my arms or legs. I really began to panic and didn't know what to do."

"Then I thought back to Sister Pamela's testimony where she said she had the same Holy Ghost power that whomever she was going to call had. It was finally at that time that I decided to call on God. When I opened my mouth to pray, it seemed like just gibberish came out. Then just like in Job 1:6, when the sons of God came to present themselves before the Lord, Satan came also. He said, 'You know God can't understand what you are saying. Listen to the way you are talking. God doesn't understand that. Just like your mother told you when you had a seizure in church that even though you thought you were saying something, no one could understand you.'

"Ms. Laura, you cannot imagine how frustrating that situation was. I just began to cry. I knew I couldn't move, and now I couldn't talk, so I couldn't pray. I could feel my body starting to twitch and shake. I began to pray from my heart because I knew I wasn't making any sense when I prayed out loud because I could hear myself. I began to reach deep down inside of me, and I began to talk to God within my heart. I said, 'God, I really don't want to have this seizure. I don't want to lose my boys over this either. I know You said You wouldn't put more on me than I am able to bear, but, God, I just can't bear this right now.' I opened my eyes to look at the pictures again. They were still jumping around.

"I continued to pray on the inside, Lord, I was told You can understand heart language, and if we couldn't say a word, then You would be able to understand my tears. Well, Lord, if You can understand all that, I know You can understand seizure language. I need You to help me, Lord. I need Your help right now. The doctors said that a seizure can't be stopped, but I know You can do anything.

"I laid there crying, shaking, and praying to God. It was as if God Himself had taken His finger and just placed it on my shoulder and said, 'Be still, My child.' I could still feel my body jerking. Then it felt like the finger got a little bit heavier on my shoulder, and God said, 'I said, be still.' Within a matter of seconds, I stopped shaking, my head cleared up, my eyes stopped jumping, and I was able to move my body. I had to fight that seizure off all night, but God did just what He said He would do. He took care of me and my boys, and I did not have a seizure that night. So, when man says it is impossible, God said all things are possible to Him that believe." By that time, I jumped up out of my seat and shouted across the family room. Ms. Laura just watched with tears in her eyes until I finished rejoicing. "That was beautiful," she said. "I have to be leaving now; I will be back to visit again soon. I really enjoyed talking to you," she said. I walked her out and waited for Brooke to show up.

When Brooke came, she brought the pizza just like she said she would do. She sat the pizza box on the counter, and we sat in the family room and talked. I could not get my thoughts together or talk about the scriptures like I planned. Since I was off work for so long, all I ever did when someone came to my house was talk about the Word of God and point out things in the Bible. I wasn't able to watch television because the flashing lights on the shows would send me into a seizure or give me excruciating headaches. For the majority of my day, I just read my word and talked to God. Brooke was really concerned about me because I had lost so much weight and because I hadn't been to class in a very long time. Brooke knew I wasn't the type to miss class. Normally, Brooke and I would talk on the telephone and figure out statistics and managerial accounting problems for hours on end. I hadn't spoken to her in a couple of months, and she had begun to worry about me. We talked for a few minutes, and then she insisted that I eat something.

"Who's helping you with your bills and stuff, Leeta?" she asked.

"Well, my sister is going to come over and organize some things for me."

"I can work on that if you want me to," she said.

"Okay, I have them on the computer. But I can't look at the computer; the lights could send me into a seizure, so you just have to tell me what you are looking at," I replied.

"Okay, I can do that," she said in her little bubbly voice that she always had. "What did you eat today?" she asked.

"I had a slice of cheese," I said.

"A slice of cheese? You really should get yourself something to eat. I brought plenty of pizza and some breadsticks," she said.

"All right, I'll get a slice of pizza," I said as I got up from the chair and stumbled my way into the kitchen. "Auhh!" I screamed.

"What's the matter?" she screamed back as she ran into the kitchen to see what was wrong with me.

"It's the box; it looks like lightning bolts are shooting at me!" I said as I closed my eyes and turned my head.

"What!" she said. "There is nothing wrong with the box."

"Hey, I have never had seizures before in my life. I can't explain it. But the box looked as if lightning bolts were shooting at me. I just need to sit down. Will you help me back in there, please?" I asked.

"Of course, come on," she said as she held me by the arm and guided me to the chair.

"I think I want to lie down for a while. I'm not feeling well. Will you please turn the lights down? They are really giving me a headache," I whispered.

"Okay, you just lie down, and I am going to finish working on your bills," she said as she made her way back over to the computer.

"Leeta, I notice you have some columns in red and some in black and some things..." she started to say before I cut her off.

"Brooke, I really can't help you right now," I tried to explain.

"What do you mean, Leeta? You are a straight 'A' student in an information system bachelor's degree program," she said as if I didn't know that.

"Brooke, the person you knew in class is not the same person I am right now. I cannot help you with what you are trying to do. I know that is my stuff you are working on, but I cannot tell you the answers to your questions," I began to explain again.

"Leeta, we are just talking about columns and rows, you know this stuff," she said in a very demeaning voice.

I said, with tears in my eyes and with my heart feeling like someone had crushed it up in their hand. "Brooke, I can't help you right now. I don't even know how to turn on the computer anymore, and I can't even read at this point in my life. Just leave everything where it is, and my sister will be over to help me later this week. It is okay, really it is." At that point, she closed all my folders and just hung her head down low, and I believe that was when it finally sunk in that something actually was different about me. By this time, my pride was out the window, and my humbling experience was having its way with me. I didn't want anyone to know that I couldn't use the computer or that I couldn't read, comprehend, or anything else for that matter. I just wanted to keep it all to myself.

As she cleared up the files, the phone rang, and it was Trina checking on me. "It's Trina from your church; she wants to talk to you," Brooke said.

"Tell her to whisper; my head hurts really badly," I instructed. I had started to feel extremely sick in my body. I became weak and dizzy, and by this time, I was completely laid out on the floor on my stomach, and I could not move. I felt as if something had me pinned to the floor. I could hear Brooke relaying the message to Trina about how she needed to be quiet and how I had the lights dimmed in the house, and all that I was going through in my body.

"Hello," I said as Brooke handed me the phone.

"Praise the Lord; are you okay?" Trina asked.

"No, I'm not," I whispered.

"Do you need me to help you?" she asked

"Please," I whispered with tears in my eyes.

"I'm on my way," she said as she hung up the phone.

Brooke and I just sat in silence for the most part. She was trying to be helpful, but I didn't need her to do anything for me. I felt awful, and I didn't know what to do about it. It seemed like only minutes had passed when I heard a soft knock at the door. Trina had arrived.

"Will you get the door, Brooke?"

"Sure," she said.

When Trina walked into the house, I was still laying on the floor in the same spot where I was when she called. "How are you?" she asked as she leaned down and kissed me on my cheek.

"Not too good," I said.

"Here are her bills that I had been working on. She couldn't really help me, but maybe you can work on them. I can show you where I left off, yadda, yadda, yadda." Brooke went on to say as she picked up her things to leave. "I will put the pizza in a baggy so the boys can eat it when they come home. Leeta didn't eat anything, but I will leave it here for them. Leeta, I am going to leave now." She grabbed the pizza box and held it upside down over me as she walked.

"Get that box out of here!" I screamed. "Get that box out of here!"

"Okay, I will; I'm just trying to make sure I have everything that I need," she said in a calm voice.

"Trina, get that box out of here now!" I was absolutely frantic by now, and I was unable to get off the floor. It was as if some dark force was holding me down. By this time, Trina started trying to help Brooke gather her things. Trina walked her to the front door. They stayed in there for a while, and I was able to get up off the floor. When Trina came back into the family room looking for me, I was in my bedroom, changing clothes because my pajamas were soaking wet with sweat, and they were stuck to my back. While I was in my bedroom, God showed me a vision; the vision was a little blurb from the movie The Lost Boys.

The Lost Boys was a movie about vampires, and in the movie, one of the main characters is Sam. Sam had finally found out the key to defeating the vampires. Unbeknownst to Sam, the man named Max that was dating his mother was the head vampire. Max went to Sam's house and knocked on the door. When Sam opened the door, Max asked Sam if he could come in. Well, Sam didn't quite understand why he was asking him if he could come in since Max had been in his house so many other times before. Sam asked, "Why are you asking me if you can come in?" Max replied and said, "I don't want to come in unless I am invited." Then, Sam was like, "Sure, you are invited into my house." Well, once Max was invited in, Sam had no power against him. I said all that to say, once God showed me that vision, then God also brought back to my attention that Sister Shelley had been telling me all along that I had been inviting spirits into my house.

While I was lying on the floor, God instructed me to research Pizza Hut. When I walked back into the room, Trina was waiting for me, and I began to tell her everything that took place and about the vision that God had just given me.

"Throw away that pizza and get rid of that box. Something is going on with Pizza Hut; it must be owned and operated by someone that worships the devil or something like that," I began to go on and tell her. "God said research Pizza Hut," I told her. But the truth is God told me to research Pizza Hut, and I didn't find one thing. I had invited the enemy to enter my mind yet again. I allowed him to enter my brain and play tricks on me yet again. I just kept allowing him to play mind games with me and use me in all kinds of ways. I was stuck in what is called a mind battle. Satan and/or a different evil spirit was talking to me, and so was God, but at times I didn't know the difference between the voices.

Second Timothy 1:7 reads, "For God hath not given us the spirit of fear;" First John 4:18 reads: "...fear has torment." The point I'm making with these two scriptures is that fear is a spirit, and the fear spirit can torment a person. It is very important to try the spirits and see whether they are of God as it reads in 1 John 4:1. I was in a place where I needed to know the voice of God and to be able to distinguish it regardless of the distractions going on around me.

I was devastated about what happened, and I just wanted some help. However, things were starting to get a little weird around my house. As Trina and I talked, Sharon and Bob came over, and we began to fill them in on what had taken place earlier in the day when Brooke was over. Sharon kept complaining that she didn't like how dark it was in the house because it wasn't of God. Basically, I told her I didn't care what she thought; I needed the lights dim because they gave me a headache, and I wasn't risking another seizure for anyone.

I'm not a follower; it doesn't matter to me what people think about me. When Sharon kept saying that she didn't like the darkness in the house, I just ignored her and continued to talk. I tried to explain the situation about the box and how I was under a spiritual attack. I later found out that one of the medications I was on made me very sensitive to light.

"Sharon, God is showing me things through my dreams," I said. "You are supposed to work with me; we are going to be great women of God. God said you have to believe me, and you will work with me in all that I do, but if you don't believe me, you can't work with me," I continued to say. I tried over and over to tell her how God was showing me things in visions and dreams, but it seemed like Sharon didn't believe me. So, I said, "Remember, you gave me a couple of scriptures the other day, and you tried to explain them to me, right?"

"Yes, that is right," she said.

"Well, you know I couldn't understand them because of what has been going on with me. You said God had opened up your understanding of the scriptures, right?" I asked again.

"Right," she said.

"Here's what I believe God is going to do. I am going to go to those scriptures that you gave me the other day. And you know that I could not even read them, let alone understand them. But today, I know that God is going to reveal them to me exactly the way that He revealed them to you. And then you are going to know that God is talking to me and telling me things. Okay?" I asked.

"Okay," she replied.

So, Trina, Bob, Sharon, and I were all sitting on the floor in the family room, and I began to open my Bible and search the scriptures; I turned to the scriptures and found them with no problem. Well, the funny part about that was before I had become ill, I didn't read my Bible often. Well, I might as well be honest. I only read my Bible if I was sitting in church, and they asked us to turn to scripture. I hated reading, and I hated reading the Bible even more because it was so confusing. Therefore, for me to go directly to a book of the Bible, especially when just a week or so ago I could barely even read anything, was truly all God's doing. They just watched me as I found the scripture.

I prayed before I spoke and asked God to help me, and then I read the first scripture to everyone, and then I interpreted it just as God gave it to me. The next scripture was about thirteen verses long. I became fearful, and I could barely read the words. I closed my eyes and began to pray and ask God to help me. I made it through the scriptures, and I didn't just read the scriptures, I interpreted them as God had given them to me.

When I finished, I said, "I believe that is exactly the way God gave it to you, Sharon."

She said, "It is exactly the way God gave it to me." We all sat for a little longer. Shortly after, they left for the night. I felt confident that God was truly helping me. I had begun to know the voice of God and started to listen, even if people didn't believe me.

Sharon never did believe that God was revealing things through my dreams and visions or that God had allowed me to prophesy. Bishop always says, "Everything God tells or shows you isn't for everyone else. People will try to destroy and tear your dreams down." Like it says in Luke 4:24: "And he said, Verily I say unto you, no prophet is accepted in his own country." Matthew 10:41 says, and I'm paraphrasing, you will be blessed if you accept the prophet. "He that receiveth a prophet in the name of a prophet shall receive a prophet's reward." I could understand why Sharon didn't believe me because I wasn't able to separate the difference between God's voice and Satan's voice talking to me. So when God would speak, I would tell Sharon and the rest of my family what God said He was going to do. However, if that wasn't God speaking to me then, of course, whatever I said would happen, didn't. I guess that's why it's called a mind battle. I was literally battling (fighting) in my mind to have clarity in my thoughts. At times, I felt like I was searching for sanity and couldn't find it. Not to mention I had no idea that I was experiencing several side effects from the medication that included brain fog and confusion.

Anyway, back to what I was talking about not comprehending. I was able to attend one day in class and one study group session during my final class. When I attended class, I felt like I was on another planet. I could not comprehend what was being said or what I was supposed to do. I looked at the book, and I looked at my neighbor's notes, and it appeared as though they were written in a foreign language.

My head began to hurt. My eyes began to fill with tears. Thoughts began to fill my head as I slowly drifted off into a world of my own. I felt the clouds fill my head as the marquee began to scroll. I thought, *what is going on? I cannot believe this; I feel so clueless.* I studied, and I sacrificed, and yet, I turned out to be a dummy anyway. I realized at that moment I was no longer the same person I used to be. I spoke with Joshua, my teacher, and explained my situation, and I collected my benefits (Psalm 116:12). I called Joshua on the same Sunday that Bishop preached about benefits. I explained to Joshua that even though he had been my teacher five times throughout my bachelor's program, and even though I had made A's in the other four classes that I had him as a teacher, I no longer had that information in my head. I went on to tell him that I spoke with my group and told them to just write down what they wanted me to say for the presentation that was due on the last day of class. For the final project, we had to create a computer system for a company that actually worked using Access, Web pages, computer programming languages, and all the other things we had learned during our degree program.

"Joshua," I said, "I know I told my group members to write down what they wanted me to say, but at this time in my life, I would not be able to explain to the class how a computer program works. Actually, I am not even able to read what the paper says and understand it. I don't read very well since I was diagnosed with cerebral lupus and released from the hospital," I told him. "Not only do I not read well, I don't spell, comprehend, or remember very well either." The conversation was totally one-sided, as Joshua listened attentively to what I had to say.

"You see, God just gave me the ability to work on the computer again, and I don't do that very well either. Oftentimes when I am in front of the computer, I am sitting waiting on the computer to respond, and then I realize that I may have pushed the wrong key, or maybe I didn't push a key at all. My mind just isn't what it once was, and I need to know what I can do in order not to throw away my GPA because of this last class. I still want an A in this class."

"This is a group assignment, Leeta," he said in that calm, pleasant voice of his. "I am not concerned about how big or small your part is in the presentation; you will get the same grade as the rest of your group. I have been teaching for three years, and you are the most outstanding student that I have ever had." Tears filled my eyes as I reflected back on the sermon Bishop had just preached earlier that day. "So, do you think I need to talk to my group members?" I asked.

"Yes, I do. Your group has to evaluate your performance, and I believe throughout this program, you have contributed a great deal to your group. Due to the current circumstances, you aren't able to contribute as much as you once did. If your group has a problem, tell them to talk to me."

My heart felt like it was going to pop out of my chest; I was so excited. Bishop was right; God does allow us to collect on our benefits. After the conversation with Joshua, I went directly to the computer and wrote an email, telling my group I needed to meet with them.

I wrote and asked my group could I meet with them, and here are the emails that followed:

Email #1 from Me
I need to meet with everyone.

Email #2 from Jim Brown
I am all ears.

Email #3 from Me

Only waiting for Rebecca

Email #4 from Me

My email did not make it to Rebecca; will someone get her correct email address?

Email #5 from Me

Jim Brown wrote an email and said that since it is so hard for everyone to meet that maybe I could talk with all of you via email. Is that okay? Please reply so I know that everyone is getting this email.

Email #6 from Me

My email did not make it to Rebecca; will someone get her correct address?

Email #7 from Paul Jones

I got this e-mail.

Email #8 from Kevin Hurt

Are we going to meet before Thursday? Tonight is good for me.

Email #9 from Me

If you all don't mind, please fill Rebecca in. I spoke with Joshua, and I told him I am not worried, because the Bible tells us in Philippians 4:6: "Be careful for nothing: meaning: be worried for nothing." I told him I have had him as a teacher for five classes, and I have made an (A) in four of those classes. But I do not believe at this time that I know what I once knew in those classes. When I got out of the hospital, I could not read. I am still having difficulty with reading. I am having difficulty with comprehension and with memory loss, along with other things. I told him that I told you guys to tell me what I needed to say, and I would say it. However, I also told him even if you wrote it down for me and I stood before the class, I did not think I would be able to read it or explain it to the class. I have been in school for over two years with a GPA of 3.9, and God just recently showed me how to use the computer again and sometimes, when I sit in front of the computer, I sit there for a while, waiting for something to happen before I even realize that I have pushed the wrong button or I have done anything at all. I am often times confused, and my children are concerned about me because they can now see that I may tell them something and they are aware that I don't know what I am talking about. Don't get me wrong; God is helping me and has done a great work in me. But like I had to tell my son Tommy this morning, as he started to get discouraged, God has a purpose for my life. I gave him Psalm 27:14: "Wait on the Lord be of good courage, and he shall strengthen thy heart; wait I say on the Lord." Then I told him that Scripture wasn't for just him, but it was for me too, and we hugged and cried together.

God has allowed me to witness almost everyone I have come in contact with, from the people driving me to my doctor's appointments from the doctors and nurses at those appointments. Don't feel sorry for me; what the devil meant for evil, God has turned it into good. I thank God for giving me this opportunity to be sick. I have learned so much. There were people that the devil had told me didn't like me, and I would have never spoken to those people again. Now those same people have been over my house cooking; if I hadn't gotten sick, I would have been cooking my own food. Those same people have been driving me to church; if I hadn't gotten sick, I would have been driving myself to church. Those same people walked me to the bathroom and asked me, Did I need any help in the stall? That means, do you need me to assist you while you are in the bathroom? (Pardon my French.) Do you need me to wipe your bottom? If they didn't like me, they would have found someone else to take me to the bathroom, but if I hadn't gotten sick, I would have walked myself to the bathroom. The Bible says in John 13:34: "A new commandment I give unto you, that ye love one another; as I love you, that ye also love one another." I was not doing that. God is showing me something. I had to learn that the hard way.

Joshua said that this is a group project, and he is not concerned about how big or small my part is. He said that I could introduce the group if I needed to. He also said that we all had to evaluate each other on how well of a part we played on/in this project. He said if any of you needed to, you could talk to him. I don't care to talk about what the doctors are saying about what is wrong with me. Most of what they are saying is speculation and guessing. I'm sure you guess that this is the place where I plan to quote another scripture; you are correct. In John 3:11, it says, "Verily, verily, I say unto thee, We speak that we do know." If they can't prove it to me, one hundred percent, then they don't KNOW it, and the Bible says speak what you know. So, I am not listening. In Isaiah 53:1, "who has believed our report? And to whom is the arm of the Lord revealed?" I choose to believe the report of the Lord. And His report says, in Jeremiah 30:17, "For I will restore health unto thee." Webster's Dictionary says restore means to renew, rebuild, alter, 1) give back, return, 2) to put or bring back into existence or use. 3: to bring back to or put back into a former or original state: renew 4: to put again in possession of something. Therefore, I believe in God's report.

Email #10 from Jim Brown

Subject: RE: Checkpoint 1

At the beginning of this class, when we found out about your condition, we had agreed just to get you through. You were not present, but as a group, we agreed that this is what we wanted for you. We did not expect you to be in the class at all. We had even jokingly suggested that we tape the introduction from your hospital room just so you would be "present" and get your grade.

These past few weeks, you have shown me unparalleled strength. You are truly an amazing woman with an amazing amount of will. This may sound corny, but your story is the story legends are made out of. I've told my wife several times about how much I admire what you are doing, and it is truly inspiring. Someday when my great-grandchildren complain about pain in their lives, I will tell them the story about Leeta, who had a seizure at two in the afternoon, went to the hospital and had tests run on her, and then against the doctor's will, drove to school in her blue scrubs with IVs still in her arms. Yeah, just like any other legend, it is a bit exaggerated, but the story still holds true. You have shown amazing courage and desire, and we all acknowledge this.

Take care of yourself.

All I could do was reply with a smile to Jim. I am truly grateful for what God has allowed me to go through. But I am also grateful that He has allowed me to go through and eventually get out of it. Rebecca actually lives next door to me, but it took me a while to remember that.

"Tommy, come here, please. Take a copy of this email to Rebecca." It seems like it wasn't even five minutes later that Rebecca was at my door.

"What is going on?" she asked.

"Did you read my email?" I asked.

"I only read the first paragraph. At the top of the email, it says to fill Rebecca in, and I wanted to know; how much more there can be?" she said with a sort of frantic voice. I began to explain the email situation to her and let her know that there wasn't anything else. I had just forgotten that she lived next door and had asked the group members to forward the email to her once they had a chance. As I was talking, I was able to get a glimpse of her shirt from behind the email paper. "What is that on your shirt?" I questioned.

"What?" she said.

I said, "That is devil worship," as I looked at the female devil with the horns and tail on her shirt, inviting everyone to visit the house of voodoo and yadda, yadda, yadda. Rebecca laughed and thought I was joking.

I told her, "I have been trying to bind and prevent demons from being in my house. So, you may not bring any more into my house." She really thought I was playing as she said, "So what, you don't want me in your house?"

"You are welcome, but you may not bring any demons with you," I said in a stern voice.

"You want me to wait outside," she said in a voice that made me think she was offended.

"You may go home and change your shirt and then come back," I said as I walked her to the door and let her outside. A few minutes passed, and Rebecca was back. She had on a T-shirt that represented a church and scriptures on the back. That was much better. Rebecca and I really hadn't talked much in the past, even though we were in the same class and lived next door to each other. This day was different; we ended up talking about the Lord and the Bible. I explained to her that the only reason we have an opportunity to be saved is because the Jews betrayed Jesus. She was also confused about who the 144,000 were, so I showed her in Revelation 7:4–8, where John counts the twelve tribes of Israel and tells us exactly who they are. The book of Revelation is the "Revelation of Jesus Christ, which God gave unto John to show unto his servant things which must shortly come to pass; and he signified it by his angel unto his servant John" (Revelation 1:1).

"The only reason we have a right to the tree of life is because the Jews did not accept Christ. They did not know what they had when they had it. They didn't know a good thing," I said.

"I know God has given me things I did not deserve," she said.

"That's not exactly what I am talking about," I said while I thought of a way to explain. "I am not talking about material things. Uhhmmm, let me explain," I said. "God allows us to have material things all the time. But some things we take for granted as if God has to give them to us. Like life," I said. "I'll give you an example." Then I began to tell her about the time when God stopped the seizure in the bed for me. But of course, I didn't get the whole story out, and by the time I got to how God stopped it, "Whoa! Hallelujah!" I said as I jumped to my feet and began to shout around the room, doing the best holy dance I could before God.

Rebecca just looked at me with tears in her eyes. She was so overwhelmed with what God had done for me. She finally understood what I meant about God doing things for you that you really don't deserve. Waving my arms and praising God, I just began to tell her how I didn't deserve His grace or His mercies, but no matter how unfaithful I may have been to God, He saw fit to stretch His arms out, reach down to earth, and decided to touch me and stop that seizure. "Whoa, I feel good! Thank you, Jesus!" I continued to yell out.

CHAPTER 4

Cleaning House

The boys had not moved back home with me yet, so I would spend most of my days just listening to music and reading my Bible. I received a call from Sister Sharp, Elder Sharp's wife, and she asked whether she could come over to visit me. I welcomed the company and couldn't wait to see her. Once she got there, I was excited to tell her about all the things God had done for me and how I had been getting stronger each day. She listened and, of course, gave me lots of encouraging words. When it was time for her to leave, she asked, "Can I anoint you, shuga, and pray for you?"

"Yes, please," I answered.

"Now, you might think this is weird, but I'm only doing what God told me to do, but if you don't want me to do it, then just tell me no, okay?" she said.

"If God told you to do it, I'm okay with it," I replied.

"God told me to anoint your head, your hands, and your tongue," she said.

"Okay," I said. She began to anoint me, and when she finished, she started to pray. I didn't say a word; I just held up my hands and bowed my head. Most of her praying was in the Holy

Ghost, so I didn't understand anything she said. When she finished praying, she said, "I have to go, shuga." She hugged me, and I walked her to the door. I locked the security screen door, went back in the family room, and continued to listen to music and work on the computer.

My living room had a huge window that covered almost the entire wall. When I got up out of my chair, I saw a policeman walk past the window. I went to the security door, which was located directly next to the huge window, and said, "May I help you?"

He said, "I need you to open the security door."

I said, "Why?"

He said, "Because I have a warrant for your arrest."

I said, "Then, by all means, come on in." I unlocked the security door, and when I pushed it open, I noticed there was another policeman standing next to the house, and he had his hand on his firearm. I lifted my hands in the air, held the door open with my elbow, and said, "I don't have anything on me." The police officer closest to me grabbed the door, and they came inside the house. "May I see your ID, ma'am?" he asked. "I have to go to the bedroom and get my purse," I said. The other police officer then followed me into the bedroom so that I could retrieve my ID. I grabbed my ID and handed it to the police officer.

"Let's go back into the living room, ma'am," he said. I just followed behind him.

Once we arrived in the living room, I said, "Can you tell me what this is about?" The police officer handed me a piece of paper. I looked at the top of the paper, and I could see it was a legal document. The title of the document stated, "ORDER FOR APPREHENSION AND RETURN." As I continued to read the first line, it said, "It being found by the Court that Leeta Bigbee has escaped from Methodist Hospital to which the individual is committed under blah blah blah blah blah..." I couldn't believe my eyes; they actually had an arrest warrant that stated I had escaped from the psych ward.

"May I call my bishop?" I asked.

"Yes," one of the officers called out.

"Bishop, the police are here, and they are arresting me," I said.

"No, we aren't arresting you," said one of the officers.

"Hold on, Bishop. I'm going to let you talk to the officer," I said as I handed the phone to the most talkative officer. "No, sir, we are not arresting her, but we do have an order to pick her up and take her back to the hospital. This isn't an arrest warrant, sir; we aren't taking her to jail," he explained. "Your bishop wants to know if he can get a copy of the apprehension order?" he asked. I nodded my head. "she said yes, sir, and we have to take her now. Yes, sir, we are taking her to Methodist Hospital. Yes, sir, goodbye," he said as he handed me back the phone.

"May I pack an overnight bag before we go? It gets really cold in there," I asked.

"Yes, ma'am," he replied.

"Do you want to follow me into the back room while I pack my clothes?" I asked.

"No, just make it quick," he answered. I grabbed my things, locked up the house, and hopped in the back of the police car to be escorted back to the hospital they claim I escaped from.

MARION SUPERIOR COURT – PROBATE DIVISION

THE HONORABLE CHARLES J. DEITER, JUDGE

1721 CITY-COUNTY BUILDING

INDIANAPOLIS, INDIANA 46204

(317) 327-5063 FAX (317) 327-4512

FACSIMILE TRANSMISSION

CAD #869

9/22/04

DATE: _____09/22/04_____

TO: COMPANY NAME: _Marion County Sheriff_

INDIVIDUAL/DEPT: _Dispatch_ _327-2586_

NUMBER OF PAGES IN THIS TRANSMISSION INCLUDING COVER PAGE: _2_

MESSAGE: _A&R Mental Health_

Please pick up Leota Bejin from 9339 E 36th Place and transport her to Methodist Hospital. Identifiers are on the order.

Thanks -

Deniker

NOTE: FACSIMILE OPERATOR: PLEASE DELIVER THIS FACSIMILE TRANSMISSION TO THE ABOVE ADDRESSEE(S). IF YOU DID NOT RECEIVE ALL OF THE PAGES IN GOOD CONDITION, PLEASE ADVISE US AT (317) 327-5015 AT YOUR EARLIEST CONVENIENCE. THANK YOU.

Exhibit _____
Page_____ of_____

SEP-22-2004 11:08

STATE OF INDIANA)
) SS:
COUNTY OF MARION)

IN THE MATTER OF THE COMMITMENT OF

LEETA BIGBEE

IN THE MARION SUPERIOR COURT
PROBATE DIVISION - COURT 8
CHARLES J. DEITER, JUDGE

NO R.JO

CAUSE NUMBER 49D080409MH000995

FILED

SEP 22 2004

ORDER FOR APPREHENSION AND RETURN

It being found by the Court that LEETA BIGBEE has escaped from CLARIAN HEALTH PARTNERS to which the individual is committed under I.C. 12-26, or has failed to comply with the requirements for outpatient status in accordance with I.C. 12-26-14-5.

IT IS THEREFORE ORDERED THAT THE SHERIFF OF MARION COUNTY, INDIANA, shall take charge of and return the Respondent, LEETA BIGBEE, to the nearest State institution listed or the community mental center that has appropriate and available facilities and personnel to detain the individual, all of which is authorized in I.C. 12-24-8-1, which is found to be METHODIST HOSPITAL.

ALL OF WHICH IS ORDERED this 22ND day of SEPTEMBER, 2004.

Charles J. Deiter
Charles J. Deiter, Judge
Marion Superior Court 8
Probate Division

PHYSICAL DESCRIPTION:
Height: 6'2" Weight: 110
Eye Color: BROWN Hair Color: BLACK
Race: AFRICAN AMERICAN
Date of Birth: 11-11-67
Last known address: 9339 E. 36TH PLACE
INDIANAPOLIS, IN 46235
NEAREST RELATIVE - YELENA BRACKNEY
4-16-87 (No. 61)

Exhibit____
Page____ of____

Once I arrived at the hospital, they took me to a glass hospital room, and they placed a deputy outside the door to keep an eye on me. Within minutes, a nurse walked into the room and began asking me questions. "Why didn't you go to your doctor's appointment on such and such date?"

"I didn't know I had a doctor's appointment," I replied.

"How in the world can you not know you had a doctor's appointment when you are grown? Didn't you make the appointment?" she screamed.

"No, ma'am. I did not make the appointment. My sister Sharon is over all my affairs. I recently was discharged from the hospital, and I had no idea I had an upcoming appointment," I explained.

"Why would your sister be over all your affairs when you are a grown woman?" she questioned.

"Ma'am, it's a really long story, but if you read my chart, you will see that she is my emergency contact, and she is also my representative," I explained in a very strangely calm voice. I wasn't sure, but for some reason, I didn't get upset with her at all, even though I felt like she didn't believe a word I was saying. She snatched my file, opened the glass door, and stormed past the deputy without saying another word to me. I just sat on the bed and waited.

A few minutes later, she came back into the room and said, "Will you need a ride home?"

"No," I said. "My bishop is going to come and get me." Now here is the funny thing. I never once asked my bishop to come to get me. Once again, she didn't say much; she just grabbed the files and left the room and didn't have much to say to me. I must admit she had a much better attitude when she came back. I thought to myself, *she must have talked to Sharon, and I bet Sharon got her told real quick! And now I'm allowed to leave.* I probably sat in that room another ten or fifteen minutes when Bishop and Sister Jeanie walked in the door, ready to take me home. I knew I could count on my bishop.

As the weeks went by, I began to get stronger and stronger. By this time, I was able to walk around the house by myself and do a lot of the things that I had not been doing the previous weeks. The boys had recently moved back home with me. Before that, I spent many hours at home by myself because the boys were still staying with Sharon. I hadn't been able to stand for long periods of time. I wasn't able to cook for them, nor was I able to drive the car to take them back and forth to school. I spoke to the children almost daily, and they enjoyed that, but they were certainly ready to come home.

Once the boys returned home, it seemed as if it didn't take them long for them to get back to their normal routines. They continued right where they left off, arguing and fighting with each other all day long. Tasha was driving the boys back and forth to school for me, and she even brought groceries over so that we would have some food to eat. But once she came in and started to put the food in the freezer, she became very angry to see that there was already hamburger, chicken, and other items already in the freezer.

"You said you didn't have anything to feed the boys," Tasha screamed as she opened the freezer.

"Well, Tasha, I haven't been able to stand up to cook, and the boys don't cook, so it was just like not having any food. I appreciate you bringing over the instant and microwavable items," I explained while I tried not to get angry with her. I wasn't a prideful person, but I hated people doing things for me and then acting like they didn't want to or that I was a bother. Even worse, I hated asking people for help. I have worked at my job for over fifteen years, but I was off work the entire time without pay, and my job didn't offer any type of short-term or long-term disability.

After that incident with Tasha, I wouldn't allow her to buy anything else for me or the house, no matter how much she insisted. Soon after, the boys and I began to lose quite a bit of weight. At church on Sunday, Sister Shelley offered to come by the house to cook dinner for me. "Sis, are you getting enough to eat at home?" she asked.

"I do okay," I said as I thought about how nosy she was asking me about my business.

"Well, what are you doing this Wednesday?" she asked. "I'll be off work, and I would love to come over and cook for you and the boys. I know you haven't been able to cook for yourself, and I don't mind at all."

Wow, as I thought back to when, I didn't even think she liked me, and now she wants to cook dinner for me. That's deep. "Sure, Sis, you can come over on Wednesday to cook. That would be great."

"Okay, my mom will drop me and Noodle off on Tuesday, and we'll just spend the night if that is okay with you, and I will drive you to your doctor's appointment Thursday," she said.

"Uhmm, okay, then that sounds good. You guys come on over; I'll be home," I was kind of surprised that not only was she bringing her son, but now they were spending the night as well. "Just don't cook any of that soul food stuff," I said. "I don't want any necks, toes, feet, butts, or guts. No sweet potatoes, no macaroni and cheese, nothing green, and no kind of cornbread. Just give me some normal food."

"Okay, Sis, I know you don't eat much of anything. I'll just fry you some potatoes," she said as she began to walk away.

"Okay, sounds good," I said.

Wednesday rolled around, and Sister Shelley, her son Noodle, and her mom arrived around 4:30 p.m., and I let them all in. The visit seemed a little awkward at first because it wasn't like Sister Shelley and I were friends or anything. I led them to the back of the house where the family room was, so that we could get more comfortable. I asked them did they want to listen to some music or watch a movie. Sister Shelley's mom wanted to watch old movies; she named movies I had never even heard of before. It was actually kind of funny. They declined all my invitations, and we just sat and talked. Noodle just kind of ran around the room and played by himself while we talked. After about thirty minutes of talking, Sister Shelley's mom left.

Sister Shelley and I had a wonderful time sitting around, talking, and just getting to know each other. We actually had a lot in common. I didn't know that Sister Shelley wrote poetry, nor did she know I wrote poetry. She had a poem about her deceased daughter that was just beautiful; it brought tears to my eyes. Sister Shelley was very deep with her poetry. I truly enjoyed the way Sister Shelley had a passion for poetry, life, and the Bible. Although I didn't understand her passion for the Bible at that time. I also didn't realize how I would grow not only to understand her passion for the Bible but to appreciate it and develop my own passion.

Just as she did when she came before, she would go around the house and point out items and tell me I needed to remove them from my house because they represented unclean spirits. I just didn't understand where she was getting all this from. I enjoyed the fellowship with Sister Shelley, but I must admit I was glad when the next day rolled around so she could leave. I grew tired of hearing about spirits, demons, witchcraft, and so forth.

After Sister Shelley's visit, I spoke with her on a regular basis. "How are you doing today, Sister Leeta?" Sister Shelley asked.

"I'm doing well," I replied.

"Did you pray today?" she questioned.

"No, not yet," I answered.

"Sis, that is your weapon; you cannot allow the enemy to take your weapon away from you. You need to pray and read your Word every day," she said.

This girl is really extreme, I thought to myself. "Okay," I said, "I will get some prayer in as soon as I get off the phone from you."

"Make sure you do," she said, "That is how you get your help. And don't forget to get all those spirits out of your house, Sis— and don't let them come back in," she said.

"I won't," I sighed because I really didn't know what else to do or say.

"I'm for real," she said. "You have to listen to what I am saying. I know you got rid of Tommy and Timmy's stuff, but you need to make sure you got rid of everything, even the stuff you like. Because if you don't, one day you are going to wake up and you are going to hear a demon laughing at you, and you are going to find a monster book or something under your couch cushion one day."

"Okay, Sis Shelley. I have to go," I said.

"Okay, love you, Sis," she said as she hung up the phone.

That girl is really off, I thought to myself while shaking my head as I got off the phone. I told myself that I was not going to spend much time talking to her because all she ever seemed to talk about was spirits, demons, and stuff like that. I know that demons exist, but it is just not that deep. She really needs to get a grip.

The boys and I normally pray together when it is time to go to bed at night. Then we get up and hug as a group, and then we hug each other one at a time and tell each other we love one another, and then go to bed. That is just our time together as a family with God at nighttime, and it takes about three to five minutes. We pray for one another and for others around the world, and for our loved ones.

After we pray and the boys are gone off to bed, I normally walk through the house and I plead the blood of Jesus through the house. What that means is I go through each room in the house and say, "The blood of Jesus" in each room. I lay my hands on the doors and on some of the windows and say, "The blood of Jesus" throughout the house. What that is doing is protecting my house from anything or anyone that is trying to enter in and trying to harm us by symbolically spreading the blood over the windows and doors as they did when the children of Israel were in Egypt (Exodus 12:13). Well, that is all fine and good for people or spirits trying to enter in that are trying to harm us, but what about the spirit that we invite into our homes ourselves? That is a good question, isn't it? It took me a while to realize it, but that is what Sister Shelley was trying to get me to understand.

That night when I went to bed, I did my normal routine: I prayed, kissed and hugged the boys good night, pleaded the blood, turned on my fan, put the covers over my head, and went to sleep. When all of a sudden, I woke up to HAHAHAHA-HAHAHA! It was a very deep, loud laugh. It was a laugh I had not heard before. It was a man's voice, and I knew a man did not live in my house because, believe me, if a man lived there, I would know it. I snatched the covers off my head and sat up in the bed very quickly and thought, *is that the fan making that noise?* Then the Holy Ghost answered me and said, "You know that isn't the fan making that noise. You know exactly what it is." *It is a demon!* I thought.

"A demon," I screamed as I jumped out of my bed and began to physically run through the house and search for the beast. "Where are you? Where are you?" I screamed! "Help me, Lord! Help me find him, Lord! Help me, Lord! I need to get him out of my house. Help me, Lord; please help me!" It was about 3:30 a.m., and the first thing I wanted to do was run into the room to snatch the boys out of the bed and run out of the house to protect them.

I can't do that; that would be too much confusion, and they wouldn't understand, I thought. Protect them from what? Where is the demon? My mind began to race. The spirits are all in the house because I have heard them, I thought. You have the greater One in you, I thought to myself. I just walked back to my bed and just waited, I must admit, not patiently, though. I sat with my knees inward toward my chest and my arms wrapped around my legs as I cupped my elbows with my hands. I began to talk to God to help me to be able to explain the scriptures and the importance of ridding our house of the spirits to my children.

Several thoughts went through my head as I rocked back and forth in that bed. Sister Chelle had gone over a scripture with me in the lobby of the church just a couple of days before. She couldn't remember how it went, but she kept saying, "Sis, it says something about an unclean spirit has left a man, and it searches for dry places." So, I decided to go and look that scripture up on the computer, and I prayed and asked God to help me to understand what it meant so that I would be able to explain it to my children. I had been so sick after getting out of the hospital that I wasn't really able to read well or comprehend well what I read at that time. If I had to guess, my reading comprehension level was probably at a third- or fourth-grade level, although I was currently in school obtaining a bachelor of science degree, maintaining a 3.9-grade point average. Believe me. I needed much prayer at this time in my life.

I continued to read my Word and study the scriptures and pray for comprehension. "Thank you, Jesus," I said as I located Luke 11:24–26 on the computer. "I feel like I am now ready to talk to the boys," I said to myself. I had been awake since about 3:30 a.m., and it was now 7:45 a.m. It felt like days had passed since the laughter had awakened me.

I picked up the phone to call my mother to tell her what had happened. "I plan to talk to the boys when they wake up about all the things we have to get rid of. We are going to start with Scooby Doo," I said.

"Scooby Doo?" she questioned. "What's wrong with Scooby Doo?"

"What do they chase ninety-nine percent of the time?"

"Ghosts," she said with a surprised voice as if she had just discovered something new.

"Yes, they do," I said.

"That is still one of my favorite shows," she said.

"I didn't say you had to clean your house. I just said this is what we have to do over here. Everyone else can keep on doing whatever they want to do; this is just what is good for me and my family. You know, like the scripture says, 'as for me and my house' (Joshua 24:15). This is what we are going to do. Well, I hear the boys waking up; I have to go."

"Okay, hon. Love ya, bye," she said as we hung up the phone.

My heart started to race, and my hands started to shake. *What are you afraid of?* I thought to myself. I had never experienced anything like this before. I just didn't know how to approach this situation, and I didn't want to mess up. "Boys, come here, please," I said with a calm but shaky voice.

"Hi, Mommy," they said as they ran into the room and leaped up into my bed.

"What's up?" Tommy asked.

By now, Timmy was all wrapped up in most of the covers and is huddled up next to me with his ice-cold feet rubbing up and down my legs. "What, Mommy? What is it?" Timmy said in a hyper voice.

"You guys need to turn off the TV and go eat breakfast; I want to talk to you," I said.

"Why, what did we do?" they both scream out almost in unison.

"Nothing. You didn't do anything. Just go eat, and I will tell you about it when you finish. Now, go eat," I commanded in a pleasant but stern voice. The boys left my room and ran off into the kitchen. "Huhhh," I said as I took the biggest, deepest breath I could take while the tears ran down my face. "Lord, please help me. I feel like I am at such a loss here. I just don't know what to do. I don't know how to handle this situation. I need Your help!"

"You need me, Mommy? Are you okay?" Tommy called out from the kitchen.

"No, thanks," I said, "I'm okay," I called back as I wiped my tears and pulled myself together.

"Come on, boys, have a seat in the family room. I need to talk to you," I said as they walked in from the kitchen after breakfast. I laid my Bible on the floor, and I said a small silent prayer again as I sat Indian-style on the floor. I didn't say that prayer because I didn't think God heard the first ten or so prayers—I just wanted to make sure. "Tommy, you know how sometimes you get into trouble in school, and you say that you just can't help it?" Tommy nodded his head. "And Timmy, you know how sometimes you say you feel like you just can't help yourself when you mess with your brother all the time?" Timmy nodded his head. "You know how it seems like I can't stop screaming and yelling at you guys all the time, and I get so mean sometimes?" They both looked at each other and really, I mean, really nodded their heads. "I think that has something to do with what we bring into our home and what we watch on TV and what videos we watch."

"What do you mean, Mommy?" they asked.

"Well, let me explain. Listen to this Scripture," I said, and then I gave them the interpretation that God gave me. "When a bad spirit, like a demon, has gone out of a person, it goes and tries to find a place to rest, like a new person. If the unclean spirit does not find a place to rest, the unclean spirit then says, 'I will return to the person that I was with in the beginning.' When he goes back to the person that he was with in the beginning, he finds that the person is clean, meaning there are no more demons or bad spirits in that person. So, the demon or bad spirit goes and gets seven of his evil and wicked friends meaning other demons that are worse than him, to go back and live inside of the person that he left in the beginning. Then the person will be worse off than he was in the first place because he now has eight demons inside of him instead of just one like he had in the beginning."

Timmy and Tommy were sitting in front of me with their mouths wide open. "Tell us more of the story, Mommy. Tell us more!" they screamed.

"It isn't a story, baby. It's in the Bible. It is God's Word, it is the truth, and that is what we have been doing in our home. Now it is time for us to clean house."

"Clean house?" Timmy says.

"We have to get rid of all demons, bad spirits, unclean spirits, and anything that is not of God. I'll show you what I mean." I turned my Bible to Psalm 101:3 and began to explain to the boys the meaning of the scripture. "It says we should not put anything that is wicked before our eyes." They sat there and looked absolutely puzzled. I began to pray on the inside once again. "Okay, guys, anything that represents unclean spirits, witches, ghosts, devils, monsters. Do you know what I mean?"

"Oh, now we do," they said in unison as they looked at each other.

183

"Okay then, let's get started. I need you to go in your rooms and pull out anything that has any of those things on it. Grab some trash bags and get all the toys, movies, video games, books, sleeping bags, toothbrushes, pencils, erasers, marbles, board games, clothes, shoes, and whatever else you can find. Just pull it out and throw it away."

"Okay, Mommy," they screamed as they took off running into their rooms. I took off in the other direction, headed for the kitchen to look for cups and dishes that may have cartoon characters that may have any demonic connotation. "Wow, look at that. We have three bags full of stuff," Tommy said. "What are you going to do with all that stuff?"

"Throw it away," I said. "Oh, we forgot the movies in the movie closet," I said as I turned around and looked at over 250 VHS movies stacked up neatly on the shelves with over fifty still wrapped in the wrapper, and that didn't even include the games. "You are going to throw away our movies?" Timmy said, with tears in his eyes.

"Baby, I have to do what God is telling me to do. I cannot allow ungodliness to continue to creep in unaware any longer (Jude 1:4). We have been watching things, reading things, and playing with things that represent all sorts of ungodliness, and because they are funny and/or cute, we have ignored them, and they are getting into our heads, our spirit and in our subconscious mind. We aren't even aware of what has been going on in our own house. We have to get in that closet and get rid of all of the movies that represent all of the unclean spirits, and we have to do it now." Both heads began to nod. But I could tell they didn't want to do it; they just nodded those little heads because they knew they didn't have a choice.

Once I walked in the closet, I began to pull down all the movies in the closet, and I soon began to feel overwhelmed. My eyes started to hurt, and my head started spinning. I didn't actually know what I was supposed to be doing in that room. We had so many movies and games in that room I couldn't even remember watching half of those movies. I fell to the ground on my knees and cupped my face with my hands, and just began to cry.

"What's the matter, Mommy?" Tommy said as he walked up behind me and laid his hand on my shoulder.

"Help me, Lord!" I cried. "Help me, Lord!"

"Ghost, witches, spirits, monsters, demons," God spoke in a still, calm voice to my spirit.

"Thank you, Jesus," I said as I got up off the floor and wiped the tears from my face.

"Are you okay?" Tommy asked.

"I'm fine; let's finish."

So, they began picking up the movies off the floor, and I continued with the movies still on the shelves. We put them in the garbage bags, and the boys called the titles off, asking me whether they were okay to keep.

"What about *Monsters, Inc.*?" asked Timmy.

"Nope, it has to go. Now stuff like that with 'monster' or 'ghost' in the name, then you guys should know it has to go. Okay?"

"Okay!" they screamed as they went back to searching through the movies. I picked up Cinderella, and I just scooted it over neatly on the shelf and stacked it back up when Tommy said, "Mommy, *Cinderella* has an evil stepmother in it."

I said, "Okay."

He said, "Evil—you said anything that wasn't of God had to go."

I said, "Okay, thank you, Mr. Tommy, thank you."

Then a few more movies went by, and I picked up the Little Mermaid, and Tommy reminded me of something else. "Why are you keeping *The Little Mermaid*?" he asked.

"What's wrong with *The Little Mermaid*?" I asked.

"There is a witch that lives in the sea," he said as if to say, "Duh!"

There are several children's movies with hidden demonic connotations; for example, Cruella DeVil is the villain in both *101 Dalmatians* and *102 Dalmatians*; her name is actually spelled exactly like devil. Additionally, while she is in her jail cell, the number listed on her hat is 6660, which we all know 666 is the mark of the beast. Several movies allow the enemy to creep in unaware, and if they make it cute enough or funny enough, then people feel that there is no harm in it, and most don't even notice it.

In the movie the *Lion King*, when Simba is an adult, he, Timon, and Pumba are in a field looking up at the stars. Simba walks off by himself and goes to the edge of the cliff, falls down to the ground to rest, and hangs off the edge of the cliff. When he falls down to the ground, the force of the fall creates a puff of dust. If you freeze the movie and turn your head slightly to the left, it would appear that you can see the word sex spelled in the clouds of dust.

On the cover of *The Little Mermaid* VHS cassette, where Ursula and Ariel's dad King Triton are around the castle, the top of the castle (the castle spires) very closely resemble a penis. Also, in the movie, the minister that is officiating Ariel's wedding ceremony appears to be displaying an erection. Many movies that our children watch or have watched have hidden connotations, and we as parents should watch the movies before our children ever see them. Not only should we watch the movies, we need to pay attention to what is going on in these movies and what is being displayed before our children. There are books, as well as movies, that have hidden themes and some not so hidden, such as the Harry Potter books, which I never purchased for my children, promote witchcraft, sorcery, and devil worshiping.[7] Witchcraft and [8]sorcery are sins, and anyone that practices them will not inherit the kingdom of God, according to Galatians 5:20–21. Here are just a few quotes regarding the books/movies:

D. Boyd, Ph.D. (*Is Harry Potter Evil?* November 25, 2007, para 16) points out that "The author, J. K. Rowling researched the occult to make her characters come alive in the minds of readers. According to Iowa Licensed Master Social Worker William Schnoebelen, former Church of Satan member, Potter characters execute satanic ceremony and technique as practiced today. Schnoebelen, also a former instructor of witchcraft, says, 'Potter imitators are blind to the en-tities that respond from an unknown beguiling arena. It seems

7 **a:** the use of sorcery or magic, **b:** communication with the devil or with a familiar (*Merriam-Webster's Online Dictionary* 2007).
8 The use of power gained from the assistance or control of evil spirits especially for di-vining: NECROMANCY 2: MAGIC (*Merriam-Webster's Online Dictionary* 2007).

so enchantingly fun and innocent, but they are trafficking in evil spirits. The books definitely draw kids to witchcraft.'"

Former Satanic mystic, Johanna Michaelson, says, "There is a beautiful side of evil—deceptive, subtle, adorned with all manner of spiritual refinements, but no less from the pit of hell than that which is blatantly satanic." (Ellen Makkai, "HARRY THE WIZ IS THE WRONG BIZ," *CREATORS SYNDICATE, INC.* Nov. 2001)

Children should not repeat everything they hear or see, such as quotes from witches, warlocks, demons, and anything that goes against the teachings of God. It is wrong and will not be allowed into the kingdom of heaven.

Psalm 101:3 states, "I will set no wicked thing before mine eyes: I hate the work of them that turn aside; it shall not cleave to me." That scripture is saying I will not put anything wicked in front of me, and the wicked thing will not cling or attach itself to me. We as people need to be more aware of what we are bringing into our homes and especially what we are allowing our children to watch, even if it is funny or entertaining.

I continued to clean the closet out. I picked up the movie *Halloween*, and I was just dumbfounded. I just couldn't seem to remember what it was about; then, the Lord spoke to me and said, "Read the name." "What does Halloween stand for?" Then these words started to roll in my head like a marquee: witches, ghosts, goblins, and spooks. Okay, now I remember. The same thing happened when I saw the movie *Ghost Ship*. It was as if God said, "Just read the name; what does it stand for?"

I still seem to be having some difficulties getting through the movies. "Lord, I just can't remember the movies, and it has just been too long since I have seen some of them. I really need some help. If it is not right and I need to get it out of my house, just allow me to feel it in my spirit, Lord." I continued to pray within, and what I mean by that is I just had several prayers running through my head. But God knew my heart, and He knew that I wanted to rid my house of all items that were ungodly and that I had a desire to do right. So, from then on out, every time I picked up a movie, if I was supposed to get rid of a movie, a weird feeling would come over me. It was smooth sailing from then on out; I didn't have any more problems. I was at a point that even if it didn't have demonic connotations, I would rather be safe than sorry. No movie is worth me dealing with unclean spirits in my home again.

After hours of working and packing up all the things, we had about five 55-gallon trash bags full of toys, clothes, video games, board games, sleeping bags, collector's cards, movies, and much, much more. Well, then I was stuck with the dilemma of what to do with all those things. I didn't want any of those items to make it into the wrong hands because I believe with all my heart that those items did have spirits connected to them, and I did not want those spirits to do as the scripture said, leave my house and go searching for a dry place to rest, find none and come back to my house and bring seven more unclean spirits and then reside in my home. I had no idea how many spells, sorcerers, witches, warlocks, demonic connotations, and demonic trafficking were in all that stuff that we had just packed up. Were there demons connected to each item? Had they already brought back seven of their wicked friends, and had they been lurking around in my house? This was just too much for me to even think about. So, this time I was determined to put these spirits out and keep them out. I had tried putting them out two other times, and they came back. Did I tell you about the other two times I had to put the spirits out of the house?

Well, here it goes. One time I went to the women's retreat. I had been kind of grouchy, and I didn't even feel like going to the retreat. I just didn't feel like being bothered by the people. I just went because my mother and Sharon kept on nagging me to go. The retreat was to get away from your everyday life and just give you a chance to get closer to God. I was having a difficult time at home and at my job, and to top it all off, I was sick in my body.

Additionally, Tommy wasn't doing well in school; actually, he hadn't ever done well in school. It wasn't that he made bad grades or anything. Well, now that I think about it, he didn't make good grades either. He just kind of did whatever he wanted to do in school. For example, I would receive at least three phone calls a week from school concerning Tommy. Now the week I am speaking of was during summer school. Tommy had been cutting up so badly in school that he was forced to go to summer school, or he would have had to repeat the second grade. Tommy loves to perform. He would dance and sing and stuff like that all the time. We have caller ID at work, so often, when the phone rang and I recognized it was the school, I would start to cringe in my chair. I just knew he had done something wrong. I didn't want to even answer the phone because if I had to leave work, my boss would give me a hard time due to the fact that I didn't have a lot of leave since I was always off work sick.

"GSA. May I help you?" I said as I answered the phone while my heart was pounding.

"May I speak with Ms. Bigbee?" The voice on the other end of the line said.

"May I ask who is calling?" I said as if the caller ID had not already let me know who it was.

"This is Mrs. So-and-so calling from her son's school," she said.

"This is she," I said. I had to say all that just to give me enough time to calm down and catch my breath.

"Yes, ma'am. I am calling you about Tommy; I have been having some problems with him. He has been acting up all week, but I didn't want to bother you. However, today I just had to call you," she said in a frustrated voice. What is it about parents? We know our children do wrong but seems like we just don't want to hear about it. Well, maybe it is just me, but I sure didn't want to hear what Tommy had been doing all week long. I just felt like saying, "If he had been acting up all week long, then why didn't you call me all week long?" But the truth of the matter is, if she had called me all week long, I would have been complaining that she called me too much.

"Well, today, while we were having a reading lesson, Tommy just took it upon himself to stand up on top of the desk and started singing a song," she said in a serious voice.

"No, for real, what did he do?" I asked again.

"I'm not joking, Ms. Bigbee. He did do that, and after he finished, he decided he was tired, and he got down on the classroom floor and decided to take a nap," she frustratingly. "I'm on my way to the school," I said as I hung up the phone. So, there were things of this nature going on, and I just didn't feel like going to the retreat. But I went anyway.

Well, while I was at the retreat, a spiritual attack came over me, and I wasn't able to move my hands as well, and I started having bad headaches. An evangelist named Sister Shannon came over to me and said, "You need to get the spirits out of your house." I just kind of looked at her. I didn't know who she was, and to my knowledge, I hadn't ever seen her before in my life.

She walked up to me another time during the retreat and just laid her hands on my head, and began to pray for me. She said, "Go into the dark places of your house and physically tell the spirits to get out of your house. Yell at them. Tell them to get out. Open the door and sweep them out with a broom and anoint your house with oil and pray and physically put them out of your house," she said.

"Yes, ma'am," I said. I guess she knew I had spirits because I had testified at the retreat about having snakes in my yard—I mean hundreds of snakes all over the place. We would go into the shed to pull the bikes out for the boys to ride, and the snakes would be wrapped around the bikes.

Maybe she knew about the spirits because I testified about the boys being outside riding their bikes while I was in my bedroom on the telephone. I had recently mopped the kitchen, so the kitchen table had been moved against the wall, and the kitchen was just one big open space. When the boys rode their bikes, I often left the garage door open. I heard the boys screaming, so I ran into the kitchen to see what the problem was. When I came into the kitchen, there was a grey-and-white three-and-a-half-foot tall pit bull in the kitchen chasing the boys. I dropped the telephone, ran toward the dog with my hands stretched out as if I was a defensive player on a basketball team, trying to block the dog from shooting a basket. I really tried to distract the dog, but the dog wasn't interested in me at all; he wanted the children. I ran into the garage and grabbed a broom; I started fanning the broom at the dog to direct its attention away from the children. The dog finally directed its attention toward me, and I told the children to go lock themselves in their rooms.

The boys were crying as they ran down the hall, screaming, "There's another dog in the garage!" While the boys were outside riding their bikes, the dogs started chasing them; they ran in the house and left the house door open, allowing the dog to run in after them. I quickly ran over to the garage and slammed the door; while locking one dog out, I had also locked one dog in. "What was I to do? The television show said, "If you are ever attacked by a dog, hit it on the nose." Then I thought, *what if I don't hit it hard enough? I could really make this dog mad, and it would eat me alive.* As I stood there with the broom in my hand, looking like a hockey player, the dog walked right past me and went and took a comfortable seat on my bathroom floor. The dog was so big, I couldn't even close the bathroom door to lock it in the bathroom. I slowly tiptoed out of the kitchen the opposite way and went down the hall and locked myself in my bedroom, and called 911. No one was hurt, thank God.

On top of that, I already knew I had spirits in my house when she told me about them. I knew because I would wake up in the middle of the night, and I would hear them talking and laughing and playing. The first thing I would do when I heard them was jump up and look around as if to say, "What is that noise? Or who is that talking to?" Well, then I started to become a little more subtle. When I heard the noises, I would just lie in bed without moving and open my eyes slowly to make sure that I was fully awake.

Once I was fully awake, I would look around the room very calmly to make sure that the TV, the radio, or anything like that wasn't on. Then I would gently get up to ensure I didn't make any noise. I snuck around the house in stealth mode to make sure nothing was on in any other rooms in the house, and of course, nothing was. But as I made it into the rooms where the noise was coming from, the noise would stop. So, I was very aware that the spirits were in there, doing whatever they wanted to do.

I did what Sister Shannon told me to do, and I commanded them to go, and I swept them out. I went into all the dark places and anointed my house. The spirits left, and I knew they were gone because my children were better, and I wasn't sick in my body anymore. Overall, my entire home life improved. Well, a few months went by, and the situation started to deteriorate once more. The same things started to repeat themselves. I could hear the sounds waking me up out of my sleep again, and I knew exactly what it was. Well, this time I went to someone at my church for help. I approached my assistant pastor Elder

Graves after Sunday morning service. At that time, I still attended Living Word.

I cannot lie; I was a little afraid and embarrassed because I didn't know what he was going to think about me when I told him I had spirits running around in my house. I had been sitting in church all morning, trying to think of a way to tell him about it.

"Uhhhhh, praise the Lord, Elder Graves," I said, with my shakey voice. "How are you?

"I'm doing pretty well, Sister Bigbee. How are the boys?" he answered, kind of rocking back and forth.

"Oh, they are okay. Uhhhhh, Elder Graves, I was wondering if you and some of the elders could come over to my house," I said as I took a deep breath and a sigh. "Uhhhhh," then I said in a quick whisper, "I have some spirits in the house." Then I just put my head down and waited for his response.

"Okay, how does tomorrow sound?" he said as he continued to look at me. I was so relieved. I just didn't know what to do, and I was thinking that I was going to have to explain or maybe he wouldn't believe me. "What time?" I said with excitement.

"I'll have my wife call you," he said. I walked away that day with a big Kool-Aid smile, just like the one on the Kool-Aid man pitcher had when he used to burst through the wall when the kids would scream, "Hey, Kool-Aid!" I was just overjoyed. I could not believe that this time I was finally going to get rid of the spirits once and for all.

Elder Graves had helped me out on several occasions. I would go to him during my associate's degree program and tell him how I would not have to read one book but still got A's throughout the entire program. He is a very good teacher; I also sat in his Sunday school class whenever I could roll out of bed to make it to Sunday school.

He and his wife showed up at my house the very next day, prepared for demon slaying—well, at least that is what I thought. "Praise the Lord," I said as I opened the door to let them both in. "Praise the Lord! How you doing, Sister Bigbee?" he said as he held his arm out for his wife to go in the door before him. She walked in the door with a pleasant smile on her face, wrapped her arms around me, and gave me a nice, tight hug. "How you doing, honey?" she asked.

"I'm okay," I answered.

"Well, let's get right down to it," he said, with that calm, pleasant voice he had. Elder Graves is a very slim man. He was probably about six feet five inches, and if I had to guess his weight, I would say he weighed about 180 pounds. His skin color was like coffee with just a dab of cream. He was very mild-mannered, and his voice dragged a bit when he spoke. Now his wife was quite the opposite of him. She was a bit shorter, maybe five feet, three inches, a bit heavier, and her skin tone was like coffee with a lot of cream added to it. She spoke with a tad bit of laughter in her voice, not slow at all like he did. I guess it is true that opposites attract.

"I notice you have several candles and incense around the house," he said as he walked from room to room, casing the place like a detective. "Yes, sir," I replied.

"Often, we don't know where candles originate from. We don't know what types of spirits, sorcery, witchcraft, or voodoo was prayed over or put into the candles and incense," he said as he continued to walk through the house. "The candles aren't lit, sir," I said, "but I have burned candles and incense before and had no clue of where they originated from," I said as my mind began to think back on all the millions of candles and incense I had burned in the house.

"Don't blame yourself, Sis. You didn't know," he said as he continued to look around the house. "Who blessed your oil?" he asked.

Feeling good about myself, "You blessed it," I said.

"Oh, okay, I didn't remember doing that. I bless several bottles of oil for the saints," he said. "Let me anoint everyone, and let's pray before we get started. Then let's anoint all the rooms," he said.

They began to pray, and I bowed my head and just listened to what they were saying. I know how to pray, but I didn't know what to pray for during that particular situation. I wanted to make sure I got rid of all the spirits, so I didn't want to mess things up. They just prayed for us that we were clean, so we would be able to rid the house of all unclean spirits.

In Matthew 10:1, it says, "And when he had called unto him his twelve disciples, he gave them power against unclean spirits, to cast them out, and to heal all manner of sickness and all manner of disease." I knew we had the power to cast out spirits; I just didn't want to mess up that power by praying the wrong prayer. He anointed each room, and then they began to go around the house in each room and cast out and rebuked unclean spirits out of each room. I didn't say or do much at all. I just followed behind them, watching and observing. I didn't feel like I had much power at all. I wasn't afraid; I guess I just really didn't know what to do.

Remember in Acts 19:14–16, where the seven sons of Sceva tried to cast an evil spirit out of a man, and the evil spirit answered and said, "Jesus I know, and Paul I know; but who are ye?" Then the evil spirit jumped on them and sent them running out of the house naked and wounded? Well, let's just say I didn't want to end up like that. I knew I hadn't been studying my Word or praying like I was supposed to, and I really wasn't trying to cast out any spirits and end up running down no street naked, so I just kept my mouth shut and watched.

They finished, we said our goodbyes, and they left. Our home life was much better. Tommy stopped getting into trouble in school. Timmy calmed down and stopped the baby-talking and whining. I quit screaming and yelling at the boys, and things just got better. Then a few months later, we were right back where we started, and I didn't know how we got there. I could hear the noises in the middle of the night again. The boys were back to arguing and fighting as if they hated each other, just as in the beginning. Tommy was back to fighting and getting suspended from school, and Timmy was confused, compulsive, and hyper. I became more hateful than ever before, and I needed to put a stop to this nonsense once and for all. So, those were the other times I tried to put the spirits out of the house.

I told myself, this time would be different; the unclean spirits would not return to my house. We took the bags outside to where we placed our trash, then Tommy and I anointed the bags. I allowed Tommy to anoint the bags because he, too, had the Holy Ghost. I did not want those spirits jumping on Timmy like they did the seven sons of Sceva, either. So, Timmy stayed in the house. I went around to the four corners of my property in the front yard and anointed the property. Then I went to the backyard and did the same, including the fence. I went inside the mini barn and anointed it. Tommy and I prayed for ourselves just as Elder Graves and his wife did when they came to my house in the past, and then we went back inside the house. I then stashed Timmy in the car for protection. We literally screamed and demanded each and every spirit leave our home. We searched for them in all the dark places and swept them out of our home, just as Sister Shannon from the retreat had told me to do previously.

Finally, we both walked outside down to the curb where the trash sat. We stretched forth our hands over the bags, and we began to pray over the bags and asked God not to allow anyone to find or get their hands on anything that was in the bags. If someone found the toys, games, clothes, shoes, and movies that were opened and unopened, they would have felt they hit the jackpot. However, the unclean spirits that were attached and associated with all that stuff would have led those spirits right back to me, with seven more spirits more wicked than the first, and I could not allow that. Or even worse, the spirits could find a new resting place and start wreaking havoc on a new family's house that didn't have the ability to fight them off like we did. Therefore, I did not give that stuff away, nor did I want to sell it or risk anyone finding it.

We prayed with sincerity that the bags wouldn't rip or tear and that those spirits would be cast into outer darkness where there would be weeping and gnashing of teeth, just as the Bible speaks of in several scriptures. Then we prayed in the Spirit and made some groans and moans because we didn't know what to pray for, as it says in Roman 8:26: "Likewise the Spirit also helpeth our infirmities: for we know not what we should pray for as we ought: but the Spirit itself maketh intercession for us with groanings which cannot be uttered."

Infirmities can also be moral weaknesses, and at that time, I had a weakness that I needed help with. I did not want those spirits back in my house, and I had the power to cast them out according to Matthew 10:1. Once we put the items out of my house this time, we wouldn't be bringing them back in.

CHAPTER 5

Do What I Told You to Do

August 2005

What? Write a book? I know you can't be talking to me, God. What kind of dream is this, God? I thought as I tossed and turned, partially awake. I tore up the hospital room in the dream, so I knew this was not a true dream. I know I didn't tear up the hospital room while I was in the hospital. I woke up out of heavy deep sleep. I lay there in that bed for a while before I believed that God was actually talking to me about writing a book. I had questions like: "How could You be telling me to write a book, God? I don't even like to read. Who will proofread the book? What will I write about? This is crazy." I had no clue what to write about. "Tell me again, God. Do you want me to write a book?" I lay in the bed a few more minutes and just waited on God to answer me.

All of a sudden, words and sentences started popping into my head, and I felt the need to write them down. I didn't know what else to do, so I began to write. It was like a story coming out of me. I had to hurry before I lost the story. I grabbed my laptop and just began typing. All at once, I knew it was true. When my hands started moving faster than I could think and the story started pouring out of me, it was true; I was actually supposed to write a book.

I worked on the book for hours every day. I typed day in and day out for weeks at a time. I had visions and dreams, and God gave me more and more to put into the book as the days went by. I dreamed about my life and the wonderful things I would accomplish. I dreamed about what Tommy would become in life and what his accomplishments would be. I dreamed about the things Sharon would do in life, and then I dreamed I would end up back in the hospital. *What? Not back in the hospital, Lord. Why? Not me; what is going on?* I questioned the Lord as I went down on my knees in prayer. *Why do I have to go back to the hospital?* In the midst of praying, a calm came over me, and I changed my entire prayer. "If it is Your will, Lord, I will go. Just please help me to be okay with whatever Your will is because I really don't want to go."

The morning God showed me in a dream that I would be going back into the hospital was the very same morning that I would be going back into the hospital, and I knew it. I started to prepare for that day. I had to leave a message for whoever would come and find me, and I knew it would be Katherine. She was a lady who attended my former church; she has seven children, six boys, and one girl. Katherine cooks good food all the time for those kids and her husband too. Later that day, Katherine called and told me she would bring food over so that I could have dinner, and I knew it would probably be something

I didn't like to eat. But I didn't want to be rude, so I said I appreciated it, and I did appreciate the help and her concern. I was sure it would be something like greens, cornbread, sweet potatoes, macaroni and cheese, and fried chicken. What was I going to do with all that food, anyway?

Now, I would eat the fried chicken, as long as it wasn't dark meat. Katherine and I grew up together. That girl was really funny, and she enjoyed joking around and making people laugh. She always brought tons of food over to eat. She did that the last time she came, but at least my sister Sharon was over, and she was nice enough to eat up all the food for me. Sharon was very good at helping me out when it came to eating my food that I didn't like.

When I found out Katherine was coming, God told me exactly how I was going to end up back in the hospital, and I wrote it down on cards. Katherine was to send her daughter up to the door, she would wait at the door, and I would take the bag of food from her and take it into the kitchen. Then I would go in the kitchen and get the Tupperware dishes from the kitchen from the last time she brought food over and bring them into the living room. While I was walking into the living room with the Tupperware, I would fall down into a seizure, and the bowls would fly up in the air. The little girl was going to go back outside to go and get her mother and tell her what was happening in the house. Katherine would come inside the house and see me lying on the floor, and then she would have to send her daughter out to the car for the cellphone, praying for me the whole time. That's the way the situation went down, except I didn't expect to feel all the pain while going through what I was going through. I expected it to be just like the dream, kind of an out-of-body experience, and it would seem like I was just watching a movie. Wrong! That is not the way it happened. I had written down the events on the cards and taped the cards to the mirror in my bedroom so that my family would find them while I was in the hospital.

While the enemy was working with my mind (remember I told you, in the beginning, I felt like I was losing my mind), I began to mix up the dreams, and I didn't know at times if it was God speaking to me, me adding things in the dreams, or the enemy planting things in my dreams. It really didn't matter, though, because no one believed me about any of it. Like I said before, Jesus said in Luke 4:24, "And he said, Verily I say unto you, No prophet is accepted in his own country," and I certainly was not accepted.

"Mama, what is Leeta's mother's number? I came over here to bring her some food, and she fell out having a seizure. I don't know what to do," Katherine said as she spoke with her mother.

"Call Mother Smith," her mother said.

"Okay, what is the number?" Katherine asked

"555-5555," her mother said.

"Thanks," Katherine said. She called Mother Smith to get my mother's number.

"Praise the Lord, Sister Mills, I'm over Leeta's house dropping off some food, and she fell out on the floor and had a seizure. Now she is just lying on the floor, not moving," Katherine said, with nervousness in her voice.

"Just let her lay there," my mom instructed.

"Well, she's been down there for about ten minutes, I guess," Katherine said.

What is she talking about? I am not supposed to be lying here more than five minutes after a seizure. What is Mom talking about? I thought to myself as I laid on the floor with my body all twisted up. *Don't listen to her, Katherine; call 911, I* thought.

Katherine hung up the phone and began to walk around the house. She started to pray for help, as I laid on the floor, my body twisted in pain. *What the heck did Mom tell her? I* thought to myself. *She knows that you are not supposed to lay unconscious for more than five minutes after a seizure. God, this is not working the way You said it would. You said my mother would get nervous and call 911. Or did I say that? Did I make that part up? I* thought. *I am getting a little confused and adding stuff to the visions. Is this even a vision from God? Did Satan plant this thought in my head? I hate it when I do that. Why don't You stop me from doing that, Lord? Just allow me to do what You told me to do, and don't allow Satan or me to add anything to the visions and dreams. That is what messes things up when I add my own stuff to the visions; that is how the visions get all confusing. My brain keeps moving, like now, I am lying on this floor all tangled up, thinking about how I should just go with the flow. How am I getting to the hospital? Right, my point exactly. I shouldn't concern myself with it; You said I was going, and that is all I should concern myself with,* my brain continued to race with thoughts.

"Hey, baby, how are you? I'm over at Sis Bigbee's house dropping off this food, and she fell out on the floor in a seizure... I don't know... I just want her to get up... I want to call the ambulance... I am scared... I am going to call her mother back... I'll talk to you later." I wasn't sure who Katherine was talking to, but I figured it was her husband.

"Sis Mills, she is still unconscious. Do you think I should call them now?"

"How long has she been lying on the floor?" my mom asked.

"She has been out probably for thirty minutes," Katherine answered.

"What is she doing?" Mom asked.

"She isn't doing anything. She keeps jerking every once in a while. I keep rubbing her and praying for her, but she mumbled that she needed an ambulance," Katherine replied.

"Yeah, you should probably call," Mom replied.

"Okay, bye," Katherine said.

"I'll meet you at Methodist Hospital," said Mom.

"All right, bye," Katherine said.

"911, what is your emergency?"

"She is having a seizure."

"What is the address?"

"The address, uuuhhh, I don't know the address. She doesn't have a home phone; she only has a cellphone. Go next door, Patty, and ask what the address is," Katherine instructed her daughter.

Patty came back in the house just in time enough to see me tossing and turning on the floor in a seizure. I felt like I had enough of those seizures. I was sick and tired of having them, and my body had enough of flopping around on the floor. Patty wasn't afraid at all; she handled things like a trooper until the ambulance arrived.

"What's going on in here?" the emergency technician said as he opened the front door.

"She has had several seizures," Katherine said as she sighed with relief.

"What is her name?" he asked as he walked over and looked down at me on the floor.

"Leeta," Katherine answered.

"Leeta, can you hear me?" he said as he flipped on the light and two or three others walked in the house.

"The light is too bright; turn it off," I screamed out as I took off in another seizure.

"Wow, what is that all about?" one of the medics asked as they watched me seize on the floor.

"Ms. Bigbee, calm down; you are going to hurt yourself if you don't stop. Calm down," one of the medics yelled out.

"Turn the lights off, nooooooowwwwwww..." I said as I took off into another. These seizures were very different, and my body was bouncing all over the floor and making me very tired, not to mention sore.

The medics moved all the tables in the living room out of the way so that I would not hurt myself, and they went outside to get a stretcher to put me on. I really didn't want to go to the hospital another time, but God had already told me this was going to happen. I knew I had something to do, so I was ready to do whatever it was I had to do for the Lord. But what did I have to do for Him? I didn't even know yet. "Hey, who turned her over?" The medic asked as he came back in the house with the stretcher.

"She turned herself over when she was seizing," another medic answered. As they tried to grab me and put me on the bed, I felt myself pass out; it was the weirdest thing. I could hear everything they were saying, and I could feel everything they were doing to me.

"Okay, she has passed out now; we can take her out," the lady medic said after she had taken my pulse and heart rate. They lifted me onto the bed, strapped me down tightly, and wheeled me out the door into the ambulance. As I was wheeled out the front door, I saw Rebecca and her husband standing on their front porch, looking unusually worried. Katherine grabbed the front door and pulled it closed as she and Patty walked out of the house. This was a very eventful day, to say the least; August 29 will certainly be a day that I will not forget. As I was wheeled to the ambulance, I shouted, "Please remember me; they are going to try to tell you that I had a stroke, but I didn't. All my test results are going to come back negative. Just remember me. Please believe me that the things I say are true." Now that I look back at everything that happened, I must agree with my family; I did sound a little deranged.

The ambulance stayed in front of my house for some time while the ambulance technician asked me questions. "What is your name?"

"Leeta Bigbee."

"Do you have insurance?"

"Yes, my card is in my purse."

"Where do you live?"

"9339 E. 36th Place; all that information is in my purse on my license."

"Do you know what year it is?"

"2005."

"Do you know who the president is?"

"George…" was all I could make out before I became unconscious.

"Ms. Bigbee, can you hear me? Ms. Bigbee… Her pulse is really weak; let's get moving."

"Where we going?" the driver asked.

"We're going to Methodist, and we need to move fast. You're not going to die on me," he said as he pushed down really hard on my index finger. "Oh, no. Let's go, guys; I'm losing her," he said. That is all I recall in the ambulance as I began to take this wonderful roller-coaster ride. My hair was blowing through the air, and I wasn't even afraid, even though I hate rollercoasters. It was the most pleasant ride I had ever been on; it was as if I was riding through the sky. I was with the birds, and the air was fresh, and it was glorious. I could feel when I went down the slopes and over a bump; my body would jump up and lay back down slowly. I could not believe I was actually enjoying a roller-coaster. I couldn't see who was riding next to me, but I felt very comfortable with him. He let me know everything would be all right. I felt one more bump, my body raised up off the seat, and I opened my eyes, and I was back in the ambulance.

"Ms. Bigbee, Ms. Bigbee," he said as he was forcing a tube into my nose.

"Yes," I said as I reached up and grabbed the tube.

"Hold on, ma'am. You rode all the way here unresponsive. You need this," he insisted.

"I am breathing fine," I said, "and please don't forget about me; they are going to tell you I had a stroke. Just please remember me. Believe me when I tell you that the words I say are true. The entire set of tests will come back negative."

"Look, lady, you rode the whole way unresponsive. Okay, just let me do my job," he said in a very nasty voice.

"Sir, I'm not trying to be rude. I'm just trying to let you know what is going on," I said. "Please, just remember me."

I covered my eyes from the light so I wouldn't have any more seizures.

"Black female, thirty-seven years old, 125 pounds, unresponsive the entire ride... " he said as he turned me over to the ER staff. The ER staff didn't seem to like me any better.

"Ms. Bigbee, remove the cover from your eyes, ma'am," the voice spoke out.

"I can't; the light makes me have seizures," I explained.

"I have to look into your eyes to examine you, ma'am. The ER room isn't very bright; you'll be just fine," she said.

I slowly pulled the covers down from my face. "I just need to look into your eyes to see if your pupils are dilated," she said as she shined a small flashlight into my eyes and sent me into a seizure, almost throwing me off the table.

"I need some help over here!" she screamed out.

These seizures were like nothing I had ever experienced before. Whenever I would start to seize, my entire body would start convulsing; it would almost bend in half. These seizures were very violent, and my arms and legs were all over the place, hitting and kicking any and everything that got in their way.

After every seizure, I would go into an almost coma-like state. I would become so exhausted that I could not move. The nurses shined the light into my eyes a few more times, sending me into several more seizures by the time I was hooked up to monitors and IVs and all kinds of other machines.

I'm not sure how much time had passed, but Sharon had arrived. "Sharon, come here," I whispered. "You have to go to my house and get all of my notebooks and bring them to me." I had notebooks about all the dreams, the visions, and the notes for the book.

"Why do you want me to do that?" she asked.

"They're going to put me in the psych ward," I said.

"Why would they put you in the psych ward, Leeta?" she asked.

"I don't know why they are going to do it, but God showed me the butterfly effect, and He allowed me to know they are going to put me in the psych ward. So will you please just go get everything?" I asked.

"Okay," she said, "but this doesn't make any sense at all."

Sharon must have called my mother and Bishop because, by the time she came back, they were all there. They sat around and talked to me while the doctors ran tests. To their surprise, every test they ran came back negative; they couldn't find anything wrong with me, just like I told them. Bishop and Sister Susie stayed in the waiting area as I explained to Mom and Sharon what was going on.

"There are some cards taped on my mirror at home in my bedroom that I would like for you two to read. Don't take them down; just read them. I believe I am going to be in a coma for five-something. I don't know if it is five years, five weeks, five days, or what; I just know that it is five. Everything is going to work for me in fives. If I am unable to speak, I will use my right hand, and one finger means yes, two fingers mean no, and three fingers mean I can't understand you or I can't answer the question with yes or no. I explained all of this to the nurses and doctors and asked them to pass the word on, just in case I was unable to talk after a seizure.

"I need Sister Jeanie to come down here to sign the power of attorney, so she can handle all my finances since she was the one that started with my finances." While I am going through all of this, I need to listen to Marvin Sapp's "I Believe." I'm going to stop breathing at some time or another (not knowing that I had already stopped breathing in the ambulance). I believed Bishop and Mom were going to be there since they didn't believe anything that I said, or at least I hoped they would.

"I was talking to God, and I said this is my Job experience, and I began to complain about how I was just like Job. I had been suffering in my body for a very long time. I had been off work for a long time without pay. I had filed for bankruptcy and had to give up my home after eight years and my car, as well. I didn't understand why God chose me to be just like Job. Then with a very calm voice, I heard God say, 'You are nothing like Job; because I allowed you to keep your children. They will live to be teenagers.' The words I heard God speak were what made me believe everything would happen in fives because Timmy was only eight years old, and in order for him to be a teenager, that would be five years from now. Believe me when I tell you that the things I say are true. Now you have to do everything like I said because I don't want to miss my blessing," I instructed.

My mother and Sharon were writing down everything that I said, but if you could have seen the looks on their faces, you would have known they thought I was crazy. Truth be told, they acted like I was crazy. They questioned almost everything I said.

Bishop and Sister Susie came in to visit while Mom and Sharon went to my house to read the cards. It did not take them long to return. My mother was her normal belittling self. "They didn't mean anything, and you didn't put any dates on them," my mother said, in that uppity kind of snotty way she can talk at me.

"I can't put any dates on them because I don't know when they are going to take place," I said.

"Yeah, but you could put the date that you wrote them so you wouldn't forget," she said.

"I'll never forget the day I wrote them. It is today—August 29—the day I ended up in here," I said. She just shook her head and walked away, letting me know yet again what a disappointment I was to her.

Aunt Lo had arrived with her notary stamp, so she could notarize the power of attorney for Sister Jeanie. But Sister Jeanie still hadn't arrived, even though Bishop had called her over an hour before. Or, so I believed he had called her. My aunt Lo really didn't care for Bishop. She let me know that while they were in the waiting area, he made it known that he thought I was faking being sick. It didn't bother me, though. I knew I was under spiritual attack, and everyone wouldn't understand what was going on with me.

Bishop came over to my bed. He was chewing some bubble gum, and the smell of the bubble gum caused me to go into another seizure. The smells, lights, and noises that cause people to go into seizures are called an aura, which is a subtle sensory stimulus or a warning sensation that precedes a seizure or other neurological disorder. That was the first time a smell had actually caused me to have a seizure. All the times at the church when Sister Diana asked me if I smelled anything, I had no idea why she was asking me that. I never smelled anything until this time.

After that seizure, I was completely out of it, unable to move or communicate with them. "Can you hear me, Ms. Bigbee? Give her 10cc of Dilantin, stat," he instructed. I could hear footsteps all around me. I wasn't able to open my eyes or my mouth. It was as if some force had me completely bound and unable to communicate with them. "Ms. Bigbee," he repeated as he opened my eyes and shined the small flashlight inside long enough to set me off violently into another seizure.

"Make them stop, Lord, please make them stop. Please, Lord, make them stop." I prayed while my body tossed and turned on the bed. As my weary body finally came to a halt on the bed, the questions began again. "Can you hear me, Ms. Bigbee? I really need you to answer me," he said as if he was getting frustrated with me.

"Why won't they look down at my hand, Lord? I told them I would answer them with my fingers if I could. They completely ignored everything I told them. Please let these be over soon so I can go home, Lord. I did what You said; I came back to the hospital."

I prayed as the question continued. "Jesus, help me! What is going on? What are they doing to me? Lord, I can't breathe. Help me, Lord! I prayed as my body lifted up off the bed, and I gasped for air. As I fell back down toward the bed, I could feel myself drifting into unconsciousness.

"The Lord is my shepherd; the Lord is your shepherd, and you shall not want." I could hear Aunt Lo praying with all her heart as I woke up to find that she was the only one left in the room.

Come to find out, Bishop wasn't able to reach Sister Jeanie to get word to her to come to the hospital.

"Leeta, think about what you are saying; Sister Jeanie wasn't the one that started out with your finances in the first place. I was," Sharon said.

"Oh yeah, you are right, Sharon. You were the one that started with my finances," I said. "So, you should be the one that signs the power of attorney." It was little things like that when I couldn't recall or remember that made my mom and Sharon not believe anything I said, no matter how many things came to pass. We signed the papers that I had drawn up for the power of attorney, and everyone stayed and visited for a while.

The doctor on call made his rounds, and it was my turn to be examined. "Hello, Ms. Bigbee, how are you this morning?" he said.

"You tell me; you're the doctor," I replied. We had been in the hospital so long it was now after midnight. I couldn't believe I had been there so long. The cliché goes, "Time flies when you're having fun," but time also flies when you are having seizures all night long.

"We're doing all we can to find out what's going on with you. Your family tells me God talks to you. Is that right?" he asked.

"Yes," I answered.

"How does He talk to you? Do you see Him? Is He with us right now?" he asked.

"No, I don't see Him. What kind of question is that?" I asked. "And of course, He is with us right now. He is everywhere all the time."

"Well, do you hear voices speaking to you, telling you to do things?" he asked.

"No, do you?" I asked. He chuckled as he began the next question. "What I mean, Ms. Bigbee, is can you hear God's voice on the outside of your head, or is it inside of your head?"

I said, "It is in the inside of my head. You know, kind of like how your conscience talks to you and lets you know things. Or sometimes He tells me things in my dreams. Have you ever had a daydream, Doctor?" I asked.

"Yes," he answered.

"Well, sometimes He shows me things in one of those like a vision. You know what I mean?" I asked.

"Yes, Ms. Bigbee, I know exactly what you mean. I hear you are pretty intelligent," he said.

"I do okay," I answered. "Why did you say that?"

"What is in your notebooks?" he asked.

"Stuff," I answered.

"Are you doing a project for God?" he asked, "I'd like to take a look at them if that is okay," he said.

"No, it's not okay!" I said in a stern voice.

"I may have some other questions for you later; that's all. Nice talking to you," he said as he walked away.

I can't believe Sharon told him about the notebooks, I thought. "Sharon," I said as she walked back into the room, "the doctor came in asking some really weird questions. You need to take my books and stuff back home and hide them," I instructed.

"What? I thought you wanted them. You said they were going to put you in the psych ward," she said.

"I guess I was wrong. God showed me the butterfly effect, so I just figured I was going to the psych ward. I must have mixed up the dream. Please just take them back home and put them away," I ranted.

"Okay, whatever you say, I'll do it. It's getting late, so I better be getting home to Bob," she said as she reached over and kissed me on the forehead.

A little time had passed, and I pressed the call button for the nurse. "May I help you?" she asked.

"I need to go to the bathroom," I said.

"I'll be right there," she answered. The nurse came back with this silver, ice cold-looking bedpan. "Here you go, Ms. Bigbee," she said as she reached over to slide that thing underneath me.

"Uuuhhh, I'd rather walk to the real bathroom," I said as I looked down at the bedpan.

"Do you think you can make it to the bathroom?" she asked.

"As long as you let me hold on to your arm, I believe I will be okay," I said. She began to assist me in getting out of the bed. It was a struggle, but I made it. My frail and weak bones trembled and shook as I slid my feet across the floor to head to the bathroom. My bed was located directly across the hall from the bathroom. The only thing separating the two was a nurses' station. We slowly moved through the maze of wheelchairs, trash cans, and other items that blocked our path.

If felt as if the trip was taking a lifetime. I was exhausted from just walking the ten to fifteen feet to the bathroom. The journey was over, and I had finally arrived. While trying not to sit down for fear of germs, I straddled myself with my knees bent, focusing on doing one of the best squats I had learned in fitness class. I grabbed hold of the toilet paper dispenser to regain better footing. Aaahhh, what a relief; that feels so much better. After cleaning myself up, I washed my hands, grabbed a paper towel to turn the water faucet off so my hands would not get all grimy and germy again, grabbed the door, and "WHAM!?" Out on the floor, I went into a full-fledged seizure.

"I need some assistance over here!" the nurse screamed as she tried to get me off the floor.

A few moments later, several nurses were able to get me into a wheelchair and back into the bed. With every bit of sound, noise, or smell, I would go into another seizure. I called that night my boring Scriptures of Job. What I mean by that is when I was reading the book of Job, I wanted to hurry up and get to the good part, where God blessed Job and gave him back all that he had lost. I didn't want to read the scriptures where Job was complaining about his pain and how he cursed the day he was born and all of that, which I thought was boring. I wanted to hurry up and get to the good part. I called those scriptures the boring scriptures of Job, and that night I went through my boring scriptures of Job and wished I had enjoyed reading a little more so that I could have known how Job made it through those really rough times.

I continued to have (what I found out to be) pseudo-seizure episodes throughout the entire night. The slightest noise, smell, or light would send me into another seizure. Therefore, I had probably two hundred seizures that night. Whenever I had a seizure, I would go into a pseudo, coma-like state, as I am told is normal. The doctors and/or nurses would perform what is called a sternum rub on me. The sternum rub is when you take your hand and ball it up into a fist and rub it extremely hard up and down the sternum to provoke the individual back to re-sponsiveness. The sternum rub would exasperate my body to the point where it would rise off the bed, and I would gasp for my breath, and then my lifeless body would fall crashing back down to the bed. These seizures weren't like any I had experienced before. I guess that's why they were called pseudo since they were similar to seizures but not seizures. Every little noise was setting me off. I wasn't comfortable laying down, sitting up, or standing: I was certain that I was definitely in my boring scriptures of Job.

When Job was going through his physical sicknesses, he had boils from the crown of his head to the sole of his feet. Boils are very painful, and they hurt just to touch them. If you can just picture that for a moment, that means Job was unable to sit, stand, or even lie down without pain. Job must have been miserable, and that is why he even cursed the day he was conceived. But when I was reading about Job, I didn't want to read all that stuff. I just wanted to get to the good part about how he became rich again. I didn't want to hear about him moaning and complaining and praying to God about taking away his pain. I didn't care how he got out of all that mess; I just wanted to read about what the reward was. The sad part about it was I should have read it because now I needed to know what to do so that I could petition the Lord and that I could get out of my dilemma. I needed the help of the Lord, and I needed it now.

Even though I sounded crazy while on my way to the hospital, things happened as I said they would. All of the test results came back negative. I didn't actually understand what was happening to me. I felt like garbage, but nothing seemed to be wrong with me. Was I making this entire thing up? I guess I could not have made up riding to the hospital in the ambulance, unresponsive the entire time. I stayed in the hospital for over three weeks, undergoing tests.

I had requested no visitors for the rest of my hospital stay. Because by this time, I was completely aware I was under spiritual attack. Sister Shelley had been back to my room to visit, and she explained that maybe she didn't explain things well to me because of the extreme way I was acting, and she thought it best to stay away from me. Sister Shelley wanted to stop visiting, even though she had been visiting every day that she was at work at the hospital. That made me sad.

When I became aware that I was in a spiritual fight, I began asking God to teach me how to fight in the spirit. In Romans, Paul said to covet the best gift. However, I didn't know what was the best gift, so I asked God for all the spiritual gifts. I didn't know which gift I needed to help me fight, so I asked God daily for all the gifts. I recall one day when I was speaking with Sis Sharp. She said, "Shuga, don't ask for all the gifts. The Bible said to whom much is given, much is required." But it was a little too late because I had been asking nonstop. I had very strong discernment, prophetic dreams, and some interpretation of dreams. But I wasn't very good at discernment. I could discern if there was a spirit, but I didn't necessarily know if the spirit was in a person, on a person, or just around a person.

One day while I was in the bathroom brushing my teeth, my mother and Sharon walked in, and I started screaming at the top of my lungs and calling my mother Judas. I think I could discern a sick spirit on her, but I didn't know how to take it. I thought it was a demon spirit or something since she had spoken so rudely to me the last time she was at the hospital. I just freaked out, and I asked them to leave. Sharon and Mom said they were not leaving and began pleading the blood over me.

So, I pulled the emergency cord that is in the bathroom (which goes back to my original request that I didn't want any visitors. Because I knew I was acting bizarre). Being under great spiritual attack will have anyone acting bizarre and paranoid. After I pulled the cord, all the nurses and everyone came rushing in to see what the problem was. My mother grabbed her blessed oil and smacked some on my forehead really quick, and started hugging me and praying. Now, I really began to freak out because I began to think if they are demons, or have demons, or whatever, how can they touch me and plead the blood over me? Then I began to question my own discernment and gifts. "Do I really know how to discern spirits? Did I misinterpret your Word, God? Is Satan messing with my head again?"

The entire situation was chaotic and stressful. They escorted my mom and sister out of the room in tears, and I couldn't have been any happier. Not that they were in tears, but that they were gone. Now you know I looked a mess with toothpaste running down the side of my mouth and ranting about spirits and so forth. I know I must have scared them to death. I can't believe how confused, paranoid, and scared I was. I felt as if what was going on wasn't real. So many weird things were happening, and they seemed unbelieve at the time. It felt as if someone was playing a cruel joke on me. I cried every time I thought about it. I got back on the bed, wiped my mouth, and began to read my Bible again. When all of a sudden, my hospital door opened, and three huge police officers came in with a psychiatrist. They started toward me and then stopped mid-stride and held their hands up toward me. I had a pair of scissors in my hand because I was working on putting tabs in my Bible, and I guess they thought I might try to stab them or something.

"Ms. Bigbee, we are going to take you to the seclusion room, okay?"

"What is the seclusion room?" I asked.

"It is the psychiatric ward, and I am the psychiatrist on duty today," the lady answered.

"I'm not going anywhere; there is nothing wrong with me. Why are you doing this to me?" I said as I began to get angry because I told Sharon the first day I arrived in the hospital that they were going to put me in the psych ward, but she didn't believe me. Not to mention at the time I told her, I wasn't even acting crazy and/or having any delusional thoughts or behaviors. Now five days later, they want me to go to the psych ward.

The hall was filled with my family members, and they were all looking into my room, some with tears in their eyes and total confusion on their faces. Some looked afraid, and some just stared in disbelief. They were not alone; I couldn't believe it or understand it either. *Why were they taking me to the psych ward? I just didn't understand—what type of behavior I had exhibited that warranted getting me committed? I was in my room minding my own business. I requested no visitors (but some were allowed), and I was taking notes while reading my Bible.* I genuinely couldn't understand what I had done. Was I that messed up in the head that my family saw no other solution than to have me committed to the psyche ward? I had undoubtedly put a hurt on them. All my aunts, sister, mother, and even my grandparents were standing out there, looking at me, until finally, someone closed the door.

"Hold on, let me see if God wants me to go," I said as I sat back down on the bed and began to pray and ask God if I should go to the psych ward. And wouldn't you know it, sure enough, just like the first day I came to the hospital, God told me to get up and go. "Okay, I need to go with you, but let me get my sheets and covers," I said as I sat down in the wheelchair. I buried my face in the pillow that I had grabbed off the bed. As they wheeled me past my family, I did not utter a word to them since they were nice enough to get me committed to the seclusion room, which I later found out was the padded room. I was wheeled past them down the hall and onto the elevator.

As I arrived at what looked like Fort Knox, I was signed in. I didn't understand why I had to be there, but I was being obedient to God, so I went anyway. When I got into my room, they wanted to take my Bible and my blessed oil which was extremely confusing to me. I gave them the items and just dealt with all of them.

In all reality, there were some behaviors that were a bit strange. I did smear blessed oil over all the furniture, floors, and walls in my hospital room. I guess that's what God meant in the beginning when the dream showed me that I tore up the hospital room. As we arrived at the room I was assigned to, one of the police officers said, "Ma'am, we needed to check out your body to make sure you did not cut yourself with the scissors." Being utterly frustrated, I grabbed my gown, raised it above my head, and started to spin around in a circle with only my panties and a mobile heart monitor on. *Really*, I thought. *Did I cut myself with the scissors I was using to cut the post-it notes so that I could mark my Bible?* Looking back on that day, I did seem a little bit deranged at the time. But the situation and the spiritual battles I was having kind of called for it.

There wasn't a clock or calendar in the room. There were blinds up to the window, but they were closed and locked in between two plastic sheets of glass for safety reasons. So that no one would use the glass, the strings, or the blinds to hurt themselves. Therefore, I could not see out the window to tell if it was day or night. All I had in the room was me and my thoughts.

The door was solid wood, and it was deadbolted from the outside, and believe it or not, they didn't give me a key. There was a very large plastic observation window that was on one side of the room. The window was for doctors and students to come to observe and learn from and about the committed patients. There was also a camera located in the corner of the room close to the ceiling, out of reach. I kept telling myself it was all a horrible dream and it would be over soon.

The days seemed to take forever to end. I had informed the staff that I didn't want breakfast or lunch because I was fasting until 4 p.m. daily, and I only wanted to eat dinner. I also instructed that I would like to drink fluids throughout the day. There wasn't a call button or anything in the room to contact the doctors, nurses, or staff. However, after a day or so of being in the padded room, the staff stopped bringing me fluids and dinner.

I began to think about people in the Bible who were bound and needed to be set free and what they did to come out of bondage. I stood up on the window sill and began pacing back and forth. In my mind, I was marching down the walls of Jericho. I sang songs like Paul and Silas did while in prison. I alternated back and forth from pacing and singing in an attempt to o whatever I could to try to get out of that room. But nothing seemed to work. When I went in there, they did not tell me how long I had to stay in the room. I figured it would be September

5th because I believed all things were happening in fives. So, the next five was September 5th. However, I didn't have a calendar, and neither could I look out the window to see if it was day or night. So, I didn't know when September 5th was. They didn't allow me to have bathroom breaks, and there was no bathroom in that room. Therefore, when I had to use the bathroom, even though there was a camera in the room. I went over and squatted down in the corner of the room to use the bathroom; at least, I did that the first time I went to the bathroom.

After not eating for days, I was too weak to get out of the bed. Not sure why they stopped feeding me. When the nurses or doctors would come into the room, I would tell them I would not be taking any medication. Maybe that is the reason they stopped bringing food and drinks. I had specifically told one nurse that I wanted dinner and fluids, but I did not tell all the nurses. After all, when was the last time a patient had to ask for meals in the hospital? They are supposed to feed the patients! Okay, let me calm down. Now, where was I? All the other times I had to go to the bathroom, I laid in the bed and just went on myself because I was too weak to get up. I laid in my own filth for days, and no one came to check on me. I wasn't brought any water or food for the rest of the time I was in the padded room. I had already told them I would not allow them to put anything in me, as far as medication, a thermometer, or anything like that, so I guess they felt they didn't have a need to come and see me. But what they forgot was I couldn't get out to go to the bathroom or get anything to eat. I was so sick in that room that I truly believed I was going to die.

The reason I instructed the doctors not to give me any medication was because I finally became aware that I was not in a medical battle. Every test they ran came back negative. None of their machines, X-ray, MRI, EKG, EEG, and so on, no matter how advanced, could detect the presence of a spirit (demon). Therefore, I didn't want to take a bunch of pills just to treat my symptoms and end up with a bunch of conditions that I never had in the first place as a result of the side effects from the medications I didn't need anyway.

There was this one time when Trina was visiting with me at the hospital a few days before I was moved to the psych ward. Now that I think about it, this is the incident that helped land me in the psych ward. Anyway, Trina and I were talking, and three doctors came into my room with several different pills. As they placed the pills on the table one by one, they explained what the pills were for. "This is for your heart condition, this is for your high blood pressure, this is for your diabetes, and this is for your seizures, yadda, yadda, yadda." I allowed them to finish talking, but then I asked, "If all my test results came back normal, how did you decide which pills to give me? Did you just go to the cabinet and pick your favorite color? If that's the case, then let me pick my favorite color. Bring me a bunch of pink pills." They went on to tell me the importance of why I had to take the medication, and I still refused. Subsequently, they stated since I refused to take the medication, I tried to commit suicide by not taking the medication.

While I was lying in the bed in my own filth, there were several times that doctors and nurses came in to try to get me to take medication. I cannot tell you what they said or what they did to me, but I would not allow them to give me any medication. I had been wearing a portable heart monitor, and the doctors were monitoring my heart the entire time I was in the padded room. While I was lying in the bed, a nurse came into the room. As soon as I noticed the nurse, I said, "When I would do good, evil was present."

And she responded, "And if you resist the devil, he will flee from you."

At the mention of that scripture, my body totally became relaxed, and I said, "Thank you."

She then asked, "Why haven't you eaten anything?"

I said, "They won't bring me anything to eat."

She asked, "What do you want?"

I said, "Something to drink like apple juice."

"I know what is going on," she said. "Why haven't you been to the bathroom?" She added.

I said, "If you say you know what is going on, then you should already know I have." She then walked over to the foot of the bed and touched my feet. "Yes, you have," she said. The bed was soaked, and I'm sure it smelled also because I had not been out of the bed in about three days, so she could tell that bed was my new toilet. The sad part is I had requested no visitors. Therefore, my family, friends, and/or my church family could not come in and ask questions as to why I laid there in my filth for days.

As she walked out to go get me something to drink, she came back with a drink and a syringe. She walked over to me and said, "I have to give you this shot because you need this medicine." I said, "Okay." She would be the very first person I allowed to give me anything, but I just trusted her because she made me feel relaxed by quoting the scripture when she first arrived. "You have to let it all go in, and don't let any of it come back out." She then reached over and gave me a shot in my arm and put her finger on my arm in the spot where she gave me the shot to ensure all the medicine stayed in my arm. I just laid there and took it all in. I totally trusted her.

When she came back in the room with another nurse, I had a small amount of energy from the shot, and I had already gotten myself out of the bed, and I was trying to get clean myself up by wiping off with the sheets from the bed.

The nurse that was with her spoke up and said, "No, no, don't do that; let's do it the right way."

They walked over to where I was standing and held me by my forearms and began to walk me down the hall to the bathroom. Once we reached the bathroom, they held on to me and walked me over to the shower. I felt horrible and could barely stand up. They scrubbed me down while they gave me a shower. I had not eaten in days, and I was so weak I could barely stand. My head was spinning so that I felt I might pass out. I felt T-horrible, which made it impossible for me to participate in my own shower. My friend Tachina would say that word meant terrible and horrible at the same time. You make the "T" sound and then say the word horrible, and it comes out T-horrible, and that is just how I felt. They did talk much during the shower; they helped me shower and then threw what seemed like a ton of baby powder at me, slipped a gown on me, and slowly escorted me out of the bathroom.

Once we exited the bathroom, there was a hospital bed waiting for me directly outside the bathroom. To my surprise, they were escorting me to the heart critical care unit. For some reason, the only medication that I allowed the nurse to give me made my heart rate drop to 29. It appeared I may have had an allergic reaction to the medication. However, if it wasn't for the shot that I allowed her to give me, there is no telling when I would have gotten out of the padded room. I don't know how long I stayed in the padded room, but I do know I wasn't treated humanely.

By the time I came to, I had a lady sitting in a chair next to my hospital bed watching me. I called her a babysitter. From that point on, I had a babysitter. Every few hours, a different person came to babysit me. I later found out I was on suicide watch, which was funny (not really) to me since they were the ones that tried to kill me. I love myself, and I have never tried to hurt myself. The entire hospital stay felt very surreal. The majority of the time I was in the heart unit, I was in and out of consciousness. I even called for a sister from the church to come and bring me a Bible. I sat up long enough to tell her she looked like an angel, and then I passed out again.

After several days had passed, I was well enough to stay awake. I was able to eat and do all the things that everyone else did, and I felt much better too. Thank God for the blood. I called some people and told them I was in the hospital and had a few visitors. After about five days, it was time for my stay in the heart critical care unit to end, and the psychiatrist came to visit me. This time it was a doctor I had not seen before, and she asked me whether I would sign myself into the psych ward voluntarily. It was a bizarre request, but I agreed. I believe I agreed in order to show my family and pastor that I wasn't crazy.

Once I got into the general population part of the psych ward, I then understood why I signed myself back in. I had work to do for God. People were following me around for days, and I couldn't understand what they wanted from me. Then one day, I opened my mouth and started saying the thoughts that were in my head.

I would go into the recreation room to listen to my music every day, and daily the same lady would come in the room and sit down with me and just listen to the music. One day when she came in, I just started talking to her about her life. Normally I would tell people things about the music I was listing to. I would tell them who was singing, what the song was about, the words to the songs, and stuff like that. So, today I told the lady, "I am not sure if it is drugs or alcohol, but I think it is both. But your daughter is going to allow you to see your grandchildren." The lady just looked at me, and her eyes began to tear up. "I think you have three grandchildren," I added. "I'm not sure if it is two boys and a girl or two girls and a boy, but I think it is the first." The lady just sat there and looked at me.

I then said, "How old are your grandchildren?"

She looked at me with the saddest face and said, "I don't know; I have never seen them before." I felt like crying with her, but instead, I said what God had laid on my heart for me to tell her.

"God said you are going to get a chance to see your grandchildren." And then I knew God was talking to me, and I was in the psych ward to encourage and tell people what God wanted them to know. It isn't as if God could not tell the people himself. But when a person doesn't spend time in prayer getting to know the voice of God, it is very easy to disregard what God says or think the voice is not God's voice. Just a bit of wisdom for you, Satan will never tell you something that is good for you.

While sitting at a table in the lobby, a nurse came and sat down next to me. "Where are you from?" she asked. "I'm right here in Indy," I said.

"Then why do you have that accent?" she questioned. For some reason, I was talking like I was from the islands or Jamaica somewhere. Because of my newfound accent, my family had it made up in their mind that I was 100 percent certified crazy.

I said, "God gave it to me. If you say something in your native tongue, I can tell you what it is you are saying." I knew from her accent that she was not from here; she sounded like she was African or Jamaican. She said something that was so long that it scared me.

I looked at her, and I said, "You have asked me a question, didn't you?" She shook her head yes. At first, I tried to guess what she asked me, and she shook her head no. "Let me go and take a shower and allow God to tell me what you said to me, okay?" I asked.

"Okay," she said. When I went to take a shower, I asked God for forgiveness in just thinking I could interpret what she said on my own. I believe I was forgiven because it was as if God had smacked me upside my head and said, "She asked you what religion are you." There were several times I felt as if I could do stuff on my own without the help of God. For instance, I felt as if I had the gift of tongues and the interpretation of tongues.

After I got out of the shower, I felt refreshed and ready to lean not to my own understanding and acknowledge God in everything. I went back to her, and I told her, "I am not going to tell you what you said to me just yet; I am going to answer your question. I am not of a religion; I am of a faith—the apostolic faith. We believe in the teaching of the apostles and living by what Christ taught the apostles. We also believe we should live our lives as Christ taught them and as the apostles taught others, as it is documented and explained in the Bible. Just as the apostles taught, we believe in being baptized in Jesus' name and being filled with the Holy Ghost as the Spirit of God gives utterance. You asked me what was my religion?" She then just shook her head as if to say, "Yes, that is what I asked you." I continued to tell people what thus saith the Lord every time God put a thought in my head or gave me a dream about someone in the hospital. During my stay in the psych ward, the only medication I was given was a stool softener. I was not given any psychiatric medication, nor was I diagnosed with a psychiatric disorder. I stayed in the hospital for a total of twenty-one days.

CHAPTER 6

Sanctification

November 2005

I finally went back to work after being off sick, and things felt like they were getting back to normal, or were they? It is amazing the things that go on while you are in a storm. A little less than a year and a half had passed since I first passed out in church. By this time, I had lost my very first home and my very first SUV in bankruptcy. The boys and I were living in an apartment, and I was driving a super dull and plain used Ford Explorer. I felt as if I was going backward in life. Things seemed to be repeating themselves. The boys were acting up in school and at home. I began to get sick again. I also began missing work because of being sick. Tommy was lashing out in school and getting into trouble with his teachers. Timmy started to regress and was acting babyish again and struggled with the class work. I began to question myself, asking, what happened? Had we fallen into the same old trap again? What had we done wrong this time?

I couldn't have ever dreamed how so-called friends would turn their backs on me. Seems like the sicker I became, the farther away my friends would run. It felt like God was actually setting me apart this time, like in a sanctification process. Maybe I wasn't supposed to be a garbage can any longer for my friends to tell me about all the garbage in their lives. Maybe I wasn't supposed to be dumping my garbage on anyone any longer, either. Maybe this time, I was actually supposed to be getting my life together.

Maybe I was supposed to be living a sanctified life instead of just going through the motions. Maybe I was supposed to stop wondering who is doing what and what is going on with this one and that one. No more back-biting and fault-finding. Just maybe this time, things were supposed to be different. Maybe in order to get out of that type of atmosphere, I had to get away from those types of people. Since I refused to change my atmosphere on my own, God decided to help me. Just maybe, that is what I was supposed to be doing this time, just maybe. So, this time when the people I thought were my friends turned their backs on me. I had a whole different mindset and a totally different attitude.

There was a time when I would take it very personally if I put a lot of effort and time into a friend, and then that friend treated me wrong. I thought they should have to pay for doing me wrong. A prime example is that I had a friend who went out of town, and she had another friend that was kind of obsessed with her. Let's call the obsessed one Sandra and the other one Nancy. Nancy is a kind-hearted divorced workaholic, exceptionally goal-oriented, doesn't have any children, lives alone, and she doesn't do a lot outside of work.

Sandra, on the other hand, is totally different. Sandra still lives at home with her parents, acts extremely immature, whines all the time, wants her way, and wants to be babied by other people. So, Sandra created a goddess out of Nancy, and I was trying to tell Nancy about it, but Nancy wouldn't listen. Or maybe she liked it and just didn't want to do anything about it.

Eventually, the situation got out of hand, and Sandra was treating me like garbage. She had concocted this little fantasy in her head that Nancy and she were the best of friends and how I was jealous of their friendship. Sandra thought they needed to keep their little secret about being best friends from me and just a bunch of other petty mess. So, one day I just blew up and let Sandra have it. Well, of course, she was crying like a big baby. By this time, we had another friend named Lanisha who joined the ranks, and she was the peacemaker, trying to keep the peace between the three of us. Well, there was a time when Nancy was actually living it up on her way to the Bahamas while I was staying at her place because mine had mold in it.

I was talking to Nancy while she was in Miami, waiting to catch a connecting flight to the Bahamas. During the conversation, she told me that Sandra was upset when Sandra drove her to the airport that morning for her trip. "Why," I asked.

"Because of you," she said.

"What?" I asked, "Why me?"

"Sandra said things are different between the two of you. She said you just don't seem the same anymore," Nancy said.

"Something is wrong with that girl. I wrote her an email telling her if she calls people foo; or if she says fool; it is the same thing whether she drops the 'L' or not, and she has not spoken to me since," I said. "That is her fault if she is mad because I told her the truth. She just needs to get over it," I added. "Why didn't you answer me when we talked, and I asked you how your ride to the airport was?" I questioned.

"I just didn't want to get in the middle of it," she said.

"In the middle of what," I asked.

"Sandra said you are always sick, and you are telling everyone that you don't want to be bothered while you are sick, and she doesn't like that at all."

"Don't tell me any more about Sandra, or I am going to get angry," I said with a stern voice.

"Okay," Nancy said as she continued to tell me about her flight.

Later that evening, I talked to Lanisha, and I rehashed the conversation that I had with Nancy. "You will never believe why Sandra was upset with me," I said. "No, that's not it," I said as she tried to guess. "According to Nancy, she was mad at me because I was sick. I told you that you would never guess it," I said as she sat puzzled on the other end of the telephone. I continued with, "She was angry with me because she said I have been sick every single day." Lanisha just didn't believe that Sandra would get angry over me being sick. She told me she was going to call her and ask her if that was the case, and she did just that. And to her surprise, she found out Sandra was actually upset with me because I was sick. Lanisha said she told her that the boys and I were living in a mold-invested apartment for the past eight months, and we were actually very sick every day while we were living in that environment.

Thinking back to that time, the funny part was while I was living in my old place with the mold, Sandra was coming over to my house and pretending to care about me and calling me daily. The funnier part was when I would get sick; I would tell Nancy and Sandra that if I was feeling sick that day, I just wanted to rest and be left alone, including no phone calls.

Well, Sandra would always call and leave messages. I didn't have a voicemail service like we do today, but I had an actual answering machine. Every time Sandra would leave a message, I could hear her talking on the machine, and it would wake me up. Even though I asked her not to call and leave messages, she would do it almost daily. Now that I look back on it, I realize she would do it for the fun of it because she knew I wanted to rest and that I could hear the machine. One day, I woke up, and she was sitting in my living room and had been in my house for over an hour. The boys had let her in. I just couldn't believe it.

After a while, I stopped allowing Sandra to take advantage of me. I refused to let her passive-aggressive behavior rule my life anymore; and she didn't like that much at all. So, she turned her attention toward Nancy. Then she started telling Nancy how beautiful she was, winking at Nancy, blowing kisses, asking her can she rub her feet, and other weird "friendly" behaviors. I tried to tell Nancy that wasn't normal, but she just wouldn't listen. So, by the time Nancy went to the Bahamas, it was in full force—total obsession!

Lanisha said that during her conversation with Sandra, she said that in addition to me being sick every day; she was also upset that I had told someone's business about them filing for bankruptcy. If she had attended church like she should have, then she would have known that person stood up in church one day and testified about filing for bankruptcy. I was getting more and more upset that Sandra was lying through her teeth, and Lanisha was trying to keep the peace while Nancy didn't have a clue about what was going on. The situation was seriously like one big soap opera.

That girl had concocted some things in her mind and ran with them. I didn't want to hear any more peace-making speeches from Lanisha either. I was done with Sandra, and I didn't want to hang with her anymore, and I had already told her so.

One thing I didn't have a problem with was speaking my mind. Bishop once asked me the question, "What is the difference between a .38 revolver, .38 long barrel gun, and a .38 snub nose gun?" I said I didn't know, and he answered, "They all use the same bullet." He continued with if I wasn't sick, I would be a pistol. I have gotten much better now, but I didn't have a problem telling people how I felt back then.

Therefore, when I found out Nancy was keeping secrets from Sandra about hanging out with me and talking to me on the phone, I told Lanisha I was going to go back to my old habits and ruin Nancy's life. I had planned to cut off all her lights, her home telephone, and her gas and then resign from her job with her computer, all while using her email address and password. I would then change her email password and put a password on all her utility accounts, so she would have to go to each company and show her ID in order to get her utilities turned back on. Then I was going to move out of her apartment and never call her again. I had planned to do it all on a Friday so that when she came back from the Bahamas on Monday, it would all be done. Several times that week, Lanisha really had to talk me out of doing all of that to Nancy. I hated Nancy at that moment.

I could not believe that she let Sandra bring all of this drama into my life after I had already told her that girl was obsessed with her.

I later wrote Sandra the longest email telling her off. I first tried to tell her off on the phone, but she hung up on me. I just about drove myself and Lanisha crazy, thinking about it. Sandra and I were calling and emailing Lanisha every day with more drama. Lanisha later became frustrated with all of us and demanded we hash out our differences. So, when Lanisha got Sandra to call me, Sandra wanted to apologize and be friends. As soon as I heard Sandra's voice on the phone, I went straight off on her. I went on to scream that I didn't even want to breathe the same air as a great pretender like her! The entire time we were living a drama-filled life; Nancy was in the Bahamas living the good life.

Well, needless to say, I had some pride to swallow and some apologizing to do to Sandra. Of course, Nancy was none the wiser. She never knew her life was about to be turned upside-down. Now you know I had to tell her, right? One day, God allowed me to see what would have happened if I had done all of that to her. Nancy told me that we would be friends for life; I had postponed my master's degree program to wait for Nancy until she finished her bachelor's so we could go into the master's program together. Then I planned to throw a graduation party for her, but of course, our "we will be friends forever" fell through about three or four weeks later.

Within that time, the boys and I moved out of Nancy's place and got our own apartment. Tommy was now in the sixth grade in middle school, and Timmy was in the third grade. Due to the distance, we moved away from the schools, and Timmy could no longer ride the bus to school like Tommy. I had to drive Timmy to school. I had been prescribed new seizure medication because of the seizures that started a year or so ago. One of the side effects of the seizure medication was extreme confusion. While on the mediation, I got lost while driving Timmy to school. At that time, I had no idea that the confusion was from the medication. I actually thought my brain was turning into mush like the doctor told me it would.

I called Lanisha and asked, "Are you asleep?"

"No," she answered.

"I cannot find the highway to take Timmy to school," I said.

She said, "Take 86th Street."

"I don't know which highway to take," I said.

"465," she said.

"I don't know where 465 is," I said as tears ran down my face and my son sat in the back seat, oblivious to what was going on. When Lanisha realized I was crying, I believe she understood that I was confused and I didn't know where I was going. "Oh," she said, "Go to 86th Street, get in the left-hand lane, turn left onto 465 South, yadda, yadda, yadda." Later on, Lanisha called me back to make sure I made it to work safely, and I told her that I had.

The next morning as I continued to feel confused, I called Nancy and asked, "Are you asleep?"

"I'm already at work," she responded.

"Okay," I said as Nancy cut me off and immediately started complaining about her job. I interrupted and said, "Well, I called to see if you could take Timmy to school today." She didn't acknowledge my question and just kept talking about all of the situations at work and how they were mistreating her on the job. I was so overwhelmed with my own situation because I still needed to find Timmy a ride to school that in the midst of her rant, I cut her off and said, "I don't have time for this right now."

She said, "Oh, okay, bye." I think about two or three weeks went by with me trying to call her back. She dodged all my phone calls and didn't respond to my voicemail messages. I had no clue what was going on and why she was dodging me. Then I sent her an email to ask what the problem was and why she was avoiding me. I basically asked her why she couldn't be woman enough to tell me that she was mad at me instead of avoiding me for weeks. In the email, I went straight off! Nancy still planned to attend my master's program after all of the drama. During her bachelor's program, she needed a tutor. So, in the email, I let her know that if she joined my class, I would stress her out with drama until she failed. Then I added, "You know I'm smarter than you, so you know I'll do it."

At this point, I didn't even know why she was mad at me. I had called her back after I found Timmy a ride to school that day to listen to her complain about her job, and she wouldn't even take my calls. And this was after the "we would be friends forever" statement. After she avoided me for weeks, I felt like I wanted to fight her. Why didn't I listen to my spirit when it told me to cut her off months earlier, but no, I had to listen to Lanisha. What in the heck was I thinking, by listening to a person over listening to God? Note to self; listen to God in the beginning, and then you won't have to go through all the drama.

Basically, I gave it a little more time, and then I called Nancy and did what God had told me to do: I asked her whether I could talk to her, and I pleaded and told her that I would not go off. She finally took my calls. She knew me well enough to know that just because I said I would not go off didn't mean anything. I would go off in a heartbeat. I was just good at losing my temper when someone pushed me too far. When she came over, I was doing another spiritual purge of all the unclean spirit-filled household items that I had bought again that should not have made their way back into the house. During this opportunity to talk to her, I apologized and told her everything that God had for me to tell her. The last thing I told her was what I was going to do to her while she was out of town in the Bahamas.

I told her about all the rejections she had in her life and how her family had rejected her, along with her ex-husband. I told her about how bad all of that made her feel. She stood there, looking at me, with tears in her eyes which made me feel like crying also. She told me that she could not deal with me being sick and just really needed space. Therefore, I opted not to tell her about the part where God said; if I had done all those terrible things, she would have wanted to kill herself because of the intense rejection. So, I waited until the next day, and I put everything else that God had for me to tell her in an email, and you guessed it, I have not spoken to her since. She ran from me yet again; she won't even sit next to me in church. It was as if she was afraid of me. But you know what? This time I am not upset with her because I am aware that this is a God thing, and I know that God's hand is in this 100 percent.

Lanisha decided that Sandra, Nancy, and I were causing her a little too much grief, so she told me that she felt it was best that we not be friends at this time. I haven't really talked to her since that time. So, I only had three friends, and all of them were now gone. I knew God's hand was in this situation because the boys and I had also gone to visit Shelia, Sam, and the kids for a weekend, and I ended up having a seizure while I was there also. The ambulance came to the house, and my family had to drive the two hours to where Shelia lived to come to get me from the hospital and pick up the boys and my car.

Well, after that situation, Shelia stopped returning my calls and started treating me differently. Long story short, I found out some years later that she said her kids had never seen anyone have a seizure, and they were afraid, so she didn't want to deal with me anymore. Now, for me to have lost all of those so-called friends in such a short matter of time, I knew this was a spiritual thing, and God was getting me to a place where He needed to work some things out of me so that He could use me for His glory. I began to realize I needed to spend more time with God and less with messy people. There were definitely times when I was a messy person. I also realized I needed to work more on myself, so I would not be considered a messy person.

I soon realized that God was separating me from all the situations and people in my life that kept me away from fully serving Him. Which is why this time in my life was the sanctification process which is a setting apart or separation. I had to be taken away from all the cliques and backbiting and the things that kept me bound in my spirit. There were times in my life when I felt I could not live without my friends. God was successful in showing me that those types of situations were not necessary for me to exist. During my difficult situations, God showed me that He was the only one that I could lean on. I am talking about wholly leaning on someone.

This spiritual storm was by far the worst storm I had ever experienced in my life. I have labeled this storm my Euroclydon. In Acts 27:14, Paul spoke about the worst storm of his life, and it was called Euroclydon. Just like Paul, I realized I could not turn to anyone but God. During this particular storm, I was fighting for my mental, physical and spiritual health. While I was in the midst of the storm, I felt like I knew just how Job felt. But I frequently reminded myself that God had already made me aware that I wasn't like Job at all. God spared my children, and for that, I am truly grateful. There were times when people would talk to me on the phone or visit with me, but for the most part, I was in the test all alone. I had to find a way to deal with things all by myself. I had to finally start listening to God and actually following the steps He had already ordered for my life. Sister Denise told me to get into my Word and fight the mind battles that I was having with the Word of God, and that is just what I did. I would read the scriptures that encouraged me, and that applied to my life three times a day. I frequently inserted my name into the scriptures so that they spoke directly to me. I told myself that I was taking the scriptures like medication so that I could get the word down in my heart and in my mind.

Sister Sunny at church was also one of the people that gave me some encouraging words when it came to pulling up my bootstraps and fighting using the Word of God. Sister Sunny spoke about several situations in her life as examples where she had to use the Word of God, and it worked for her. Sister Denise became a spiritual mentor to me; she took me under her wing and nurtured me back to spiritual health. She taught me how to fight the mind battles and other spiritual situations with the Word of God. She always told me, "I'm giving you the formula that works, and I know it works because it worked for me."

I could have learned a lot more a lot sooner if I would not have been so afraid as a child when Mother Martha Girly approached me and asked, "Would you like to be my daughter?" I looked at her like she was crazy and said, "I already have a mother." I was only ten or twelve years old, and I was afraid of her. I didn't fully understand the question, and I didn't know what else to say. To me, she was a scary lady. She wore a black cape and a black hat every time she entered the church. Furthermore, I had heard her preach about how she touched her son, and he came back from the dead. I also heard her preach about how she once held a baby with no pupils; she covered the baby's eyes with her hand, prayed, and the baby miraculously grew pupils. Because of our lack of understanding, my friends and I thought she was a witch doing magic. As a child, I had no idea it was the anointing of God that was so strong in her life.

However, Sister Denise did allow Mother Boyd to mentor her spiritually and allowed her to be a huge portion of her life. So, I guess I did indirectly receive some of the teachings of Mother Boyd. Some teaching is better than no teaching at all.

I decided that when I got out of that test, I would not allow anyone to dump their garbage in my spirit again and cause me to behave in such an unseemly way. I decided I would be clean and free from cliques and wickedness from now on. I don't ever want to go through a test like that one again. In order to ensure that I don't, I have to stay in the Spirit, and that is what I plan to do. I just want to keep my conversation focused on good things and not talking about people by finding fault or causing drama in relationships and by keeping a good heart and not trying to destroy anyone's character or spirit. There can't be anything wrong with that.

CHAPTER 7

Escorted Out and Treated Like the Enemy

As I walked into the sanctuary, I thought to myself, *I'm feeling pretty good*, then I looked over at my Sunday school class and saw exactly who I wanted to sit by. But almost immediately after I sat down, my head started feeling kind of funny, and instantly I knew something wasn't right. *Oh, no, what is going on?* I thought. The next thing I knew, I was shaking so hard that I shook myself off the pew and right onto the floor. Just that quickly, I was having a seizure. I hadn't had a seizure in a while since I had been on medication to control them. *What brought this on?* I thought. A couple of brothers from the church rushed over to my row, picked me up off the floor, and carried my stretched-out body out of the sanctuary. I was shaking so violently that, as they were carrying me, they must have lost their grip because they dropped me on the floor in the lobby by the entrance. Once I hit the floor, I continued to shake, and I had several more seizures back-to-back. I don't think I could have been any more embarrassed. Well, maybe that one time when

I wore a thong to church, and I had a seizure, and my dress flew up above my waist for all the world to see my blessings. But I don't think I could have been any more embarrassed than that time. The ambulance had been called for me so many times while I was at church that the head deacon scolded me and said, "You shouldn't come to church if you are sick. You need to stay at home," he added. *Don't I get my help at church,* I thought. Anyway, during the time I was on the floor in the lobby, people were walking in and out of the church and just walked around me as if I was not even there. Maybe they were praying as they passed by, but I couldn't tell. I wasn't aware of everything that was going on around me. Then when Sister Denise came through the doors, she said, "Did y'all call the ambulance?"

Minister Roads quickly screamed out, "She said not to!" Sister Denise didn't waste any time. She dug around in that huge purse of hers and found her blessed oil. She dropped her purse on the floor, opened up the oil, and rubbed it all over her hands. She braced herself as she got down on the floor next to me. She rubbed my face with her hands, putting oil all over my face, and started rebuking and casting those spirits off of me. *What in the world?!* I thought. I couldn't believe it! *Was I possessed? Were spirits around me? Were they in me? Were they on me?*

She got down on the floor in her church clothes. "Take your filthy hands off of her, you low down dirty devil! You have no dominion over her, and your assignment has just been canceled. Satan, you are a lying, defeated foe, and the Spirit of the Lord is against you! I rebuke you in the name of the Lord Jesus Christ! As she spoke, I laid on the floor, seemingly paralyzed as she prayed. All of a sudden, I jumped to my feet and just stared at her. *Is there another spirit around me?* I thought. I didn't have to say a word. I believe Sister Denise was completely led by the Holy Ghost. She didn't stop praying and rebuking spirits. "I cast down every stronghold and mind battle that the enemy is trying to use in an attempt to hinder my little sis! I lose joy, peace of mind, and victory in your life! You are delivered and set free, lil' sis!" She exclaimed as she lifted her hands in victory. Instantly I felt lighter! I began rejoicing and praising God for delivering me from that heavy weighted-down feeling that appeared to have me bound on the floor. I was so grateful to be delivered.

I walked back to my seat and didn't even sit down. Praise and testimony service had started, and I was ready to give my testimony of what God had just done for me. "Praise the Lord, Sis Leeta," the praise service leader called out. "I once was bound, but now I'm free!" I yelled out. "Said I'm free, praise the Lord I'm free. No longer bound. No more chains holding me. My soul is resting. It's just a blessing. Praise the Lord, hallelujah, I'm free." I sang out. I was so excited; I testified and sang a song.

Now, I bet you want to know how someone with the Holy Ghost could have an unclean spirit. I wanted to ask the same question. But before I do, I will tell you about a quick little situation that happened while I was at church. There was a visitor sitting next to me, one of the church members came over to us and asked the visitor to move away from me. Timmy was sitting next to me, and he was so upset. "Why did she come and move that lady away from you, Mommy?" he asked. "I'm not sure," I responded. "It's not a big deal, don't worry about it," I added. I later found out that the member was going around church telling people that I was possessed by demons, and she had to get a visitor away from me. I didn't get angry, but I was extremely disappointed and hurt. I thought, *if you believe you discerned a spirit in me, on me, around me, or whatever, why in the world didn't your Holy Ghost kick in and lead you to intercede on my behalf? Why didn't you help me?*

So, about if a Holy Ghost-filled person can have unclean spirits question. The Bible speaks that God hath not given us the "spirit" of fear, which means fear is a spirit. So, my question is; is the spirit of fear in you, on you, or around you? Many have been fearful, and fear hath torment according to the Word of God. Depression is a spirit (I'm not talking about when someone has a chemical imbalance in the brain causing depression) that will come around people and create a heaviness that will bring down the person's emotional state. In Isaiah 61:3, it speaks about putting on the garment of praise for the spirit of heaviness. This tells us heaviness is also a spirit that, to me, feels very similar to depression. Now is the spirit of depression/heaviness in you, on you, or around you? Many people talk about Satan, but they don't appear to believe in unclean spirits. If Lucifer took a third of the angels (which turned into unclean spirits) with him, how many spirits are in the world today? We know there is at least a legion because Jesus met the man in the cemetery and sent at least two thousand (if you research, a legion can be up to seven thousand) into the swine, and the swine ran off the cliff into the water and were choked. So how many more unclean spirits remain? That was a rhetorical question.

After I finished singing and shouting around the church, I went out into the lobby to catch my breath. And someone came up to me to see how I was doing and hugged me instantly. I felt the spirit of heaviness again. I didn't understand it. How could this person do that to me? They are supposed to love me. They are supposed to care about me. The Bible tells us to watch as well as pray, and I did not do that. I allowed someone to walk up to me in the church and put that spirit right back on me. Just because people are in the church doesn't mean they are saved. I went back to my seat and started to feel weird. I turned around to the pew behind me and tapped a minister. "I don't feel well," I told her. Within seconds of telling her that I had another seizure and I was back on the floor. The brothers carried me out of the church yet again. I don't recall anyone at church attempting to help much. It seemed as if they just wanted me gone so that I would not disrupt service again.

I called Sister Denise that night, "Will you please come over? I believe I still have another spirit around me," I said.

"I don't have to come over there. I can pray for you over the phone. Jesus sent His word and healed people all the time. Do you believe that I can pray over the phone and you can be delivered?" she asked.

"Yes, I believe you can do that," I answered.

"Lil Sis, you know that no one put a spirit on you, right?" she asked. "Satan is playing games with your mind and trying to keep you preoccupied about spirits and thinking God cannot deliver you. God did exactly what His Word said He would do. Do you believe that?" she added. I thought about it for a few seconds and rehearsed the situation in my mind, and I realized she was correct. No one put a spirit on me. It was all in my head. I was so paranoid while dealing with this particular spiritual battle that the thought of unclean spirits was always on my mind. I frequently thought someone was possessed by demons or that the demons were tormenting me and the boys. I would grab the boys unexpectantly and tell them to sit down. I would anoint them with oil and begin to rebuke unclean spirits. Satan was winning the battle.

I was stressed, paranoid, and overwhelmed in my mind with constant thoughts of Satan and demons. Sister Denise was working with me to help find a way to address it better. "Keep your thoughts on God, Lil Sis," she said. "I will," I answered before we hung up the phone. This mind battle is the hardest battle that I have ever had to fight.

When dealing with my health, the test results continued to come back negative. There was nothing medically wrong with me, and most people would love to hear that. But not me; I wanted the doctors to tell me something was wrong, so they could fix it. But the test proved that there was nothing to fix. It was all me. I was what was broken. My spirit was under attack, and it was being manifested with physical ailments.

I sat at home night after night, not being able to sleep because I was dealing with a restless spirit. I was restless, anxious, and often depressed. I didn't understand the test, and I didn't understand why I was still in the test. The thoughts of *why I couldn't overcome the heavy, depressed feelings, along with the feeling of anxiousness*, were constantly on my mind. I wanted out of this test so badly. I became extremely emotional and cried the majority of each day. Because I was alone all the time, it felt as if the walls of my apartment were closing in on me. I had never been so tired of staying at home in my life.

I needed the help of the Lord, and I didn't know how to find Him anymore. It was as if I had forgotten how to pray and/ or how to seek the Lord. In the past, when I kneeled down to pray, I would only pray for five or ten minutes. I had not been a prayer warrior, and truth be told, I didn't even know how to pray. During prayer, my mind would wander, and I would become distracted. I couldn't sit still for more than a few seconds because of the racing and ruminating thoughts causing constant anxiety. Having a lack of control over my own thoughts, I felt like I was losing control of my life and losing my mind. After getting into the car accident, I no longer had transportation, and I was home alone more often, and I was hating it. The boys did argue and fight when they were home, but listening to them provided a distraction from my thoughts.

My weight was going up and down, and I became frustrated about that too. I wanted so badly to be skinny all my life. The sad part is, when I look back at pictures, I was always skinny. But because of my family constantly telling me how big and fat I was, I couldn't see it. During this time, I had lost more weight than I wanted to, and I believed I looked sickly. I didn't look or feel healthy. My clothes were way too big, hanging off of me, and they looked sloppy. I had no desire to shop or buy new clothes. Depression overwhelmed me. The heaviness was exhausting, so I often stayed in the bed most of the day just thinking. It seemed as if I was the only person in the world who knew what I was going through. I kept trying to explain it to people, and it just sounded like I was complaining; I got so sick of being me and dealing with what I was dealing with.

Neither my church family nor my biological family weren't calling to talk or to check and see how I was doing. The bad part about it was I didn't want to actually talk to anyone. However, I wanted them to call so that I would know they cared. I was surprised that my mother hadn't called to check on me. I don't know why I was surprised because I was never my mother's favorite child, and she rarely ever called me. Additionally, my family had already convinced themselves that I was crazy for real. Therefore, when I would talk to my mother, it was often an unpleasant conversation. Just about every time we talked, it would end up in an argument.

I often called Sharon so that she could remind me that the earth wasn't going to open up and swallow me. "I don't know how to talk to her; she acts as if she hates me," I said to Sharon.

"She doesn't hate you; she loves you, and she's concerned about you," Sharon replied.

I guess she just doesn't know how to take me, and clearly, I don't know how to take her, I thought. After Sharon and I finished talking, I walked around the apartment and thought about why my mother hated me so much or why I felt like she did. It didn't matter how she felt about me because actions speak louder than words. Also, perception often determines thoughts, and I perceived that she didn't like me (or I wasn't the favorite), and so in my mind, that's how it was.

My mother had always treated me differently from my brother and sisters. Growing up, Sharon seemed to always be the needy one. Sharon dropped out of high school and got pregnant at an early age, and then had another baby two years later. Because she was so young, Sharon didn't have a job and depended on the system to support her and her children. Because of her situation, she couldn't afford to do anything extra for the children. My mom would help Sharon with the bills and things like that. My mother would find items at the store that she thought would look nice in Sharon's apartment and buy them for her. She would buy clothes for the kids and just help out with little things like that.

I didn't mind my mother doing those types of things for Sharon; because she needed help. I did the same type of things for her and the kids. I would help with school supplies, clothes, and shoes for the kids. I helped with the kids because I loved them and didn't want them to go without the things they needed. However, it bothered me that Sharon never seemed to appreciate it. To me, she acted as if it was my job to help take care of the kids. I remember one day I dropped by her place after the kids had gotten out of school and the kids were outside playing. They had on a pair of shoes that I bought them for school. "Sharon, why didn't you make them take off their school clothes and school shoes when they came home from school?" I questioned.

"They don't have school clothes and play clothes; they are all the same," she said.

"That's why they don't have anything nice to wear because you do stupid stuff like that!" I screamed. From that comment on, of course, we continued to argue. Sharon called my mother, and my mother always would take Sharon's side. "You two need to stop and make up," she would say. Sharon was never wrong in anything that happened between us, and it is still that way today.

There was an incident that had me burning with hatred toward Sharon. Once Sharon's two children were older, Sharon had another child, a son, and she would make the other two take care of him. My niece Stephanie wrote a poem about the situation; it was called "Virgin with a Child." The poem was so deep it made me cry. Now at this time, Stephanie was only ten or eleven years old. I tried to talk to Sharon about it, but she just didn't care. She wanted to do her own thing and was angry at the fact that her childhood ended abruptly when she had her children. Sharon made my mother a grandmother at age thirty-two, and Stephanie made Sharon a grandmother at age thirty-two. I recall a time when I told Sharon that I would never be a grandmother at thirty-two years old. After going back and forth arguing with her for a while, she finally said, "You have no idea what your children will do. So, how do you know you will never be a grandmother at thirty-two years old?" I looked at her and calmly stated, "I know I won't be a grandmother at thirty-two years old because my oldest will only be seven when I'm thirty-two." The conversation ended, and she walked away. Seems like Sharon and I were always going back and forth about something. We didn't communicate well, and we seemed to always get offended with each other, regardless of the conversation.

When Stephanie was a senior in high school, her son was one year old, and I could tell that she was very depressed. Stephanie and I used to be very close, and we talked almost daily. Stephanie was ready to leave Sharon's house, and she asked if she could come and live with me. I decided to allow Stephanie to move in with me and the boys. I went to Sharon and Bob and told them what had been decided.

"Sharon, Bob," I said, "now you know this is going to be hard on me since I am a single mother. Do you think you guys will be able to help out financially?" I asked.

"No," they answered almost in unison.

"Well, do you think you can at least buy Pampers for Tanner?" I asked.

"No," they said. "You are taking them, and now they are yours," they said as if to say good riddance.

"Okay, then if that's the case, I will be claiming them on my taxes next year," I said, thinking they would change their minds.

"Fine with us," they said.

I walked out of the room, went, and informed Stephanie. We packed up their belongings and left. Sharon and I didn't communicate much after Stephanie moved out.

Stephanie continued to talk to her mother, and I continued to take care of business raising my boys and both Stephanie and Tanner. Stephanie and Tanner went to her mother's house for the weekend. While Stephanie was there, Sharon caught Stephanie in the next room with Tanner's father at about 9:00 a.m., and guess who Sharon was mad at? You guessed it—me.

"What the heck are you mad at me for? Stephanie would have never snuck someone in my house because I don't sleep with my door closed, nor do I allow her to sleep with her door closed," I told Sharon. Once again, our lines of communication were severed. Sharon never apologized for anything; after months of not talking, she would just show up at my house and act as if nothing ever happened. As always, I would give in even with no apology because I wasn't the one upset in the first place.

A few months passed, and I received a letter from the school that Stephanie's book rental had not been paid since she started high school, and it needed to be paid, or she would not be allowed to graduate. I called Sharon to tell her about the letter. "Stephanie is living with you now, and we told you when you took her that we could not help you financially," she said.

"No, what you said was you could not help me financially with what they may need. But this is not a bill that she made while she was living with me. The book rental was due before she ever moved in with me. I don't mind paying for all her graduation expenses, but you and Bob need to pay her past-due book rental; fair is only fair," I demanded.

"We aren't paying for anything. You have her, so you can pay for it!" she said as she slammed the phone down in my ear.

"No, she didn't just hang up on me; she is really crazy!" I screamed.

"What did she say?" Stephanie asked.

"Don't worry about it, Stephanie. You will get to graduate; I'll take care of it," I assured Stephanie.

I was not going to let Sharon mess this up for Stephanie. Stephanie was in her last semester of her senior year; she was a straight A student and had already past the state standardized testing on the first try. She had two full academic scholarships to well-known colleges waiting for her. Tanner was going to live with me and my two sons, and Stephanie would come home and visit him on the weekends. I was definitely going to take care of this situation.

I wrote the nastiest letter I could think of telling Sharon about how lazy, trifling, and what a no-good mother she was for risking Stephanie's education like this. I had recently had surgery on my feet, so I wasn't able to drive. So, I had a friend drive me over to Sharon's house to put it in her mailbox.

Later that evening, I received a voicemail from Sharon, telling me how she hated me and my children. She added she hopes that me, my children, Stephanie and Tanner, burn up tonight in my house. I could not believe the message. I must have listened to that message ten times that night to ensure I heard it correctly. I believe if I could have walked, I would have run to her house that night. After that night, I didn't call or talk to Sharon again, and I never let Stephanie hear the message.

Of course, Sharon called my mother, and all my mother had to say was, "You two need to stop it and just get along." Not only do I believe my mother hated me, but I believe I genuinely hated her too. I didn't have much to say to my mother because she didn't listen to me anyway. My sister was angry at me for trying to help her daughter. I didn't understand it, but it was true, and all my mother could say about the situation was, "y'all need to get along." Never did she ever tell Sharon that she needed to fix the mess she created.

Tax time rolled around, and I couldn't wait to file my taxes. It had been a struggle being a single mother of two and taking care of two extra people. I filed rapid refund, so I could get the check back in forty-eight hours. "Hello," I said with excitement in my voice when I saw H&R Block's number show up on the caller ID in less than twenty-four hours.

"There was a problem with your tax refund with one of the social security numbers. We will need you to correct the problem before we are able to send in your refund," the lady said on the other end of the phone.

"Whose social security number is it?" I asked.

"I can't tell you that, ma'am," she answered.

"Then how am I going to know what needs correcting?" I asked.

"You need to check everyone you filed on your return and make sure all the names and social security numbers match," she replied.

"Okay, thanks for your help. I'll call you back," I said.

I went directly to Stephanie soon as I hung up the telephone. "Stephanie, I said."

"Yes, Auntie Leeta," she answered.

"Is this the correct information for you and Tanner?" I questioned as I handed her a piece of paper with their names and social security numbers written on it.

"Yes, Auntie Leeta, that's all the correct information," she answered.

"Okay, thanks," I said as I ran out of the room to go call back H&R Block. "Yes, my name is Leeta Bigbee. I received a call that there was a problem with my tax return and that I needed to correct the problem. So, I'm calling to change my son's name on my tax return. I used Bigbee as his last name, and social security must have his father's last name on his social security card," I explained.

"Okay, ma'am, what is your son's name?" she asked.

"Tommy Hicks," I answered.

"We will make that change and process your return, thank you," she said.

"Thank you," I replied as I hung up the phone. *That's a relief,* I thought. The very next day, the phone rang, and it was H&R Block again, and the conversation was very similar to the last conversation. "May I speak with Ms. Bigbee?"

"This is she speaking."

"I'm calling from H&R Block, and there is..." I stopped her before she could finish the sentence, "Don't tell me; there is another problem with my taxes," I uttered in frustration.

"Yes, ma'am, there is," she said.

"Okay, then it has to be my other son's name. Change Timmy's last name to Sims, and change Tommy's last name back to Bigbee," I instructed.

"All right, ma'am; that should take care of the problem, and I'll get this filed today," she said.

"Thank you," I said as I hung up the phone. *I sure hope I don't get another phone call. My check should be here by now,* I thought. It couldn't have been more than thirty minutes later, and the phone rang again. "May I speak with Ms. Bigbee?"

"Speaking," I said.

"I'm calling from—"

"Please don't tell me there is a problem with my refund," I said while almost in tears.

"Yes, ma'am, there is, and I'll tell you now that if we keep trying to send it through, they will reject it and investigate you," she said.

"Alright, here is what I would like for you to do: change Timmy's name back to Bigbee. I have filed with Timmy and Tommy's name as Bigbee for years. So, please remove Stephanie and Tanner's names from the return altogether and just file the return," I instructed. I hung up the phone and went into the room where Stephanie was.

"Stephanie, do you think that Tanner's father could have claimed him on his taxes?" I asked.

"No, I don't," she replied. "He doesn't even work."

"Okay, thanks," I said. I left the room, and after months of not talking to Sharon, I decided to call her. "Hey, Bob, is Sharon home?" I asked.

"Sharon!" he screamed.

"Hello," she answered.

"Hey, Sharon, did you all file Stephanie and Tanner on your taxes?" I questioned.

"Yeah, we did," she replied.

"Why would you file them on your taxes, and you know they didn't live with you at all during the year? Not only that, we talked about it, and you and Bob knew I was supposed to file them since I would be supporting them one hundred percent financially. You clearly stated you would not help me financially!" I screamed.

"Well, it was an accident," she said.

"How can it be an accident when they asked you if the people lived with you the entire year? You had to lie and answer yes, and you call yourself filled with the Holy Ghost?" I screamed even louder.

Next thing I know, I am listening to a dial tone. "I can't believe it. She screwed me over, and I am the one getting hung up on again. How many times do I have to go through this?" I screamed. I called my mother to try to get her to talk to Sharon, and of course, she thought "we" had a problem. We probably went about six months without speaking, and then one day, out of the blue, Sharon saw me at Wal-Mart and said she couldn't take me being mad at her and that she had no idea why we were even mad at each other in the first place. No apology or nothing, typical Sharon, as always.

Shortly after that, Stephanie ended up moving back home with her mother; it didn't seem like I was able to help her. Stephanie dropped out of high school during her senior year last semester with straight A's and two full academic scholarships. It wasn't too long after she moved back home that she was pregnant again.

Lately, since I had been sick, Sharon and I had become closer, but I think she believes I am a little off, like crazy. My mom had previously told me that Sharon is jealous of me, so I guess now that I am crazy, there isn't anything to be jealous of. After being in the psyche, I stopped concerning myself with what people thought of me. If I worried about what people thought, I would be in way worse shape mentally. I've already been to the psych ward a few times, so having people think I am crazy doesn't really bother me. I just have to make sure I don't go crazy for real worrying about what people think.

Now my mother's relationship with my brother is a totally different story. He just can't do any wrong in her eyes. Kevin, now he is a real people person. He could probably talk a homeless person out of their cup. You know how people say kids normally grow up to be what they were when they were little? That is just how we turned out. For instance, Sharon was always a loner; she loved to read as a child and never would go outside and socialize. Needless to say, she is the same way today. She seems to get jealous when she tells me, "I don't have friends like you do." She often says she doesn't have any friends, but she doesn't want to socialize and/or fellowship with anyone. She normally stays to herself, and she still loves to read. Kevin would pick with Sharon and me all the time. He would do little things to us. For instance, when we were younger, he threw a comb and hit Sharon in the head. The comb stuck right in the top of her head, and blood started pouring down her face. There was a different time when we were kids; Kevin was twirling me around by holding on to one of my arms and one of my legs. My mom sees him and says, "Let her go." Kevin did exactly what she said. He let me go, and I went flying into a bedpost and busted my head as well.

Kevin would walk around with little stick pins, and if you weren't looking, he would sneak up behind or beside us and stick us really quick in our back, leg, or arm. While one of my stepbrothers was washing dishes one day around Christmas time, Kevin walked up behind him and hit him in the back with a Christmas ham. Seems like Kevin never knew when to stop playing or when his actions were actually hurting others.

One time my mom's ex-husband saw me squatting in front of the back door. If you can picture this, I'm squatting down like kind of in the fetal position but still standing on my feet, with my arms wrapped around my legs and my head resting on my knees. He approached me and said, "What are you doing?" I said. "Are you coming?"

"What are you doing, girl?" He asked again.

"Are you coming?" I asked again.

He was a big man, and I was a very small child, probably only about forty pounds, even though I was about in the second or third grade.

He said, "Girl, if you don't tell me what the heck you are doing, I am going to beat yo' behind."

I said, "Kevin is in the backyard smoking some grass, and he said to let him know when someone was coming. So, I need to know if you are coming." He reached down, grabbed me by my collar, snatched me from in front of the back door, and tossed me over to the side. He then ran out of the house to the back-yard to find Kevin in the backyard pulling grass and wrapping it up in toilet paper. Not sure where Kevin had seen someone smoking grass before, but he wanted to try it. Kevin was always into something.

Oh, yeah, and don't let me forget the time when he said, "Mama."

"Go to bed, Kevin," my mom said in a groggy voice.

"But Mama," Kevin whined.

"Boy, you better get out of here and go back to bed!" she screamed.

"Okay, but Sharon and Leeta are going to burn up in the bed," he said calmly as he began to walk back to his room. My mom and stepfather jumped out of the bed and raced into our room to find that Kevin had set the bed on fire with us in the bed. Kevin would steal money from my mom and stepfather, not change like I would take out of the drawer. He would take twenties and tens out of their pockets and purses.

Now that Kevin is an adult, he is a recovering addict. He has been arrested for theft, and his ex-wife swears he used to hit her. I don't know if he really did; I never saw any bruises. But he doesn't discipline his children very well. He disciplines his chil-dren kind of like the way he used to treat us. If they misbehave, he may punch them in the chest or in the stomach. It doesn't matter what Kevin does; my mom will never see it as wrong.

When I was a child, I had the smartest mouth in the world. I could cut you up with my tongue. I would get a swift backhand in the mouth all the time for getting smart with my mother. Often, I didn't even realize I was saying something wrong; it was just natural for me to talk that way. Now, if it was me, I could never do anything right in my mother's eyes. I was very inquisitive, and I enjoyed playing with my baby dolls. As an adult, I have been told the way I talk is offensive, and told most times, I don't even realize it. But I am trying my best to change my tone and not be offensive, even though it isn't intentional. My family is the one that mostly complains about my tone. My family is also the people that say, I don't realize I am doing it. So, if I don't realize I have a bad tone or that my tone is offensive to my family, how do I change it? It appears that anytime I communicate with my family, it is offensive no matter what I'm talking about.

Also, as an adult, I still am extremely inquisitive; I love to research, question, and examine just about everything. People often say I think I know everything. I don't think I know everything, but there are many things I do know. The reason I know so many things is because once someone mentions something that I am unaware of, I will often go research it and study it until I become familiar with it. Before the internet was so popular, I would often say I was a wealth of useless information. My friends will frequently email or call me and ask me legal questions, forensic science questions, political questions, questions concerning divorce, the constitution, and the list just goes on and on. Many times, I know the answer, and if I don't, if it piques my interest, I'll research it and find the answer.

I would guess all the playing with the baby dolls is what made me the nurturing type that I am. I find myself not only caring for my children but other people and their children as well. My house or apartment was always the one where all the kids came to sleep over. In my friendships, I find myself always trying to nurture or care for someone. The majority of people I meet need something from me, and once I have helped fulfill that need, they move on. We all grew up to be exactly what we were as children.

It still bothers me that I don't seem to be enough for my family. No matter what I did, it was never enough. I remember when I bought my first house, the first and only compliment I remember getting from my mother was that I picked a nice house; then she started telling me all the things she felt were wrong and how she would have done it differently if she had bought the house. When I graduated from college with the highest honors, Summa Cum Laude, and I received the outstanding professional award, all after I had been in the hospital and told I would be a vegetable by the time of graduation, she didn't even make it to my graduation to see me walk across the stage. I asked Sharon to bring my children, so they could see me walk across the stage, but they didn't make it until the graduation was over. No one was there to cheer for me after all my hard work. I guess it just wasn't important enough. I had to learn to be my own cheerleader and strive for things on my own. I guess that's how I turned out to be independent. Over the years, I found out that I can only truly count on myself and God.

CHAPTER 8

Mind Battles

January 2006

Before the car accident occurred, the boys and I had been in the house for days. I was still off work on sick leave and low on funds. I had been reading several books and watching a bunch of movies trying to understand God and the plan he had for my life. I had spent over 4000 dollars on movies, books, and CDs in an attempt to see and/or hear a message from God through them. My family was growing more and more worried about me because they felt like my behavior was extremely erratic. Looking back on the situation, I would have to agree with them.

I was excessively paranoid about unclean spirits. Several times throughout the day, I would grab Timmy and/or Tommy and sit them down at the kitchen table, smear blessed oil on their foreheads, and rebuke unclean spirits. I perceived that I was under constant attack from Satan, and he had now caused my children to act out. Once again, I knew I needed to clean my house of any unclean spirits the boys may have brought into the house. Running around like a maniac, I went from room to room, grabbing toys, books, movies, clothing, and whatever else I could get my hands on that Satan or one of his demons could be attached to. I threw away all types of items, like hanging pictures, clothes, shoes, my eyeglasses, my retainer, dishes, food, and the list goes on. My head was spinning, literally. *I think I'm losing my mind,* I thought over and over again. My thoughts were so erratic because the mind battles were so severe. I was confused and frustrated, and I was running out of options. I was searching for answers in books, movies, and music, and I didn't find any. I was reading the Bible all throughout the day, and some of the scriptures seemed as if they were speaking directly to me. However, they weren't speaking clearly, which is what made me turn my attention to books, movies, and music for clarity.

After watching so many movies and being in the house for several days without any contact from my family and friends, I began to think maybe we were already dead. Maybe we were trapped on earth and unable to transition to heaven for some reason. Once I had watched enough movies convincing me that we were dead, I wouldn't eat any food for fear that it would keep me trapped on earth. I tried to convince the boys that they didn't need to eat food either. I explained to them, "Guys, we are already dead, and we are just waiting on our new bodies. We won't be hungry for long. Just try to hold out," I added.

I wasn't aware that the boys were in contact with my family and updating them on what was going on. The really sad part about it is that Timmy believed me; he thought he was dead. Our ceilings were eighteen feet tall, and Timmy asked, "Since I'm dead, can I jump over this balcony down to the first floor?"

"Sure," I answered. Before, Timmy could make it all the way up the stairs, Tommy grabbed him and said, "Don't do that. You will get hurt or die for real."

"We are already dead, right, Tommy?" Timmy questioned. According to Dictionary.com, a battle is "a hostile encounter or engagement between opposing military forces."[9] I was constantly battling to determine the opposing views that plagued my mind to understand the difference between right and wrong, true and false, and between fiction and non-fiction. I am so grateful that Tommy had the wherewithal to speak logically and soundly to Timmy. I'm also extremely grateful that Timmy listened to him even though they both somewhat believed me when I said we were already dead. Honestly, I believe the only thing that saved us (besides God) was that they weren't really clear about what it meant to be dead.

The boys weren't so convinced that not eating would help us to transition to heaven. "We are really hungry, Mommy," Timmy complained.

"How is not eating going to keep us out of heaven?" Tommy questioned.

"I don't have all the answers, guys. I'm trying to figure it all out," I replied. "Lord, please don't charge my ignorance to my heart," I prayed as I put a few chicken wings into the oven. When the wings were almost done cooking, I reached into the oven and pulled it out with my bare hands to check on them. "Mommy!!!" Tommy screamed.

"What?" I answered.

"You grabbed the hot pan right out of the oven with nothing covering your hand," he said frantically.

---

9 https://www.dictionary.com/browse/battle?s=t

"It's not hot, Tommy," I said calmly. "See, it's not even done yet," I said as I put the chicken back into the oven. Noticing that I didn't get burned furthered my belief that we were already dead. Therefore, I chose not to eat once the wings were done. "Tommy, help me take these pictures to the dumpster, please," I yelled out to Tommy as I continued to grab pictures off the wall that I felt were keeping us from transitioning. I played the music throughout the apartment very loudly in an attempt to elevate my mind and ward off evil spirits. "Timmy, you just stay right here, and we will be right back after we go to the dumpster," I ordered. Timmy sat down in a chair in the kitchen.

When I opened the apartment door, there were two young men walking up the stairs headed to the apartment across the hall from ours. Tommy and I walked past them and continued down the stairs to the dumpster. When we returned to the apartment, Timmy was standing in the kitchen, shaking and crying. "What happened?" I asked. He didn't respond; he just continued crying. "Tommy, those two men we just saw were demons!" I screamed. "They came into the apartment while we were at the dumpster and just killed Timmy!" I said while hugging Timmy and crying. "Tommy, they killed us too; we just thought we walked outside to the dumpster. It's like in the movies when people see things over and over in different views or dimensions," I ranted. "Come here, guys, huddle up. Let's do a group hug," I said as we all huddled up in the kitchen, rocking back and forth to the music while crying. "Calm down, guys. It's all going to be okay. Just listen to the music," I said. "People made different songs because they were going through things in their lives," I added. The music was blasting, "this could be it, guys. This could be the way we transition. Help us, Lord! Help us, Lord! Sing it with me, guys," I pleaded. "Help us, Lord! Help us, Lord!" We all chanted. "We need you, Lord, please accept us now, Lord, please deliver us, God," I sang out with tears running down my face and with my voice shaking.

With my eyes closed tightly and still hugging the boys as hard as I could, I yelled out, "I believe, Lord, I believe." *This has to be how we transition*, I thought. "I don't know what else to do, Lord," I continued to cry out. "You all are not singing and praising God enough!" I scolded. "Just start calling out things to God about how you feel and what you want and create your own songs," I said. "You have to believe God is going to do it!" I yelled out as I began to squeeze each of them tighter while in the huddle. I wanted to ensure that when God began to transition us, we each transitioned together and that we all stayed together. By this time, we all were calling out to God for help with tears running down our faces. We hugged each other tighter and tighter as we all pleaded, "God, please transition us to heaven right now." While still in a huddle, I opened my eyes, and you guessed it, we were still standing in the kitchen. We did not transition, to my disappointment.

"Okay, guys, that's enough. Let's get cleaned up and get ready for bed," I said as I slowly released my death hold on the boys. "Why didn't we go to heaven?" Timmy asked.

"Yeah, why didn't we?" Tommy questioned.

"I'm not sure, guys, but I will find someone to help us," I answered. I felt so confused and mentally drained. I didn't understand why we were still stuck on earth. I began to think about how people in the movies would transition from earth to heaven when they were having problems. I finally figured it out. *A Ghost Whisper was what we needed*, I thought. I thought about it long and hard all throughout the night. My mind raced, trying to figure out who could be a Ghost Whisper. No one had ever told me they were the Ghost Whisper. I had to do some thinking about how people in my life have acted and behaved and so that it could help me to figure out who I should contact. *Would people even be able to see us since we were already dead?* I thought. The more I thought about it, I believed a lady at work could very well be the Ghost Whisper. It took forever for me to fall asleep because I was so excited about getting up in the morning and going to my job to speak with the Ghost Whisper.

When I woke up, I thought, *feels like I didn't sleep at all.* It felt very similar to when they put you to sleep for surgery. One minute you are talking to them, and the next, it feels like you are waking up while also feeling like you never went to sleep. I proceeded to get out of bed and start preparing the house for whoever would find it after we transitioned. When I took a break to contact Ortis, which was a person from my old church that had helped republish his mother's book. I called to inform him that he would now be responsible for completing and publishing my book. "Hey, how are you, Ortis?" I said as he answered the telephone.

"I'm good. Who is this?" he asked.

"I apologize; this is Sis Bigbee. I'm calling because I know you published your mom's book, and I was calling to tell you about my book. I have left several notebooks and reading material lying around in the apartment that will help you complete the book. I had been doing a lot of reading, trying to figure out how to deal with the spiritual battles that I found myself in. I also tried to research how to transition after death. "Ortis," I said, "are you still there?"

"Yes," he answered.

"You have to come into the house and go through my notes and the computer in order for you to complete my book without any problems," I added.

"Why do you want me to be the person to complete your book?" he questioned. "Why aren't you completing your own book?" he asked.

"Well, I am dead already," I answered. There was nothing but silence on the phone as I spoke to Ortis. "My sons and I have been killed, and our bodies will be in the apartment but don't worry about that at all," I added. "I will leave the door unlocked for you, and as you come in, just move around us and please ignore the blood. But you can't touch us because you will disturb the evidence," I stated.

"Sis Bigbee, I don't think that is a good idea for me to come into your apartment," he said. "I don't feel comfortable doing that," he added.

"It's really not a big deal," I said. "However, if you don't want to be used by God, then don't come. Maybe I was wrong in thinking you were the one that God had selected to complete my book. Have a good day," I said as I slammed down the telephone. That conversation made me feel more confused than ever. I felt like God was speaking to me and telling me what to do and what not to do, but things just weren't adding up. *So, how will my book get completed if I am dead, Lord?* I thought.

"Hey, guys!" I yelled out. "We are going to go to my job to find someone to help us transition to heaven. "How do you know who to ask Mommy," Tommy asked. "I'm not really sure, Tommy, but I felt as if God is directing me to a lady at work. If it isn't her, maybe she knows who I am supposed to go to so we can get help," I explained. As we gathered our things and proceeded to leave the house, I didn't even grab my keys. I believed God would just start the car without the keys. As we walked toward the door, I decided since I was dead, I didn't need to open the door. I'm sure I can walk right through the wall, I thought. "Wham!" Was the sound that rang out as I literally walked face-first into the wall. "Are you okay!" Timmy screamed out.

"I'm fine, Timmy, just a little confused," I answered. Since I had been diagnosed with cerebral lupus, I felt that maybe my brain just wasn't working the way it once did, and I was just not hearing God clearly. "Come on, Mommy, let's use the door since we haven't transitioned yet," Tommy said with a baffled look on his face.

Once we walked outside, we waved at several people that were driving by, and no one seemed to notice us. After no one waved back, I was 1one hundred percent sure that I was on the right track about us being dead. "They can't see us waving," I said as Timmy and Tommy waved at people in their cars. "Wow, they can't see us. We are dead! I told you she was right, Tommy," Timmy yelled out while Tommy just walked to the car quietly. When I arrived at the car door, I felt even more confused because the door was locked, and for some reason, God had not opened the door for us. "I have the keys right here," Tommy said. Feeling confused yet again, I slowly took the keys from Tommy, unlocked the doors, and we all got into the car.

I started the car and turned the music up almost as loud as it could go as we began our trip to find a way to transition out of this world. As I began driving through the apartment complex, there were several ambulances and police cars in the apartment parking area next to mine. "Look, guys, look over there. Do you see all the ambulances and police cars?" I asked. "Yes, we do," they yelled out. "That is actually our apartment. I know it doesn't look like it, but being dead, it kind of works like a three-dimensional world sometimes. Often times in movies, people talked about feeling like they were outside of their bodies and how they could actually see themselves doing stuff. But don't worry, the police have found our bodies and they will notify everyone. I told you we are on the right track," I said with excitement.

I finally reached the exit gate for the apartment and made a right turn onto 71st Street. I was elated because it felt like things were finally starting to add up. As I turned the corner, I sped up and zoomed down the street in great anticipation. It was a cold winter day, and I was going a little bit faster than the speed limit. The street was only a two-lane street with one lane going in each direction. As I drove down the street, I noticed traffic in my lane had come to a stop at the traffic light ahead, and it looked like there were about five to ten cars stopped in my lane. I was driving too fast to stop, fearing we would slide on the ice or just not have enough time to stop without hitting a car. I glanced over into the oncoming traffic lane and noticed there were no cars coming. I chose to go around all the stopped cars, and I crossed over into the oncoming traffic lane.

I probably passed about two cars when I noticed a city bus had turned at the light from the cross street ahead and was now in my lane. Well, technically, I was in the wrong lane, but I was unable to switch back into my original lane due to traffic. Now, there is a city bus headed straight toward us. Realizing that we would probably crash head-on into the bus. I reached over and turned down the music. "Hey, guys," I said as I saw the bus coming closer toward us. "I think we are about to transition. So just close your eyes and relax. It's gonna feel like we are about to go on a roller coaster ride," I explained. I then turned the music back up as loud as it could go, closed my eyes, took my hands off the steering wheel, and began clapping to the music.

What is that noise, I thought. *Sounds like the car is scraping the trees*, I thought. "Mommy, are you okay?" A small voice from the back seat called out. I glanced behind me and noticed Tommy hanging from the backseat of the car on the passenger side while still in his seatbelt. I remember trying to turn my head from side to side to see why he looked as if he was hanging instead of just sitting in the back seat. Timmy was not in a seatbelt but instead directly behind my seat, literally sitting on the backseat driver's side window inquiring if I was okay. As I drifted in and out of consciousness, I looked out of the driver's side window to see nothing but the grass touching my window. I quickly realized the car had flipped over, and we had crashed into a tree. My thinking was foggy and unclear. I was struggling to see because the car seemed to have smoke in it. I thought the car was on fire. I have no idea how I ended up with the car flipped over and in the midst of the trees. As I looked around the car, I noticed the airbags deployed, and that was the reason I struggled to see through the smoke. A man had climbed up the undercarriage of the car and reached in through the passenger side window to release Tommy from his seatbelt and pull him out through the window.

I continued feeling light-headed and drifted in and out of consciousness. "Are you alright, lady? Are you able to talk? Can you hear me? I'm a nurse," the voice cried out as she reached through the window, grabbing Timmy by the arm and lifting him out of the car through the same passenger window that Tommy was lifted through.

I can hear people screaming out several things, but it isn't clear what they are saying, I think to myself, as my body lay tangled up in the airbags and rubbish. I began trying to communicate with the nurse through sign language as my hands began to wave franticly through the fog and smoke.

"She's deaf; does anyone know sign language?" the lady screamed out after she had climbed into the car with me to stabilize my neck. "I'm here to help you; just hold on. I'm here; don't move," she said. "Did anyone call the ambulance? I believe her neck is broken," she said as she put the brace on to stabilize my neck.

I can easily get myself into a mess, I thought. I could see the feet of so many people running back and forth to my car. There was smoke everywhere, and I felt as if I could hardly breathe.

"Can you hear me? I'm a nurse. I'm here to help you. Just hold on. I'm here; don't move, please. Please, someone, call the ambulance!" she screamed from inside the upside-down car.

As I laid there, I did a mental sonogram and realized I wasn't hurting at all. The nurse stayed in the car with me the entire time until the fire department came. The fumes in the car were so bad she could barely breathe and kept coughing. She kept turning on the car to open up the sunroof. I could see some sort of flame or something under the hood of the car, or at least that is what it looked like. I kept telling her to turn off the car, and so did the fire department, but the sunroof would only stay open if the car was on. The nurse was very helpful.

The fire department finally came and began working on ways to try to get me out of the SUV. I am not exactly sure why I was stuck in the truck. My legs and hips were kind of twisted around, but I didn't feel like anything was broken. Since I had the smallest hands, I had to help the fire department maneuver the driver's side seat so that they could cut the seat and me out of the car. At the time of the accident, I was only about 105 pounds, and their hands were too big to fit into all of the compartments.

By this time, the nurse who crawled into my car with me had crawled out, and a fireman had taken her place. I could see several firemen surrounding my car. Still drifting in and out of consciousness, I opened my eyes, and I saw the sky. Then, the next time I opened them, I saw several trees. It is absolutely amazing that so quickly, something so devastating could happen.

The SUV ended up flipping over exactly where the stopped cars were sitting in my lane. I remember there were at least ten to fifteen cars in front of me, and I have no idea how I did not hit any of those cars, but I didn't hit any of them. I later obtained the police report. I called everyone that helped and let them know that we were alright. I can truly say God works in mysterious ways! God is a good God, and there is no fault in Him.

After the accident, every day I leave the apartment, I normally see my windshield and my hubcap still sitting on the

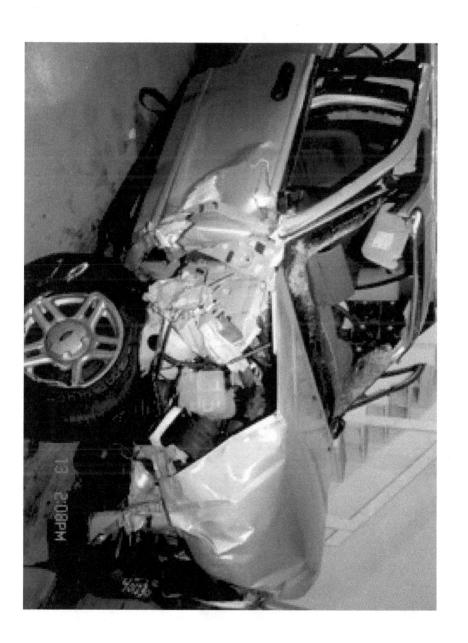

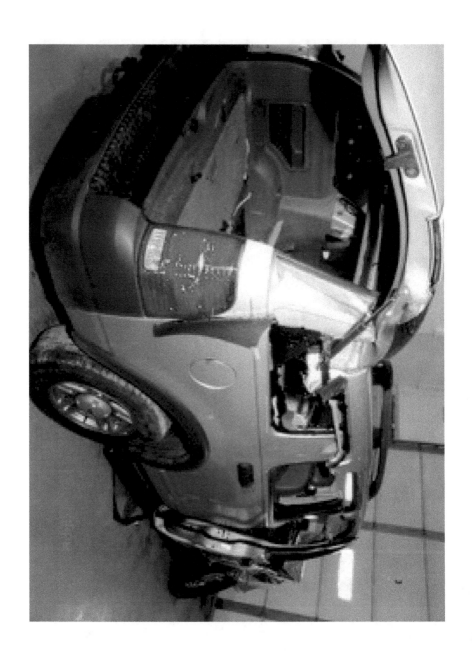

ground next to the tree we hit. I believe it served as a reminder of what happened to us and how close we came to death. Reminding us to be grateful for what God did for us. Since my friends were no longer talking to me, I felt very alone and had no one to talk to about the car accident or my state of mind during the time of the accident.

I vaguely recalled how the boys escaped from the car until, during church one Sunday morning, Tommy stood up and testified about it. He spoke about how God had spared our lives during the car accident. Before he testified, he told me that Sharon didn't want him to talk about the accident, but I told him to go ahead and tell everyone about God's goodness. Tommy testified, saying, while I was driving, I drove into oncoming traffic, and we were headed into a head-on collision with a city bus. I then passed out and, therefore, could not control the car. I did think it was very weird because I actually did pass out. I missed the entire accident.

Tommy said the car veered back into the right-hand lane, where we should have been driving all along. The other cars were sitting still, waiting for the light to turn green. Soon after our truck had veered back into the right-hand lane, the cars suddenly moved. Our truck began to flip over. Timmy was ripped from his seat belt and was loose in the car as it began to flip over. Tommy stated it flipped over three times, but he quickly added it didn't hurt at all. "It felt like we were in a bubble," he said. Then the truck flipped onto the driver's side, knocked down several small trees, and came to a screeching halt as we finally hit a large tree.

It was then that my mind drifted off, and I began to think about when the fire department covered me up with a security blanket. Then they shattered all the windows, cut the roof off the SUV, and used the jaws of life to cut me out of the car. They removed me and the entire driver's seat from the car while I was still sitting in the seat and while the car was still flipped over. The nurse stated earlier that she thought I had a broken neck. I believe they cut me and the seat out of the car to ensure not to cause any additional damage. While I was being rolled away on the stretcher, I saw several family members and my bishop. "I'm going to be in a coma for five months or five weeks, or five days," I screamed out. "Please take care of the boys," I added as I was rolled off on the stretcher and into the ambulance.

After what seemed like about five minutes, the doors to the ambulance flew open, and the EMS grabbed the stretcher out and rushed into the emergency room, and began speaking to the nurse, "This is Leeta Bigbee, single, black female, age thirty-eight, was in a single car accident where the car flipped over an unknown about of times and crashed into a tree. There was an off-duty nurse on the scene and in the car assisting the patient before EMS arrived. According to the nurse, the patient was in and out of conscienceless while still in the car. Patient appears to be speaking and understanding okay. The patient stated she was not in any pain at this time," the EMT called out to the nurses as they lifted me from the stretcher onto a rolling hospital bed. "We are going to take care of you, Ms. Bigbee. Please, just remain calm," one nurse said. "Do you feel any pain?" she added.

"The pain I feel is coming from this brace you all put around my neck. It's very uncomfortable, and it hurts," I complained.

"We will remove the brace just as soon as we do your X-rays and MRIs," she answered.

"I'm not getting any X-rays or MRIs," I screamed. I said, I'm not in any pain, and there is nothing wrong with me. I am not willing to pay 20,000 dollars for a bunch of tests just so you all can tell me what I already know. I'm fine!" I ranted in frustration.

"Ms. Bigbee, you don't understand, you were in a very bad car accident, and you lost conscienceless, so it is imperative that we ensure there are no head injuries and/or internal bleeding," the nurse explained.

"I don't care!" I screamed. "I am not having any test done; I am fine," I said. "I know Satan is using you, and you are trying to stop me from transitioning! But I believe God, and I am not going to allow your demons to stop the plan that God has for my life!!" I screamed.

"Please, Ms. Bigbee, no one is using me. I'm just doing my job. And my job is to make sure that you are okay. Please let me help you," the nurse pleaded as she continued pushing the rolling bed. "You may try to silence me, Satan, but I'm going to speak with boldness to come against you and your demons. I rebuke you in Jesus' name, and you have no authority over me. I will not take any test," I said with authority. A few minutes later, we arrived at a room where there were glass doors and an armed sheriff's deputy standing outside of the room. The nurse leaned over and whispered something to the deputy. *I saw her whispering to him. They are both working for Satan,* I thought.

When my family members came into the room, I started to do a praise dance while I was in the hospital bed. "I'm so glad you all made it!" I began praising God, and I screamed out because I was excited that other family members were dead and that we were going to transition together.

"Of course, we would be here," Aunt Luv stated. "You were in a really bad accident, and you need to have some test run to make sure you are okay," she added.

"I know they probably told you I was in a bad accident, but I really wasn't. I'm already dead," I explained. "Aren't you dead too?" I asked.

"No, Lukes, we aren't dead. Please, they need to run some tests to make sure you are okay," she said with tears running down her face.

"Oh, I see now. You have allowed Satan to use you, too, Aunt Luv," I said as I shook my head in disappointment. "You and all these nurses are trying to stop me from transitioning into heaven. When I first saw you, I was so excited because I thought you, too, were dead and we were going to transition together. But now I see Satan is just using you to try to trick me," I stated.

"Please, Lukes, you are not dead, don't say that, please. The doctors and nurses really are here to help you," she said as tears continued to roll down her face.

"I rebuke you, Satan," I stated as I put my hands over my ears and refused to listen to any more lies from Satan. "Please, Lukes," Aunt Luv said as I stuck my fingers in my ears and started singing blah, blah, blah so that I could not hear anything else she tried to say. Aunt Luv turned and hurried out of the hospital room

Just a few short seconds later, several family members came into the room to convince me that I needed to allow them to run test on me. "I'm already dead, I calmly stated to each and every one of them. The nurse came into the room and tried to speak to me. I quickly put the covers over my head, stuck my fingers in my ears, and began telling her, "I'm not listening because I know you are trying to stop me from transiting. I rebuke you, Satan, and all of the demons you brought with you!" I chanted over and over. Within a few minutes, my room was silent. I took the covers off my head and looked around, and no one was in the room but me. "Ha! You lying, defeated foe! You can't trick me, Satan! Paul, you know, Jesus, you know, and you know me too!" I screamed so Satan and his demons could hear.

As I was looking out the glass walls and doors that surrounded my room, I saw Sharon walking toward the door. "Hello, honey, honey. How are you doing," Sharon said as she walked into the room.

"You already know," I said.

"Yes, I do," she added. "You have to allow them to run some test, honey. You really were in a really bad car accident, and I promise you I would not lie to you.

"Sharon, listen, I guarantee you I will be transitioning out of this room by 9:00 p.m. I was not in a car accident. We were killed back at the apartment yesterday. I was driving to go find someone to help us transition. We crashed directly into a bus and were not hurt at all. So, you see, we were already dead. So why would I let them run tests and leave you all with the bills. If I am not dead, then why am I not in any pain? You said I was in a really bad car accident. Then why didn't I feel it?" I ranted.

"You didn't feel it because you passed out before it happened," she added.

"You have to be careful, Sharon. If you allow Satan to use you, you won't be able to make it to heaven. I am trying to help you. Satan is very tricky and can have you believing stuff that isn't true," I added.

"That's exactly what I was trying to tell you," she said. "If you are dead, then why do you have an IV in your arm?" she asked.

"I'll tell you why! They are trying to stop me from transitioning!" I screamed as I reached down to rip out the IV. "Don't do that!" she screamed. "Please let them help you, Leeta. You aren't thinking clearly," she pleaded.

"Okay, I'll leave it in, but it is not going to stop me from transitioning to heaven. God knows my heart, and He knows I am sincere about serving Him and that they put that IV in my arm in an attempt to tie me to this earth, but they can't keep me from transitioning!" I ranted. While I was speaking, the nurse walked into the room. "We need to flush your IV, Ms. Bigbee. It is clogged up," she stated.

"Okay, go ahead; it's not going to make any difference," I said. Within seconds I was asleep. "Thank you so much, ma'am," Sharon said. "I don't know why she is talking like this. I don't understand it at all."

"Looks like maybe she is having a manic episode," said the nurse.

"Oh, no. I rebuked that in the name of Jesus! We are not claiming that at all," Sharon added.

"That's fine, ma'am. We are going to take her and run all the tests we need to run to ensure there is no damage to her brain, spine, or anything else. The doctor wrote an order to have her transferred to the psychiatric ward after the tests. However, we do not have any room in our psychiatric ward, so we will have to transfer her to University North Hospital," she stated.

"Do what you have to do, ma'am. We will be right here waiting for her," Sharon added.

What is that noise, I thought as I slowly opened my eyes. *Where am I, and what is going on?* I thought. I looked down, and I was in a hospital gown and in a bed which appeared to have been left in a lobby. As I quickly realized I was still in the hospital, I noticed I was no longer in a single room with glass windows and doors. I could see a bunch of people sitting in what looked like a lobby with a television and a person at a desk. I slowly got up off the bed, grabbed my gown, and held it closed so my blessing wouldn't be showing. I then walked over to the desk. "Excuse me," I said as I waited for the lady at the desk to look up.

"Yes," she said.

"What's going on," I asked.

"What do you mean," she questioned.

"Where am I, and why was I sleeping in a lobby?" I asked.

"All I know is you are a transfer from Methodist Hospital because they didn't have any room for you over there. You are currently in the psychiatric ward at University North Hospital. Your room number is 6, and it is directly behind you," she said as she nonchalantly flipped her hand toward my room.

"Why am I in the psych ward?" I asked with a puzzled look on my face.

"Ma'am, you will have to wait to see the doctor, and he isn't in on the weekend," she added.

"Weekend? You mean to tell me doctors here don't work on Fridays?" I questioned.

"You were asleep when you arrived last night via ambulance. Today is Saturday, January 7, 2006," she stated, "the doctor will be back in on Monday, January 9. You need to save all of your questions for the doctor," she stated as she looked back down at whatever she was working on.

"I would like to check myself out," I said.

She slowly raised her head and huffed loudly. "You can't check yourself out, ma'am; you are on a psychiatric hold," she stated.

"What! Why am I on a psych hold?" I asked.

"Once again, you need to save all your questions for the doctor. Your room number is 6; lunch is at noon; the telephone is over by the TV if you need it. Now please back away from the desk before I call security," she added.

I quickly went over to the phone to call Sis Denise. "Hey, it's me, Lil Sis. Will you bring my Bible to me?" I asked.

"Bring your Bible where?" she questioned.

"To Community North," I said.

"Why are you in the hospital?" she asked.

"I was in a car accident, but I wasn't hurt," I replied.

"You telling me the truth, Lil Sis?" she asked.

"Of course, I'm telling you the truth; why would I lie?" I questioned.

"Well, Bro Black stood up in church and requested prayer for you and the boys 'cause he said y'all had been in a car accident. But I thought he was just trying to put me in a trick bag. I didn't believe him," she added.

"Yeah, Tommy called him. He and Sis. Black came to the accident site along with Bishop. So, are you going to bring me the bible or not?" I asked.

"I can't go in your house. I don't have a key," she stated.

"The door isn't locked. I left it unlocked when I left," I added.

"Sis, I can't go in your house without you being there; someone could tell on me," she said.

"What? That is stupid. I just gave you permission to go in my house. No one else has any say so about that," I declared.

"Lil Sis, you should not be leaving your door open. Anyone could come in and steal your stuff. And you have some really nice stuff in your place," she said.

"I don't care anything about that stuff in that apartment. I was on a mission to take care of God's work. I left the door unlocked because I didn't think we were going back there," I said.

"What? Why didn't you think you would be going back?" she asked.

"It doesn't matter. I'll tell you about it later. So, are you going to get my Bible or not?" I questioned.

"Sis, I don't feel right going into your house while you aren't there. Can I just go buy you a Bible from the store?" she asked.

"Sure, make the print big enough so I can read it, okay?" I stated.

"Okay," she replied. Several people came to visit me, even my grandparents. When my sister Sharon came to visit, I told her that God had given me all kinds of abilities, and now I could play the piano. I sat down on the piano to play and quickly realized that I couldn't play at all. I'm not even sure why I thought I could play the piano. Seems like my thinking was so far off, and I couldn't seem to get it back on track.

Sharon asked if she could sit in when the doctor spoke to me, and I didn't mind. I think I believed I didn't have a choice but to let her sit in. "Doctor, we want you to keep her in the hospital," Sharon stated.

"I can't keep her in the hospital," he said. "There isn't anything wrong with her. She has been here several days, and she

THIS IS THE LORD'S DOING

is perfectly fine. We aren't even giving her any medication," he added. As he was talking, a fight broke out in the lobby where a patient attacked a nurse. The doctor, Sharon and I just looked toward the people with disbelief. "I need out of here now, Doc," I said. Just as I was speaking, Sharon yelled out, "Y'all need to keep her here and at least run the test so we can find out what is wrong with her!"

"Doctor, is my family able to keep me in the psych ward?" I asked.

"No, they can't do that," he replied. You are grown, and as long as you're mentally stable, you will be released. She may have bipolar, but that isn't a big deal. She can just take medication for that," he added.

"Oh, no, we are not claiming that! The devil is a liar!" Sharon screamed.

"Ma'am, you asked me to find out what is wrong with her and her symptoms suggest she is bipolar," he added as he shrugged his shoulders.

"Just let me know when she will be getting out, so I can pick her up," Sharon stated in a frustrated voice.

"I will be discharging her tomorrow," he said.

I ended up staying in the psych ward for a total of six days before I was released to go home.

Thinking back, Timmy was only eight years old when the accident occurred and, of course, too small to brace himself in the car as it flipped over. Therefore, we know it was nothing but the grace of God that protected him. Sister Denise later told me that the night before the accident, God woke her up and told her to pray away the death angel from my family. She also added that she stayed up for about five hours praying that night. Needless to say, we all walked away without a scratch.

As I refocused and continued to listen as Tommy testified about the accident, I sat in my seat, and I began to think about the goodness of Jesus and all that He had done for me during that terrible test. When I thought about just how far my mind had gone and how I had literally lost touch with all reality, I searched for sanity and couldn't find it, but God literally regulated my mind. I began to jump and run around the church, dancing, giving God the best praise I could give. While I was dancing and praising God, Tommy decided to join in, and we both gave God the best holy dance we could. We danced before the Lord with all our might, just like David did! Satan had tried to kill us, but God didn't allow it.

Time had passed, and it was now about a month after the accident, and I decided I needed another car because I knew, eventually, I had to return to work. Because of the mental breakdown I had experienced and due to the severe mind battles, I was on a ton of psychological medications. Therefore, I had started to experience a lot of side effects from the mediations, and the anxiety had become overwhelming. So, purchasing a car and driving was a huge battle in itself. I wanted to get the car, but I was afraid of driving after the accident. Fear had become one of the most devastating mind battles I had ever faced. I spent days thinking about the accident and visualizing the accident in my head. I frequently thought, *we almost lost our lives, and I almost killed my children.* The fear of driving and even getting back into a car was intense and often caused panic attacks and horrible anxiety.

I didn't understand why I was going through fear, panic, anxiety, and mind battles. I had never gone through this type of mind battle before. I wanted and needed a car, but fear made it, so I didn't want to drive the car. I wanted to leave the house, but as soon as I got out of the house, anxiety made it, so I wanted to go back home. I stayed awake all hours of the night with ruminating thoughts about all the things that had already and that could go wrong in my life.

I spent many days in the house, sitting in my room just thinking. I didn't know what to do about my situation. I had to encourage myself daily to push past the uncomfortable and frightening situations I feared the most. When I felt like screaming and/or pacing around the room because some strange feeling had come over me, I had to deny myself, rebuke the restless spirits, and not allow it to take over or control my mind. I had to go through the same process of rebuking spirits, praying, refocusing, and encouraging myself daily. It became physically, mentally, and spiritually exhausting. There came a time when I felt like I could no longer take things one day at a time; I had to take it one second or one minute at a time in order to get past being overwhelmed with fear, panic, and anxiety.

I placed a call to Elder Roads, knowing he had a friend that worked at a car dealership. Once getting the contact information for the dealership, I contacted the dealership to schedule an appointment and to ask if I could be picked up so that I could purchase another car. Leading up to the day of the appointment, I became overwhelmed with fear and worry. Therefore, on the day of the appointment, I called the car dealership to cancel the appointment. I knew I needed a car, but I just couldn't force myself to actually drive again. I was afraid of getting behind the wheel, thinking the worst about the outcome if I drove.

I attempted to distract myself with the fact that the beds that I had purchased for the boys were delivered today; although the boys were still living with Sharon, I was hopeful they would be home soon. I needed help assembling the beds, so I called Brother Ron. "Hey. Praise the Lord, Ron, how are you?" I asked.

"I'm good. What about you?" he replied.

"I'm good," I said. "Ummm, is there any way you could come over today to help me put the boys' beds together?"

"Sure," he said, "give me about an hour."

"Thanks, I'll be here," I replied.

After about an hour had passed, Ron showed up as promised. "Hey, Sis, what's up? You okay?" he asked.

"I'm good, just feeling a little down and anxious about going back to work and getting another car," I answered.

"Sis, you are going to be just fine," he said. "God protected you from that accident, and you will be back out driving and going to work in no time," he encouraged.

"I have an appointment today to go to the dealership to purchase a car, but I don't feel like I can do it. I want to call and cancel the appointment because I feel so overwhelmed about driving, but I'm also feeling stressed about canceling the appointment," I stated in frustration.

"Do you just want to stay home and not go to the dealership, or would you like to try to go today?" he asked.

"I don't want to go," I said as I began to pace the floors anxiously.

"Just call them and tell them you changed your mind," he said calmly.

My heart felt as if it was going to jump out of my chest as I walked over and picked up the phone to dial the number. "Hello..." I said as I was quickly interrupted by a recording.

"You have reached the voicemail of—" the message stated before I hung up the phone. "Voicemail," I said as I hung up the phone, looking and feeling extremely disappointed. "I don't want Brother Roads to get upset with me; because he set this deal up for me, and I don't want to mess it up, so I will just go to the appointment," I rambled. While I was still talking, the phone rang. It was the car salesman on the phone, "Ms. Bigbee?" he questioned.

"Yes," I responded.

"I've arrived; I'm parked right outside in front of your apartment," he stated.

"Okay, I'll be right out," I said.

"Who is that?" Ron asked.

"It's the guy from the car dealership. He's outside waiting," I said.

"Okay, then, there's no turning back now. I'll ride with you if you want me to," Ron added.

"That would be great. It would calm me down a bit. Thank you so much, Ron," I stated as I grabbed my things and headed towards the door. We both walked out of the apartment and headed to the car. The anxiety had me feeling like my skin was crawling. I rode most of the way to the dealership with my eyes closed because my stomach was in knots with fear, thinking we may crash and thinking about how am I going to drive back home if I got a 'Well, how do you like this car, Ms. Bigbee?'" the salesman asked.

"I was just thinking that this is a really nice car. What type of car is it?" I replied.

"Well, it's a 2004 Toyota Corolla. I drove it to pick you up because I felt this might be a good fit for you. If you like it, once we arrive at the dealership, I can get a copy of your driver's license, and you can take it for a spin. How's that sound?" He asked.

"Uhhhhmmmmm, it sounds kind of scary. Is there any way my friend Ron can take it for a test drive and I just ride with him?" I asked nervously.

"Yeah, I can drive it for her if that is okay," Ron added.

"Sure, if that's the way you want to do it, that would be just fine with me," the salesman replied.

Once we arrived, we went inside for the salesman to get a copy of Ron's license. Ron drove me around in the car for maybe five minutes. "Hey, can you turn around and let's go back to the dealership," I asked Ron.

"Okay, sure, you wanna drive the way back? If so, we don't have to go all the way back to the dealership; I can just pull over and switch seats with you," he stated.

"Nope, I'm done. I don't want to drive it, and I don't want to ride anymore either," I stated.

"Huh? You done, Sis? Okay, I can turn around and go back," he added.

"Thank you so much," I said. "I know I'm probably getting on your nerves, but I just feel so anxious, and I'm ready to just get it over with," I said.

"No, Sis, I understand. If you don't want to get the car, that's fine. You need to feel comfortable in the decision you make," he added.

"Oh, no, I'm going to get the car," I answered. "I just don't want to drive it right now. So, would you be willing to drive the car home once I buy it?" I questioned.

"Sure, Sis, I can do that," he answered. Ron did exactly as he agreed. Once we returned to my place, Ron parked the car; we said our goodbyes and I went inside.

Not even realizing that it, but two months had passed since I purchased the car, and I have never driven it. The car was still parked in the exact place Ron left it two months ago. *This is it*. I thought to myself. *I have to get up enough courage to drive this car, or I will be afraid forever.* I grabbed the keys and headed to the car. I was able to drive the car around the corner and back, but I was shaking with fear and anxiety. Therefore, I drove around the corner and went right back home and parked the car. The car sat for several more days.

Today is a new day, I told myself. I decided that if I had some support to encourage me, then I would feel less anxious about driving. "Hey, Sister Denise, what are you doing?" I said as I called her on the phone.

"Nothing much; I just got off from work," she replied. "Why, what are you doing?"

"Well, I got another car, and I test-drove it a little bit. But I was thinking, why don't you come over and see it?" I suggested.

"I will do just that. What kind did you get?" she asked.

"A Toyota Corolla," I answered, "It is a 2004."

"Look at Jesus. No other person can get a car with no job and no money down. I prayed today, and I asked Godspeed to be with you if it was His will that you get a new car, and He did just that," she said.

"What does that mean, Godspeed?" I questioned.

"It means God's favor and/or His blessings be with you," she answered. "And that is just what God did. Look at Jesus. I'll be right over," she said with excitement.

When Sister Denise came over, she walked right over to my car. She walked completely around the car and even stopped to take a look inside before knocking on my door, looking at the car, and she walked all around it before she came inside. "That is a beautiful car God has blessed you with, Lil Sis. He is so awesome," she said as she raised both hands in the air to give God praise.

"Yes, He is," I said.

"What's wrong with you?" she asked.

"Nothing," I said.

"Then why do you look so sad? Have you been quoting your Scriptures today?" she questioned.

"Yes," I said.

"You need to quote them every day, all day long until you feel that heavy feeling lift up off of you. Don't allow the enemy to take your mind, Sis. You are in spiritual warfare. You have to come out of this thing, Lil Sis. You can't mess around and get lost in the wilderness dealing with this thing. You just got a brand-new car, you have a beautiful home, your children need you, you are loved, Sis, and people are waiting for you to get your life back. What are you waiting for? You have to fight the good fight of faith and don't give up. Come on, start quoting your Scriptures. Start with 2 Timothy 1:7, 'God hath not give us the spirit of fear but of power, love, and a sound mind.' I mumbled along with her as she quoted the scripture. Come on, Sis, you gotta say it like you believe this thing. Go ahead and say Isaiah 41:10. I'll start it off for you, 'fear thou not for I am with thee...' Go ahead, start quoting it," she instructed.

"Fear thou not, for I am with thee, be not dismayed; for I am thy God: I will strengthen thee; yea, I will help thee; yea, I will uphold thee with the right hand of my righteousness. "God did not give Leeta the spirit of fear but of power, love, and a sound mind," I said with a weak voice.

"Keep saying it over and over again until you feel it in your soul," she said with authority. I began repeating the Scriptures until that anxious and heavy feeling lifted up off of me. I didn't know how, but Sister Denise could always tell when I was feeling anxiety, depressed, and/or perplexed in my mind. I thank God for her because she was always there for me spiritually. She kept me loaded with the Word of God and helped me to endure hardness as a good soldier. She would always tell me, "I know the formula works because I used it for myself."

"Sis Denise, would you be willing to ride around with me in the car so that I could feel more comfortable driving?" I asked.

"Oh yes, Lil Sis, I was hoping you would take me for a ride in your new car God blessed you with," she answered as she smiled from ear to ear. I drove Sis. Denise was around in the car until I no longer felt anxious about driving. I was beginning to feel like my old self again. After about thirty minutes of driving, we finally pulled up to my apartment.

"Lil Sis. You really drove that car like you were used to it. You did a great job," she said as we walked into the apartment. "I'm going to go inside with you so I can pray for you and anoint and pray over your apartment," she said. "I know you haven't been sleeping well, and I see you have lost more weight. We are going to rebuke that lying defeated foe and let him know his assignment has just been canceled, and you are a victor.

She grabbed her oil and began to put a little above all the doors and windows in my home. She also placed some on my forehead and began to pray. "Satan, you take your hands off my Lil Sis! You have no authority here. God is in control, and I rebuke you, and your assignment has just been canceled. You have no dominion here, and you cannot operate in the presence of God and His children. You are a liar and the father of lies, and I command you to leave this place and never to return again. In Jesus' name, Amen and Amen," she prayed.

Before, she prayed I had not been sleeping very well, and I had not been eating very much either. My weight had dropped from 142 pounds to 103 pounds, and food was just not appealing to me at the time, and I rarely ever felt hungry or even wanted to eat. "Lil Sis, do you remember the time when we went to the grocery store, and nothing sounded or looked good to eat? I kept pointing out food to cook, and you didn't want to eat anything," she added.

"I do remember that time," I answered. "I'm not sure if I was feeling depressed or what I was feeling. But you were adamant that it was a spirit, and you were determined to cancel Satan's assignment and get that spirit off of me, away from me or whatever the case was," I said.

"That's right, and I also remember not only did you not want to eat, but you didn't even want to grocery shop. So, from now on, before you eat, put a little bit of blessed oil on your tongue and rub some on your stomach before you eat, and once you do, pray and ask God to help you to eat your food," she said as she handed me a small bottle of oil. "Every day before you leave the house, you should anoint yourself from head to toe with oil. You needed to be covered under the blood. The oil is symbolic, and it has been prayed over, and God will honor your sacrifice and your faith to believe that the oil will heal and deliver you," she added.

As Sister Denise walked through the entire apartment praying, she touched every door post and window. "I plead the blood of Jesus. I plead the blood of Jesus to cover this place and to watch over and protect my Lil Sis. Lord, please allow your angels to encamp around this apartment so that no evil shall ever come near this place again. Oh, God, rebuke the devourer for her sake. You said you have prayed for us that our faith fails not. Oh, God, allow her faith to soar so that you will be able to operate on her behalf. Do miracles, signs, and wonders in the place and in her life God. Show yourself strong, oh, God, and let the enemy know that you have never lost a battle and that this battle belongs to you. Help her to forever give your name the glory, the honor, and the praise. Help her to walk with boldness against the enemy that desires to sift her as wheat. Allow her to run towards the giants in her life so that she may have confidence to know that you have already defeated them," She prayed as she walked all around the apartment. "Hey, Lil Sis, why are you looking so down? Hold your head up and begin to quote your scriptures again. God is moving in this place, and Satan doesn't like it. He will try to perplex you and try to make you feel depressed, but he is a liar. Start quoting your Scriptures with some authority right now. You have to learn to take authority over this situation," she demanded.

"Fear thou not..." I began as I started quoting the scriptures. My mind kept wandering off, and I struggled to stay focused. I began to think, *If anyone walked by my door or in my apartment building, they would think we were crazy. With her praying and me quoting Scriptures and pointing and waving our hands, and praising God, I'm sure we sounded like a couple of lunatics in there.*

As I refocused, I was able to block the voice of Satan out of my mind. I continued to quote my scriptures and even joined in on the prayer. Finally, the heavy/perplexed feeling passed, and I felt so much lighter physically and emotionally. When I started to feel that heaviness and/or depressed, the feeling would be so strong that it didn't feel like it would ever leave.

"Sis, pull out your Bible and just began to read the Word of God," she said. "Just open and start reading; it doesn't matter which scripture," she added.

As I was reading from my Bible, I screamed out, "Oh, my head is hurting!" My head began to hurt so badly that I felt as if I was forced to close my eyes and couldn't continue with the Scriptures. "It's a distraction from the enemy, Lil Sis. There isn't anything wrong with your head," She yelled out. Rebuke that lying spirit that is trying to give you lying symptoms of a headache," she said as she walked over and began to pray and rebuke the enemy yet again. As Sister Denise prayed for me, I could feel the headache leaving, so I continued to read the Bible. "Who are you going to agree with, Satan or God? Satan is a liar and the father of all lies!" she yelled with a loud voice.

"I chose to believe God and what He says about me," I replied. "I am healed; I am set free. Thank you, Lord, for my healing. Whom the Son sets free is free indeed!" I yelled out. "Hey, Sister Denise, what is the scripture about the Lord having healing in his wings?" I asked.

"It's Malachi 4:2, 'But unto you that fear my name shall the Sun of righteousness arise with healing in his wings; and ye shall go forth, and grow up as calves of the stall.' That's a good one, Sis. You need to add that scripture to your scriptures that you quote every day," she stated.

"Okay, Lil Sis, I'm about to leave. God has already done the work; all you have to do is believe Him. This house is clean, and the spirit of the Lord is in this place. Walk in victory, Lil Sis." She said as she walked toward the door to leave. "Thank you for everything, Sis," I said as we hugged and said our goodbyes. I closed the door and walked to my room so that I could go to bed.

After laying in the bed for a while, I still could not fall asleep, and I felt very restless. Even though Sister Denise prayed over my bed, I still had a hard time falling asleep. I grabbed my CD player and began to listen to some relaxation songs. Seems like I was in a cycle of dosing off for approximately ten to fifteen minutes and then waking back up again. When I was awake, I had a difficult time determining when and if I was actually asleep. I didn't feel as if I rested during the few minutes I slept.

I didn't feel the anxiety feeling anymore, and I was grateful for that. However, I couldn't rest. I had ruminating thoughts, and I felt extremely tense and restless. I kept tossing over and over in the bed, trying to find a comfortable position. I began to remind myself of something that I heard in church. "The good part about going through a situation is that if we are going through, we are still moving, and that meant eventually we were going to come out on the other side of it." Several times I drifted off for a few minutes at a time throughout the night. Every time I woke up, I checked to make sure my music was still playing. After I checked the music, I began to quote scriptures in order to calm my mind. I refused to complain but decided to use the awake time to pray and just simply talk to God.

While lying in the bed, it seemed like the mattress was as hard as a brick, and I couldn't get comfortable. I frequently got out of bed and placed a blanket on the floor, and I laid on top of the blanket. "Lord, this is my threshing floor, and I am here to be cleansed of any and everything that is not like you. Help me to hear your voice clearly. Help me to apply your word to my situation. Help me to run towards the things that I fear or that seem to be too big for me to handle. Allow me to slay the giants in my life just as David did. Bind fear in my life and lose spiritual boldness. Help me to have the confidence in you that David had. Show me your will and help me to accept whatever you allow. I want to be pleasing to you, Lord, and I never want to let you down again. Help us to be so close to you that I know your voice no matter how loud everything else in my life seems to be. Help me to trust you and to believe what you said about me..." I prayed as I drifted off to sleep.

Within the next few weeks, Sharon brought Tommy and Timmy over more often to visit. I felt so grateful that God was answering my prayers. I was feeling physically better, but I still hadn't returned to work yet. I felt I was ready to return to work, but I had not been released from the doctor to drive, and my employer would not allow me to drive or park my car in the parking lot. I didn't have a ride to work, so I just waited for the doctor's release. A few more weeks passed, and I began having seizures again. I felt extremely defeated and confused. *Why would you allow me to continue to go through this, God?* I thought. The seizures became so bad that my doctor had concerns about me living on my own and wrote a note informing the apartment complex I could no longer live alone. The note actually came as a blessing because I wasn't back to work, and I didn't have the money to pay the rent.

The apartment was technically the third place I had lost since I first fell out in church back in 2004. The mind can play tricks on you and have you thinking God doesn't care about your situation. However, I continued to remind myself, "I know, God, I'm not like Job. I am grateful that you spared my children, and I know all of this will work out for my good because I love you, and I am called according to your purpose."

Once the doctor wrote the note to allow me out of my lease, I tried to stay with several family members and was told no. I didn't blame them for saying no because I had some erratic behavior in the past, and I know they didn't want to or couldn't deal with me during that time. I wasn't upset, but I was extremely hurt. I felt like since I had helped so many family members, they should help me. I prayed often about my attitude. I could not expect people to act like I would act if they needed help. The situation was grim, and even though the family would say things like, "You can ask for anything because we are family," didn't mean that they would give me whatever I asked for. The truth of the matter was that no one owed me anything, and I didn't help them out in the past so that I could be paid back one day. But I often wished that's what it meant.

Since the onset of the mind battles, my mom and I didn't seem to get along. But she's my mom, and even though I felt like my mother didn't care for me right now, I reached out to her anyway. "Hi mom, uuhhhmmm, may I stay with you a couple of weeks or so until I am able to return to work and get my own place?" I asked.

"Yeah, that should be fine, I spoke with mama, and she said you couldn't stay with her, so I figured you would be calling. What are you going to do with all your stuff?" she asked.

"Why didn't she call me instead of telling you?" I questioned. "She was just going to leave me hanging too? Wow, that's deep," I said as I processed the love from my family. "I have a little bit of money, and I get a couple of hundred in child support, so I plan to get a storage unit for my furniture. I plan to put my clothes over at Aunt Ruthie's house and then just bring a few items to your house. If that's okay," I replied.

"Yeah, that's fine, but you are going to have to pay me 300 dollars to stay, and you have to go half on groceries too. Your brother is here, so you will have to stay in the family room, but you can sleep on the love seat," she added.

"I already pay Sharon 300 dollars for the boys to stay with her, and then I have to pay 125 dollars for the storage unit for my furniture. I also have to pay 300 dollars for the boys to go to before and after care. I'm never going to be able to save up enough money to move out," I ranted.

My mom didn't say a word but sat on the phone in silence. I finally just said, "Okay." It's not like I had other options. All

I could say was, "kay." I didn't have anywhere else to go, and I needed a place to stay. I can't explain the isolation and loneliness I felt at that very moment. I was in a situation where I needed help, and clearly, no one wanted to help. *My mom said she would help, but If you pay someone for something, is that help, or are that services provided? I thought.*

In February 2006, which was about two weeks after the conversation with my mom and a little over a month after the accident, I moved into my mom's house. The doctor released me to return to work the very next month. I lived with my mom until September of the same year before I was able to buy another house. During the time I lived with my mom, I was taking several different prescriptions for anxiety and depression. I was unaware that many of the symptoms that I was experiencing were due to the side effects of the prescriptions.

Because of the prescribed medications, I started to experience severe restlessness, panic attacks, body aches, headaches, bouts of anxiety, and even more depression. I was extremely overwhelmed and discouraged. I often thought about which sicknesses and/or diseases could cause the symptoms that I was having. I began to speak over myself and declare which diseases and sicknesses I had. I began self-diagnosing myself, all while speaking damnation over my life. My mother would try to encourage me, and she prayed for me daily. It was like a never-ending battle with fighting the thoughts in my head.

Over time, I began to go back to church and therapy. I took therapy seriously. When the phycologist gave me tools and coping skills to help with what I was going through, I did what I was instructed. At the church I was attending at the time, people would testify about how they didn't have to lay on a couch and talk to a therapist because they could talk directly to God. It would be statements like that which had me questioning my salvation and if I truly trusted God.

Just because a person believes and trusts God doesn't mean they don't need therapy. Going to therapy has nothing to do with your faith in God. What it could mean and does mean for me was that I needed clarity in some areas of my life, I needed help working through complex emotions, I had experienced some traumatic events that I needed to work through, and I needed coping skills to overcome challenging and/or negative thinking patterns, and I also needed to focus on personal growth and on my relationship with God and his will for my life. A mind battle is exactly what it sounds like. It is a difficult fight between opposing enemies, which could be good vs. evil, right vs. wrong, truth vs. fiction, etc., going on in the mind. The only way to get victory over a mind battle is for God to deliver a person and declare the victory over it. If God doesn't deliver a person from a mind battle, then they won't be delivered no matter how much they pray. It is what it is until God says it isn't.

CHAPTER 9

Remember Your History

June 2015

Normally, when I call my mom, she answers the phone by saying hello, and the first thing I say is, "How goes the battle?" Her response is always the same: "The battle goes on." I have used her reply to remind myself that even during seemingly peaceful times, the battle still goes on, and the enemy is still the enemy. Matthew 13:25 says, "But while men slept, the enemy came and sowed tares among the wheat, and went his way." This scripture is a reminder to all that the enemy is going to be the enemy no matter what. The enemy can and will attack while we are physically sleeping and/or spiritually sleeping. We must be one guard at all times. The battle still goes on whether or not we feel like fighting or not. If you know your enemie's strengths and weaknesses and you have defeated the enemy before, then you go back to doing whatever it was that won you the victory in past battles. I know that to be true now, but at the time, I had forgotten the tricks and tactics of the enemy, and there were times I had even forgotten there was a battle.

All of a sudden, I started having problems sleeping again. When I was unable to sleep, I became very fearful. Because going without sleep for several days is what led to me passing out in church back in 2004. To me, not being able to sleep meant the start of a bigger problem. Back in 2004, I was unable to sleep and had an extraordinary amount of energy, so I stayed awake for about eight days straight. I was told by the doctor(s) that when I fell out in church that particular Sunday morning, my brain was forcing my body to shut down. I didn't intentionally do anything to force my body to shut down, and I wasn't intentionally trying to stay awake. During that time, I just wasn't sleepy or tired at all. The last few days had begun to feel exactly like that time, and I was afraid, and I began to worry. When I ended up in the hospital in 2004, of course, I was told I was stressed and depressed about the death of my father, and my body chose to process it by staying awake. I didn't understand that answer and really didn't have many options but to just trust that what the doctors told me was true.

When I went several days without sleeping in 2006, I was diagnosed with bipolar and was told that even in 2004, when I couldn't sleep, those were more than likely manic episodes. I was confused because I was thirty-six in 2004, and bipolar is supposed to start when someone is in their late teens and early twenties. In 2006 when I wrecked the truck, I didn't feel anxious or afraid at all. During the episodes, it felt more like euphoric than anything. I felt as if I could do anything I wanted. I felt confident, intelligent, and fearless. However, I also felt confused. I felt as if I didn't know what was right or wrong, so I would just pick something to do and decide to stick with it.

Which lead me to crashing the car and a bunch of other destructive behaviors.

When I would wake up in the mornings, I rarely ever got dressed or left the house. I would stay in the bed and think about different scenarios about what would happen if I didn't fall asleep and/or what if I became manic and began to have unclear thoughts. The stress of the "what ifs" had me more anxious and afraid than I was during any previous manic episode. During a manic episode, I wasn't thinking clearly, and my behavior was very unusual. I spent much of my time thinking about how bad things were the last time I couldn't sleep, and that made me feel extremely overwhelmed and anxious.

Not only was I not sleeping, but I felt very distant from reality and people. I didn't want to leave the house, and I didn't want to be around anyone. I didn't want to talk to anyone on the phone, but I was hurt when people didn't call or want to talk to me. I'd been missing a lot of work because I couldn't focus, and I didn't want to make any mistakes at work for fear of being written up or fired. When I was off work, I didn't feel comfortable about being off work, but instead, I stressed about it frequently, thinking I might be fired. Because even though I had been with the same employer for almost twenty-six years, they had tried to fire me the last time I was in the hospital. Therefore, I believed they were always thinking of a way to fire me while I was off work due to sickness, whether it be mental or physical. On the days I did go to work, I wasn't productive because I was struggling with distractibility, lack of focus, insomnia, and fatigue. I have had several surgeries in my lifetime, and now it felt like my body was failing.

For days on end, depression, heaviness, and feelings of hopelessness were my only companions. I tried to pinpoint exactly when and why I started feeling depressed and heavy. But I couldn't figure it out, and the more I tried, the more depressed I became. I had been going back and forth to a psychiatrist and psychologist for a few years, attempting to get a handle on the depression symptoms and, recently on the diagnosis of bipolar disorder. I didn't understand what was happening because all of the mental problems I was having had just started out of the blue. Also, none of the medications that were prescribed now and in the previous years didn't work. I couldn't grasp what was going on in my life, and quite frankly, I was tired of suffering through it. "God, please allow me to die. I'm serving you, doing all I know to do to live a holy life; therefore, I am ready to die. There is nothing left for me here but suffering," I cried out to God daily, asking Him to please take my life. "I would be happier if I just died and was with you," I added. I regularly thought about the Scripture that says (and I'm paraphrasing) that to be absent from the body is to be present with the Lord. When I thought about how great it must be to literally be present with the Lord in heavenly places, I would become overwhelmingly excited. I could spend hours just thinking about how blissful heaven must be.

During one of my doctor visits, I continued to complain about not sleeping, and the doctor wanted to put me on Seroquel. "Like I said before, Doctor, I'm not going to take a medication that makes me gain weight and doesn't actually control the symptoms," I said.

"Ms. Bigbee, your symptoms are so bad that I'm afraid you are going to lose your job if you don't take this medication," she insisted. I had tried probably twenty-five different depression/ bipolar medications before, including Seroquel, and none of them took away the symptoms of depression or mania. "Seroquel is your only hope," she insisted.

"Alright, just called it in," I said reluctantly.

I began taking the Seroquel around mid-March or early April, I guess, and by October, I gained almost forty-one pounds. I went from 127 pounds to 168 pounds in approximately seven months, and the medication still wasn't working. None of the bipolar or depression symptoms were better. According to the doctor, lack of sleep was a bipolar symptom. I believe I felt depressed and/or emotionally low because I was not sleeping. I was unable to focus at work because I was tired from not sleeping. It was a vicious cycle that not one of the medications prescribed to me was ever able to control.

I was frustrated and discouraged, which led me to feel as if life just didn't seem worth living anymore. I wasn't attending church often because I had outgrown all of my clothes, and I couldn't afford new ones because I was off work off and on. Around that same time, I felt even more depressed because none of the symptoms I was being treated for were improving.

I contacted the psychiatrist in the middle of the night and left a voice. "This is Leeta Bigbee, I have been awake for three full days, and I am anxious and frustrated. You wanted me on this stupid medication, I've gained a ton of weight, and it still isn't helping," I ranted. I probably left at least a five-minute message about how urgent it was for the doctor to return my call. The next morning the doctor called back. "Hello," I stated as I looked at the caller ID, knowing upfront it was Dr. Paula.

"Ms. Bigbee, hello, this is Dr. Paula, and I received your message from last night, she stated. I didn't say anything at all. "Hello, Ms. Bigbee, are you there?" she asked.

"Yes, I'm here," I begrudgingly responded.

"Well, since the medication isn't working, I believe it would be best that you enter into an intensive outpatient (IOP) hospital program," she said.

"I don't understand why I have to go back into the hospital? The last time I was in the hospital, they weren't even giving me mental health medications, and you already have me on medications. So, why would I go back?" I asked as I became extremely frustrated.

"No, Ms. Bigbee, I'm not suggesting you go back into the hospital. The IOP is a program where you would go to the hospital every day to attend a therapy program that lasts from 9 a.m. to 2:30 p.m. During your time at the hospital, they have group sessions, counseling, art, music, and many other classes to help patients with mental health issues. There isn't a set time frame when you would complete the program. The program is completed once you receive the help you need," she explained. I thought to myself, *If I attended the program, I would be off work again without being paid for the entire time I'd be in the program.*

I was desperate and felt that my problems were getting the best of me, so I agreed to attend the IOP program. "Sure, I'll go, and hopefully, it will help," I added sarcastically. The program lasted approximately twelve weeks. During the time I was off work, my employer contacted me and actually loaned me some sick leave, so I didn't have to go without pay. Every time that I accrue sick leave, it would go directly to my employers for repayment. When my employer loaned me leave, it gave me hope that I would beat this, knowing that they believed I would return to work to repay the leave.

June 2016

Not much had changed in my life over the past year. I was still depressed, still missing work, and was now weighing 199 pounds. I went from a size 6 to a size 16 in approximately twelve months. I maintained my weight at 199 pounds because, against doctor's orders, I stopped taking the medication. I had nearly cut off all my family and friends because I didn't want to hear how much weight I had gained. I didn't go to church because all of my clothes were too small. I didn't know how much paid time off my employer would loan me, and that made me anxious.

The first thing I did when I woke up this morning was contact Sister Sun. "Sis Sun?" I said when she answered the phone.

"Yes, this is she," she replied.

"Hello, this is Sis Leeta. I was calling to see if you could come over to my house. I need your help," I said.

"Yes, honey, of course, I can come over and do my best to help you. How about tomorrow after I get off work? Will that work for you?" she asked.

"Tomorrow will be great. Thank you so much, Sis," I said.

"You are very welcome, and Lord willing, I will see you tomorrow," she replied.

Later on, that day, I was sitting on the bed, and I began to think, *What if I'm in another spiritual test and/or a spiritual battle? Could that be the reason all of the mediation that is used to treat bipolar and bipolar depression isn't working for me? What if I really don't have bipolar and Satan is back at his same old tricks, playing mind games and giving me symptoms to keep me distracted from the Word of God and all that I should be doing in the kingdom?* I continued to think about every scenario that had taken place in the last couple of years and all of the medications that the doctors have had me try with no success. *I believe this is a spiritual battle. It is happening exactly like before, with symptoms out of the blue with no positive results from the test and from any of the prescribed medications.*

Satan doesn't use new tactics, and the Bible talks about familiar spirits. I recall to my mind a time while working at the Equal Employment Opportunity Commission (EEOC) as an investigator. While conducting discrimination investigations, I, along with other investigators, had instances where we had to conduct an onsite investigation where we had to physically go to an individual's place of employment to interview them and/or witnesses that may have pertinent information pertaining to the discrimination charge that was being investigated. When I started working there, the standard operating procedure was that all new investigators would be assigned a mentor. The mentor normally accompanies the new investigators on their onsite investigations. During the onsites, the mentor is there to provide help in the form of guidance, note taking, preparing interview question(s), and other duties. My mentor was Bob, and he would normally like to leave for onsite early in the morning, around 6:00 a.m. When Bob went with me on an onsite, I normally would have to leave home before the boys left for school. Therefore, I would call them before they left the house to pray for and with them as they went about their day.

During our drive to one onsite, after I hung up the telephone from praying, Bob said, "Well, I allow St. Christopher to pray for me." I hadn't asked, but since he mentioned it, I replied, "Well, my Bible tells me I can go to the throne boldly and pray on my own behalf." After that reply, Bob didn't say another word about prayer.

Several weeks went by after Bob had accompanied me on my onsite. "Hey, Leeta," Bob said, "would you go with me to one of my onsites to a hospital?" he asked. "I have been assigned a charge where the charging party (CP) is a nurse, and she filed a charge alleging she was discriminated against based on her disability. Which is cancer; she has a brain tumor. To be honest, I need to hurry up and conduct the onsite because the doctors aren't expecting CP to live much longer," he added. I had never accompanied Bob on one of his onsites. He had always come along on one of mine to help me. *So,* I thought, *That's somewhat of an odd request. However, he had previously helped me on several onsites, so I didn't mind.* Therefore, I answered, "Sure, why not?

The day had finally arrived when it was time for me to go with Bob on his onsite. We started out driving to the hospital at about 6:00 a.m. in the morning. About an hour later, I called the boys while driving so that we could all pray together before they left the house for school. The hospital was about two and a half hours from our job, so we had a little bit of a trip ahead of us. The GPS began to say "rerouting" when we were very close to the end of our destination. "Rerouting... rerouting... rerouting," the GPS voice cried out every time we drove a few hundred feet or so. "I think I am going to turn around, Leeta," Bob said. "I know we didn't see the hospital, but it has to be around here somewhere," he insisted. After about five or ten more minutes of driving, we saw a very old-looking building located off in the distance on top of a hill. "Do you think that is it," Bob asked.

"I sure hope not," I replied. "It looks creepy," I added.

"I'm going to drive over to the building just to see if it is the hospital and if not, at least we can go inside and ask for directions," he said. As we drove closer to the building, we could see that it looked very isolated, dark, and gloomy. "This looks like the Bates Motel," I said as I sat up forward in my seat so that I could get a better look. "Yes, it does look pretty creepy," he added, "however, I see a sign, and this is the hospital," he said.

As we drove closer to the building, I could see the sign on the building. It read Children of the Corn Psychiatric Hospital. "Bob, are we at a psychiatric hospital?" I asked.

"Yes, I told you, CP was a nurse," he answered nonchalantly.

"Yes, you did say she was a nurse and that we were going to a hospital, but you didn't mention it was a psychiatric hospital," I said.

"Oh, I thought I told you that," he said with a little smirk. "It's too late now we are here, so we might as well go get this over with," he said as he pulled into the parking space and turned off the car. As we walked up to the door of the building, there were signs explaining that the building was a secure facility and you had to be buzzed in to the building and check in with the receptionist. "Okay, here goes nothing," Bob said as he reached over to ring the buzzer.

"May I help you?" a lady's voice spoke out.

"Yes, I am Investigator Bob Rollins, and I am with the Equal Employment Opportunity Commission, and I am here to conduct an onsite investigation. My contact person that I am supposed to meet with is Michael Johnson," he continued.

"Pull on the door to open it and come inside. Once inside, go through the double doors, make a right turn once inside the double doors and keep walking until you see the desk behind the security glass," she instructed.

"Okay, thank you," Bob said as he pulled the door open, and we walked inside. "Hello, I'm Bob Rollins here to see Michael Johnson," Bob stated as he walked up to a security desk and spoke through a circle of small holes that were in a clear security glass window where the receptionist sat. I stayed a few feet behind Bob as he continued to check in.

While we waited for Mr. Johnson, I looked around, and there were patients walking around and sitting in the waiting area where we were standing. There was a patient that kept getting really close to me and looking me directly in my face. I must admit, I was somewhat afraid. I had been in the psychiatric ward inside of a hospital before, but never in a hospital where the entire hospital was the psychiatric ward. I wasn't sure if the patients there were criminally insane or exactly what they were. The only thing I knew was that I agreed to accompany Bob on his onsite to a hospital that turned out to be a psychiatric hospital. I knew the hospital looked really creepy and reminded me of the SAW movies. I've actually never seen any of the SAW series movies. But I have seen the movie trailers, and when I saw people in the trailers strapped down to hospital beds being pushed down dark, creepy halls, with lights blinking on and off. After seeing the trailers for the movies, I figured I had seen enough, so there was no need for me to watch the movies.

"Investigator Rollins?" Mr. Johnson questioned as he walked over to Bob.

"Yes," Bob answered as he stuck his hand out so they could shake hands. "This is Investigator Bigbee, and we will be conducting the onsite interviews today.

"Hello, Investigator Bigbee, nice to meet you," Mr. Johnson stated as he stuck his hand out to shake mine. "Please, follow me, and I will take you to the room where you can conduct your interviews," Mr. Johnson added. As we followed Mr. Johnson, I walked very close to him and Bob to ensure I did not get attacked as we walked through the hallways. As we walked down several halls, my mind continued to replay the SAW movie trailers in my head. When they directed us to the interview room, we had to go down to the basement, where there were dim flickering lights in the hallway, and the ceiling was leaking and stained also. They put us in a room where the door had a long thin vertical window on it, and we could see out, and others could see in.

The lady that was standing super close to me in the lobby had followed us down to the interview room. While we took our seats and prepared for the interviews, I could see the lady standing outside the door. She was watching me through the door. I sat facing the door at a desk and began setting up to take notes for Bob. "Hello, I'm investigator Bob Rollins," Bob said as the first person arrived for the interview. "Please be seated," he added. Bob began to swear in the person for the interview. Even though I was supposed to be taking notes, I began to zone out a bit because the lady that had followed us to the interview room was still standing outside the door, and she was staring at me. Once I looked noticed her staring, she started jumping up and down and started swinging her arms like a monkey. As she was swinging her arms, she began making grunting noises also. She was bent over so low I could only see her face when she jumped up and down in front of the door, swinging and/or waving her arms around like a monkey. I attempted to ignore her by hunching down in my chair, and I just continued to take notes. I could see her still jumping out of my peripheral view even though I tried not to look up at her.

I don't know why, but I felt afraid of her even though she was outside of the room we were in. Not to mention, there were several others in the room with me. I worked hard at trying to pay attention to the interview so that I could get the best notes possible for Bob. But she was really distracting. I felt myself becoming anxious. As I did my best not to focus on her, I heard God speak so clearly to me. He asked, "What are you afraid of? You know that spirit; you have seen it before." I sat up tall in my chair and began to focus on the lady. I monitored her behavior and attempted to recognize her. As I began to realize that I had allowed fear to distract me spiritually. Once I calmed down and focused, I could see that the spirit in her was very familiar to me, and she was behaving exactly like a person or persons I had seen before when I had been treated in the psych ward.

Once I sat up in my chair, I looked toward the door where the lady was and directed my eyes to hers. Once she was in my view, I then began speaking to the spirit in her through my spirit. *Jesus, you know, Paul, you know, and you know me too! I rebuke you in the name of Jesus, and you have no dominion or authority here,* I said within myself. I never opened my mouth while speaking to her, but within seconds the lady was gone from in front of the door. I was then able to refocus my attention on taking notes for Bob during the interviews. We stayed in the room and conducted interviews for another eight to nine hours.

When it was time for us to leave, Bob had to check us out at the same front desk where we checked in. While Bob was talking and checking us out, I stood a few feet behind him as I did when we checked in. As I was standing there, the same lady came walking upright over to where I was standing. She was no longer hunched over like a monkey, nor was she grunting and/or howling like a monkey. She was very calm as she approached me. She smiled and said, "Jesus Christ, Jesus Christ?" I smiled, nodded my head, and proceeded to walk out the door.

As I waited for Sis Sun, I thought about the last few major spiritual battles where I dealt with an anxious spirit, a confused spirit, and a restless spirit. I began to think to myself, *is this another spiritual battle, and I was too distracted and/or afraid to realize it like I was during the onsite interview?* I waited quietly and just allowed my mind to go back and think about the tactics that Satan used in the past, and I quickly realized that he was back at his same old tricks. A great feeling of peace came over me as I regained my courage. I began to reminisce and meditate about how God had allowed me to fight and win previous spiritual battles in my life.

My meditation was interrupted by the doorbell. "Well, praise the Lord, Sister Leeta," Sister Sun said when I opened the door.

"Praise the Lord; it is good to see you. Come on in," I replied.

"What a beautiful house you have," she added. "Wow, this is a big house," she continued.

"Thank you very much. It's approximately 3,700 square feet, and I guess that is big since I'm the only one that lives here. I'll take you on a quick tour if you would like," I replied.

"Yes, I would love to take a tour," she answered.

"It has three floors; are you okay to walk all three floors?" I asked.

"Yes, I can handle the stairs," she answered.

"We are on the first level with the living room over here to the right as soon as you walk in. The family that lived here before me used it as an office," I said as she stepped fully into the house.

"Nice," she said as she walked into the living room.

"Okay, as I close the door, you can see the formal dining room to the left," I added.

"This room is very nice also," she replied.

"Follow me through the foyer, and to the right is the family room, and to your left is a not-so-formal dining room/eating area that sits in front of the screened-in patio. Right next to the eating area is the bar that separates the eating area from the kitchen. Walking slightly out of the kitchen to the left, there is a half-bath, which is across from the laundry room/mud room," I continued to talk as she walked slowly behind me.

"Girl, this house is beautiful," she added.

"Thank you so much. God really blessed me with this house. This door leads to the two-car garage, which has an extra-large built-in workbench, and just as you walk past the workbench is a service door that leads to the backyard," I said.

"And you have that cute, little sports car parked in here too," she said as we headed back into the house.

"Thanks," I said. "Okay, let's cut through the dining room, and we can go up to the second floor. I really like the upstairs foyer also but haven't decided what I plan to do with it," I said.

"Yes, because the foyer is a nice big area, and you have lots of space when you decide what it is you want to do with it," she said while smiling.

"This first room right here is my prayer closet, and to be honest, I hadn't been using it like I should," I confessed. "However, as I walk past my prayer closet, I can still feel the presence of God still lingering around and beckoning me to come in," I added.

"You'll get back to it, Sis, don't worry about that at all. It is still a beautiful room," she said as she smiled again.

"Over here is my office since I work from home Monday through Thursday, and I am so grateful to say I am off on Friday, Saturday, and Sunday," I chanted.

"What a blessing. Your decorations are beautiful," she gleamed.

"Thank you," I said. "Now, this next room is the guest room—" I started to say as she interrupted me.

"Oh, my goodness, this is simply gorgeous," she said as she interrupted. "I absolutely love this red velvet round bed," she gleamed again.

"Thank you, this bed belonged to my grandparents, and it has been in my family for thirty or forty years. I started asking my grandmother if I could have this bed when I was about ten years old. My grandmother's favorite color is red. She had a red bathtub and red sinks, and the grout in the bathroom tiles was also red. Since I had asked her for the bed for so many years, she decided to give it to me when my grandparents changed their décor. My family is big on seniority, and my grandmother has eight daughters and four sons, all older than me. So, when she decided she wanted to let the bed go and give it to me, they were all puzzled about why she gave it to a grandchild instead of one of her kids. When they started asking questions, my grandmother politely told them, 'She has been asking for the bed since she was a child,'" I explained.

"Well, it sure is pretty, and I will be on the lookout for some matching items to help really set this room's decorations off," she said.

"That is so sweet of you. Thank you very much, because as you look around, you can see I don't have many ideas for decorating this room," I replied.

"You're welcome, sweety," she replied.

"This, of course, is the guest bathroom. Since it is so close to my office, I normally use this bathroom when I'm working," I said.

"That's understandable," she replied.

"Now, over here is the last room upstairs, and it is my bedroom. The master bath is one of the things that made me fall in love with this house," I explained as we walked into the master bedroom. "Now, look over here," I said as I directed her to the huge master bath with three closets.

"This is simply amazing; look what God has done for you, Sister," she said.

I began to smile even harder as I replied, "I remember a time when I was feeling extremely emotionally low, and I confided in you about how guilty I felt for getting sick and losing our house after we had lived in the house for eight years. Then I ended up back in the hospital and lost another place that we lived in shortly after that. You looked at me as humble as can be and said, 'Honey, we lost our house after thirty-eight years.' After that conversation, which was on your birthday, I quickly learned that life wasn't as bad as I thought it was," I whispered.

"Oh, yes," she said, "I remember what God did for me. He is a mighty good God," she exclaimed as I led her back downstairs.

"Okay, now follow me down this hall, and this door leads us to the basement," I said.

"I'm right behind you, and I must admit these stairs can be challenging," she added.

"I totally agree," I said. "I hate it when I am upstairs and forget something in the basement or vice versa and have to take both flights of stairs at the same time," I said as we continued down the stairs. "Let's turn to the left once we get down the stair,s and on the left side is the home gym equipment, a seventy-inch TV in order to watch and participate in workout videos," I said with a huge smile on my face because I was just so grateful for what God had blessed me with.

"I remember your testimony at church about this house, and girl, God has truly blessed you," she said as she looked around the room.

"Okay, if we walk through to the back of the gym, we can go over to the other side of the basement, and you are in the theater room. Tada," I said as I held my arms out toward the theater room. The theater room has eleven reclining movie theater chairs, all with cup holders and some with food trays. The chair sizes range from the front to the back—small, medium, and large seats are up on the platform. Behind this wall is the popcorn machine. Stand up on the platform if you can and look down towards the front of the theater room to the 120-inch HD screen, a 3D Ultra HD black projector, three speakers behind the screen, six in the ceiling, and a subwoofer. On the walls, you are looking at a full and a partial sound wall," I said as I looked around to see if I was missing anything. "Oh, yeah, and a three-person sauna to relax and sweat away the day after the workout.

"Wow, Sis, this is just amazing," she said as she sat down in one of the large chairs.

"When I had the theater system installed, the installation guy asked me how loud did I want the system to get. I just looked at him with a puzzled look because I was not familiar with sound equipment. I think he could tell I was a bit confused because he then asked, 'Do you want to shake the house?' Immediately, I started nodding my head up and down really fast, and I became overly excited. So, needless to say, the sound system is absolutely incredible," I added.

"Sister, I know I said it before, but I do remember you testifying about how God had blessed you with this house, and it truly is a blessing from God," she said as we worked our way back up the stairs to the first floor.

"We can come down here into the family room," I said as we made our way down the hall toward the family room to sit down so that we could begin discussing why I asked her over in the first place. "Well, it seems God has blessed me financially and physically, and I am finally out of the dark pit that seemed to have had me captive," I said. "I wanted to explain to you why

I asked you over. I have been experiencing some extreme mind battles, and basically, I didn't feel strong enough to fight on my own. I felt that I needed someone spiritually strong to fight for me," I explained.

"While I was moping around feeling depressed and defeated, I began to talk to God," I said with deep emotion. "I began to open up to God honestly and just explain how I felt and how I felt like there was too much being put on me. I felt like I could not make it through this battle because I was too weak to fight, and I didn't seem to have the tools for this particular battle," I said.

"Um, um, um," she said as she shook her head.

"But in the midst of it all, God began to speak to me, and I had an epiphany. I remembered how my Euroclydon started and stopped back in 2004, and it seemed extremely familiar to this particular battle. This mind battle wasn't as intense, but I began to notice I was basically suffering with and being distracted with the exact same things," I ended as I hunched my shoulders as if to say, "there it is."

"Sister Leeta, when you called, I already knew this was a spiritual situation," she said. "As soon as I hung up the phone from you, I went to God in prayer and thanked God, first of all, because I didn't know what to do or how to do anything to help you, but I was grateful that God laid me on your heart so that I could have the chance to help," she said. "The truth is, when you first fell out in church the first time back in 2004, God immediately spoke to me and said, 'She is not sick, this is a spiritual thing,' and He instructed me to get up and go plead the blood and to deal with it spiritually. I did hear God clearly, but I was too afraid of what people might think about me if I came over to you talking about spirits. I began to question God, and I said, 'Lord, what are they going to say if everyone is praying for her healing. After you fell out in the sanctuary and they escorted you into the choir room, I decided to get up and go do as God had instructed me to do. However, when I entered the room, everyone in the room, including Bishop, was praying for your healing. Once again, I became fearful, and I said, 'God, they are all praying for her healing. What are they going to think about me if I enter the room and start talking about rebuking and binding spirits and/or pleading the blood?' I was afraid and a bit embarrassed," she said. "So, I decided to go back to my seat," she said. I just sat and listened and didn't say much at all. I had previously thought about how, back then, I was confused that the so-called Holy Ghost-filled people didn't discern that I was in a spiritual battle. But now, as I listened to her, I realized that at least one person was aware but too afraid to do anything about it.

"During that day, church continued for a while, and I could not get back focused on church. God was still dealing with me, and He instructed me to go help you. When I walked back to the choir room, you all were gone," she said. "I was told that they had taken you into Bishop's office. I walked down to Bishop's office and knocked on the door. When the door was opened, there were way more people than what was in the choir room. I must be honest; I didn't even try to reason with God or ask Him any more questions. I stayed in the room for a few minutes, and then I turned around, walked out, and went back to my seat," she said, speaking in a heartfelt tone. "My failure to help you bothered me. I made a promise to God that if He ever told me to do something like that again, I was going to be obedient and do it boldly. So, that's why when you called, even though I didn't know exactly what I was supposed to do. I knew it was spiritual, and I know God would help me," she said with confidence.

By the time she finished talking, I had a big smile on my face. "What are you smiling about?" she asked. "I'm smiling because I know that you are telling the truth. Because there was a time that I was on the pulpit ushering, and I was extremely dizzy, and I felt like I was going to pass out. I had this horrific pressure behind my eyes. I never acted any different, and I never told anyone anything about how I was feeling except God. Out of the blue, you got up from your seat, walked all the way to the back of the church, around to my side and up the side aisle, up the stairs to the pulpit, and out of nowhere, you just started praying for me. I was so shocked and grateful all at the same time. What really shocked me was when you started asking God to release the pressure behind my eyes, then I knew that God told you to come over to pray for me."

Then she began to smile, and she said, "I don't even remember that, but to God be the glory." We talked for hours and just enjoyed each other's company.

July 2017

"Ms. Bigbee, please come downstairs so we can talk to you," said the officer.

As I stood at the top of the stairs wearing nothing but a T-shirt and panties, I yelled down, "Brian, I'm not coming down-stairs, but you can come up." The officers cautiously began to move toward the stairs as they noticed there were about two inches of water on the floor. They slowly walked through the water to the staircase as they attempted to keep their eyes on me. However, I had a different plan. As the officers reached about the second step, I took off, running into the guest room where the big, red, round bed from my childhood lived. Di-gressing for a moment, I was about ten years old when I no-ticed the bed in my grandparents' room. To me, the bed looked like a bed of royalty. As a child, I would imagine myself sleeping in that bed every time I visited my grandparents. There was one time when I was a child; I went into my grandparent's room without their permission. I crept into the room just so I could sit on it and lie down for a moment. I was terrified and excited all at the same time. I was terrified because when I was a child, you didn't go into adults' rooms unless they told you to. That was just not allowed.

To Be Continued...

Epilogue

In life, we are going to have some natural situations, and we are going to have some spiritual situations. We as a people need to know the difference and be prepared for both. We are currently in a battle that doesn't end until Jesus returns. The majority of our fight is in the mind. Don't get tired of fighting, and don't forget who your enemy is or how he fights. Satan doesn't have any new tricks; he uses the same tools he did from the beginning of time. He comes to kill, steal, and destroy. Philippians 4:8 states:

> Finally, brethren, whatsoever things are true, whatsoever things are honest, whatsoever things are just, whatsoever things are pure, whatsoever, things are lovely, whatsoever things are of good report: if there be any virtue, and if there be any praise, think on these things.

You are to think on those things because Isaiah 26:3 reminds us that "Thou wilt keep him in perfect peace, whose mind is stayed on thee: because he trusteth in thee." God will protect your mind, but it is still a fight, and you have to do your part. Remember that and know that this battle is not yours, but it belongs to the Lord. Fight on!

About the Author

Leeta Bigbee is a single mother of two sons named Tyler and Trelyn. She worked in federal service a few weeks shy of thirty years. Dedicating seventeen of those years to the US General Services Ad-ministration (GSA), the last position she held at GSA was a Business Management Specialist, serving other Federal agencies in all property management needs. She spent the last twelve years of her career serving as a Federal Investigator with the Equal Employment Opportunity Commission (EEOC), working to eradicate discrimination in the workplace for all citizens. She served in the US Army and received an outstanding scholar award, and is now a Disabled Veteran. Leeta has obtained a Bachelor's degree in Business Information Systems and a Master's Degree in Management.

Leeta has served the Lord for over twenty years. She was baptized in Jesus' name and received the Holy Ghost in July 2000. Throughout the years served in and on several auxiliaries. The auxiliaries ranged from the choir, ushering, altar worker, media room, sound room, Sunday school teacher, homeless ministry, and the prison ministry, and she played the drums and clarinet for the women's and missionary choir. Leeta continues to serve and trust God and hopes that in the future, she can continue to work in every ministry that God has ordained for her.

CPSIA information can be obtained
at www.ICGtesting.com
Printed in the USA
BVHW050029110223
658309BV00010B/118